MAY
2023

Disney's
British
Gentleman

Disney's British Gentleman

THE LIFE AND career OF DaViD TOMLINSON

NaTHaN MorLeY

For Sari

First published 2021

The History Press
97 St George's Place, Cheltenham,
Gloucestershire, GL50 3QB
www.thehistorypress.co.uk

British Library Cataloguing in Publication Data.
A catalogue record for this book is available from the British Library.

ISBN 978 0 7509 9330 2

Typesetting and origination by The History Press
Printed and bound in Great Britain by TJ Books Limited, Padstow, Cornwall.

Trees for LYfe

CONTENTS

aCKNOWLeDGeMeNTS

I am grateful to the exemplary cast connected with this biography. Firstly, I owe a special debt to the Tomlinson family – Audrey, David Jr, Jamie and Henry – all who have made numerous valuable contributions and suggestions to this manuscript and allowed me to quote from David Tomlinson's memoirs. I also thank them, more generally, for their positive efforts to share the David Tomlinson legacy for new generations.

I would also like to extend special thanks to Richard Ingrams for kindly sharing his memories, along with a sizable cache of fascinating correspondence with David. Robert Sherman, the son of composer Robert B. Sherman, passed on valuable unpublished notes from his father's autobiography that described his period working with David on *Mary Poppins* and *Bedknobs and Broomsticks*.

Among others whose help and interest have contributed to this work, I would like to single out Jill St John, Bonnie Langford, Geoffrey Boycott, Gyles Brandreth, Lawrence Douglas, Frances De La Tour, Michele Lee, Griff Rhys Jones, James Kettle, Jonathan Kydd, Simon Day, Ann Bell, Piers Haggard, Shirley Eaton, Vera Day, Mary Peach, Russell Grant, Roy Snart, Judi Spiers, Barry Fantoni, Robert Longden, Jimmy Cricket, Merete Bates, Iain Sutherland, Jess Conrad, Jeffrey Kurtti, Bernard Morley, Rosanna Ritchie at the BBC Written Archives in Caversham, Beverley Matthews, the archivist at Tonbridge School, Mark Hourahane at the Leas Pavilion archive, Jenifer Hayward at the Henley Players, Kate Lees at Adelphi Films, Ben Simon and Jérémie Noyer at Animated Views, Paul Johnson at the All Angels' Episcopal Church in New York and Mark Beynon and Jezz Palmer at The History Press.

INTRODUCTION
BY DaVID TOMLINSON Jr

At the start of that iconic film *1917* set in war-ravaged northern France, I instantly spotted a special significance for my family and me. Out of 365 days, the author chose 6 April, the thirty-fourth birthday of CST – my grandfather Clarence Samuel Tomlinson – on whose seventy-first birthday I was born thirty-seven years later. That day in 1917, CST would in all likelihood have been serving in France: he was certainly there when just over a month later on 7 May my father ('DT') David Cecil MacAlister Tomlinson was born in Henley-on-Thames at the home of his uncle, CST's elder brother Richard Tomlinson.

CST was a robust individual and though the carnage of the Great War would remain indelibly imprinted on his memory, he survived it for more than sixty years, displaying little outward signs of post-traumatic stress, though heavily reliant on barbiturates prescribed by his GP to help him sleep.

So, back in 1917, some weeks went by before CST got leave to come and see the third of the four sons he had with my grandmother Florence. Unhappily, any joy from this latest arrival in the growing family had already been undermined by a shocking discovery that Florence had made about CST shortly before DT was born. That she kept it secret for many years astonished DT and his brothers. 'My mother has never been able to keep a secret,' DT mused to his great friend, Robert Morley. 'This is one secret, Dear, that she couldn't reveal,' the ever shrewd Robert observed: Robert called most people 'Dear'.

In adulthood, DT and his three brothers had had their suspicions that their father had a skeleton in the cupboard. During the Second World War in 1942, through the RAF DT learned that his elder brother, Peter, a squadron leader who had gone missing in German-occupied Holland, was alive and as well as any POW could be. DT struggled for many hours to find CST to pass on the welcome news. Then in 1954 after my birth, believing me to be CST and Florence's first male grandchild, about which he turned out to be only half right, DT later reflected that CST hadn't been that excited at the time as may have been expected.

There is invariably something going on at any time in anyone's life: DT and CST were certainly no exception. In this carefully researched book about my talented, though far from uncomplicated, father, Nathan Morley has made some further discoveries. Of course, my brothers James and Henry, and our mother have undoubtedly assisted with some details, but the end product, which we consider masterly, is Nathan's alone. This is no slavish tribute to a flawless character. The reader may well doubt the wisdom of some of the choices DT made. He could be needlessly combative and sometimes capable of picking a fight where the circumstances barely required a diplomatic solution, or indeed any remedy at all. Marrying our mum, though, was the best decision of his life. Her own assessment that in middle age, DT became rather more like his emotionally fragile mother than his mostly unimaginative father was astute.

So, at DT's graveside after his coffin had been lowered into the ground, I said a few words of thanks to the small gathering of family and friends, acknowledging that he was far from perfect and capable of fussing unnecessarily about silly little things that really didn't matter. The positive was that, in the words of his brother Peter, DT was 'always very good at the big things'. As siblings do, they had argued and hadn't been speaking to each other when in the mid-1970s Peter had a heart attack; a chastened DT immediately contacted him and they made up. That was what prompted Peter to say what he did; DT was invariably good at the big things. Supported, of course, by my mother, his biggest thing was to gain an understanding of the autism that had made life such a struggle for my brother, William, in his early years. Doing the right thing by Will became my parents' greatest achievement.

DT died twenty years ago, and it is thirty years since, with Margaret Morley, he produced *Luckier than Most*, his own memoir of the life he led, adopted by James Kettle for Miles Jupp's solo performance about DT from the very first song the character of Mr Banks sings in *Mary Poppins*. We were agreeably surprised that James and Miles thought DT's memory deserved a 'one-man show'. I had seen Miles perform on stage and TV and noticed similarities in his understated approach to breezy, subtle comedy. It seemed natural for someone who had played the sort of parts that I could imagine my father doing in his youth to portray him in *The Life I Lead*.

In retirement and old age DT's life was enriched by the friendships he made with a younger generation of comedy talent and in the literary world. Sadly the inspirational Beryl Bainbridge is no longer with us. I mention in particular Griff Rhys Jones and Richard Ingrams for the memories they have expressed and in Richard's case for sharing some of the letters that DT wrote him in the last decade or two of his life, of which we were hitherto unaware. The contemporary memories of a wide circle of friends and acquaintances that Nathan has unearthed will enable any reader of his book to gain an insight, as have we and other close family, into the complex character who was my father.

1

Growing Up

There were no esteemed adventurers, footballers, explorers, politicians or literary notables in the Tomlinson clan. But likewise, there weren't any crooks, reprobates, or horse thieves. 'Although,' David Tomlinson once revealed, 'I'm proud to say my aunt was married to quite a well-known Shakespearean actor of the Irving School called Lauderdale Maitland,' a bespectacled character known for his vigorous work at the Lyceum, where he often appeared as the popular hero.[1]

David Cecil MacAlister Tomlinson – known as 'DT' in the family – opened his eyes to the light of Henley-on-Thames on Monday, 7 May 1917. Henley Registration District Office archives reveal he was a healthy, normal baby with a tuft of brown hair, fair, pink skin and strong lungs. He arrived as the First World War raged bitterly in the filth and mud of the Western Front. That same morning, the people of Henley were in a state of flux given the *Daily Mirror* warned of compulsory rationing in the face of 'Germany's plans to starve us into submitting to a premature and humiliating peace'. In the midst of this mayhem, photographers in London trained their lens on Queen Alexandra, who, clad from head to toe in black, performed her first public function at the Albert Hall since the death of King Edward.

David's roots were purely middle-class, like many of the characters he portrayed on the screen. His father, Clarence Samuel Tomlinson – invariably referred to as 'Clargy' or 'CST' – was 34 and a true Victorian. Born in leafy Chiswick, West London, in 1883, he left school with acceptable grades and entered the legal profession, eventually becoming a solicitor of the Supreme Court, practising from a plush office at 161 New Bond Street. By all accounts, Clarence lived a life regimented by routine. He smiled in the friendliest fashion and could be charming, but was also dominating, impatient and, much to the dismay of his children, always 'seemed to be in a hurry'. When he was not giving orders from the depth of his sitting-room chair, Clarence's deepest creative energies were invested in searching for the perfect piece of beef. 'This was the only perfection he ever sought,' David recalled. His mother, Florence, on the other hand, a young beauty of Scottish descent, was 'kindly, good-natured and friendly,' and repressed her own impulses in the belief that she had a duty to keep the peace. Born Florence Sinclair-Thomson during the twilight years of the Victorian period in Calcutta in 1890, she blossomed into a graceful woman, with impeccable dress sense and style.[2] Her needlework was flawless; she played bridge and, most importantly, ran an efficient household. Family records show Clarence and Florence tied the knot at St George's, Hanover Square, on 26 June 1913, just a year before the world plunged into its first global war. The ceremony was brief but joyous, a frugal reception and honeymoon followed. Florence's first pregnancy began soon thereafter, with Michael, David's eldest brother, born in 1914. Peter – his second brother – arrived two years later.

For a brief period, the family rented an apartment near Olympia in London but when Clarence found himself being called up by the Royal Army Service Corps in September 1916, Florence and the children lodged with Clarence's brother, Richard. He lived on St Andrews Road opposite the home of Hannah Scott, the mother of the celebrated explorer Robert Falcon Scott, a woman still wracked with grief after the death of her son in the Antarctic in 1912.

Clarence rose to the rank of lieutenant, serving on the Western Front but, like so many others, was forced home a year later invalided with 'trench foot,' a painful skin disease caused by prolonged standing in mud and water. Nobody knows what the war cost him emotionally, but his grandson David Jr can guess, 'Having come home from the trenches with his nerves shot to pieces, for the remaining sixty years of his life, he took a massive dose of barbiturates each night to help him sleep. If he woke in the night, he'd top up the drugs with a slug of gin.' Despite the injury, his army service continued briefly with a posting to a local camp before a medical discharge let him return to the legal profession.

David was scarcely a toddler when the family upped sticks for Folkestone, the epitome of the upscale seaside resort that boasted a racecourse, pleasure baths and cliff-top promenade. Local records show the Tomlinsons had several addresses before settling at Wellfield Road, a large property set back behind a small front garden, within shouting distance of the sea. To the outside world, they represented the model of successful upstanding Edwardian middle-class people, leading a life paced to the easy elegance of the time. Neighbours, although always treated with friendliness, were kept firmly at a safe distance. David had a comfortable childhood, and remembered that anyone who had grown up in Folkestone and gone to public school hardly knew the working classes existed:

> I had no idea until I was in a barrack room with thirty-five of these chaps. There I was quite helpless and these other soldiers, all perfectly equipped to cope with life, all had to explain the simplest things to me. It opened my eyes.[3]

Florence was aided at Wellfield Road by four young 'live-in' servants – Ethel, Lena, Vi, and Louise – all sisters from nearby Hythe that looked after the burdensome household tasks. David held a special affection for Vi, who he remembered as 'wonderful, warm and affectionate' – the pair would often sneak off to the seaside and watch the world pass by, with their legs dangling over the pier. A sweet, bookish girl, Vi took David under her wing, becoming the closest thing he ever had to a sister. Together they observed pensioners painting gauzy landscapes where fishermen unloaded their catch and old men shading under umbrellas avoiding the stew of humidity.

'David and his brothers would have grown up immersed in entertainment, with the inter-war years seeing another regeneration of the town that offered amenities for all,' says local historian Mark Hourahane. The seafront was prettified with a new promenade, rotunda, swimming pool and the Marine Gardens Pavilion to cater to a world inhabited by the leisured and retired. 'Two Victorian bandstands remained on The Leas, where the Leas Cliff Hall was built for indoor concerts and J. Grant Anderson opened a repertory theatre in the Leas Pavilion and eventually founded the Indian National Theatre.' Also along the seafront – and across the road from the Tomlinson family home – sat the picturesque Pleasure Gardens, whose theatre was famed for hosting Kent's first moving picture show.

Although there was plenty of music to be found in the resort, David reckoned the Tomlinsons were 'probably the most unmusical family' in town. He recounted:

My father's attitude to singing was rather like dogs. He had a desire to lie down on the floor and moan. It was always funny to see him turn on the radio; he had a sort of nervous trick of doing it when he came into the room. And the moment he heard any sort of sound – music, talk or in particular male singing, he'd switch it off immediately. All you heard was a little zip of sound.[4]

But Clarence, it seems, wasn't completely allergic to the arts. During one memorable summer, Mrs Patrick Campbell, a one-time darling of the Victorian theatre, was invited to lunch with the Tomlinsons – an occasion cemented in family folklore, because, according to the tale, the celebrated actress perched the young David on her knee. The Tomlinsons were also friendly with another Folkestone family called Bentin, who were sufficiently well-to-do for their sons Michael and Tony to be sent to Eton. 'Michael became a very successful comic actor, though he added an 'e' to his surname,' David Jr notes:

Even as children, Michael and Tony Bentin were fascinated by the occult and the after-life. The whole family hosted a séance to which all the Tomlinsons were invited. Florence shook with laughter throughout; CST, who had witnessed quite enough death and destruction in France, was less amused and testily dismissed the whole thing as nonsense.[5]

How many traits David would inherit from his father is a matter of opinion. Like Clarence, he was a shrewd judge of men, never suffered fools and had a burning sense of right and wrong – but on the other hand, David could be infuriatingly stubborn and curt. It was rather from Florence that he received his salient characteristics: warmth, ambition, patience, resilience and a huge passion for life.

Given Folkestone was just about far enough away from London to make a daily commute arduous, the Tomlinson family adopted a few unusual living habits. Instead of commuting to his New Bond Street office, Clarence spent weekends with Florence and the boys, arriving on Friday evenings and departing for London on Mondays, where he resided at the sumptuous Junior Carlton Clubhouse in Pall Mall, a popular bolt hole for Members of Parliament, lawyers, and the aristocracy.

To compensate for her husband's absence, Florence heaped love and attention on her sons and the family grew with the birth of Paul in 1921. Around that time, David was enrolled in the Feltonfleet Preparatory School for Boys, where much to his delight, drama lessons featured high on the curriculum. But soon enough, Clarence, fearful that David was going 'soft', decided that his young boy needed a firmer hand and packed him off to Hillcrest school, an establishment where Charles Dickens might have been hard-pressed to describe the sadism and brutality.

A surviving well-leafed curriculum shows that for an annual fee of 70 guineas, 6- to 14-year-olds received a 'thorough all-round grounding to prepare boys for the Public Schools and the Navy'. Hillcrest's prospectus painted a delightful picture of an institution situated amid salubrious pine-woods, enjoying a climate recommended by doctors as highly suitable for growing children:

> The school building stands on gravel soil in an elevated position, with light and airy classrooms and dormitories and a well-fitted gymnasium. There is a good playing field with a garden attached, and part of each day is devoted to games under expert supervision.

'All utter poppycock,' David scowled in later life. Hillcrest would forever be seared into his memory as a dank, dark place where pupils were subjected to gratuitous torment. The school moved from Folkestone to Heathmere in 1922 under the watchful eye of headmistress Miss A. Brackenbury-Hall, a woman puffed up with self-importance, assisted by her beleaguered clerk J. Coleman Dixon and a gaggle of 'visiting masters'. David reckoned Brackenbury-Hall was at her best when meeting parents, but loathed by pupils:

> In the mornings we were lined up in a freezing corridor stark naked, whilst Miss Hall, dressed in black clothes seemingly from the previous century, very lean and angry looking with a pallid complexion and watery eyes, stood brandishing a cane as we were forced to jump into a freezing bath.[6]

Brackenbury-Hall, whose very name sounded like something out of a Victorian melodrama, presented the young David a glimpse at the rotten, corrupt side of human meanness:

> The headmistress, her cronies, and her staff would sit at the top table filling their faces while the boys had porridge and our own treacle – no milk. The one strong point of the school was the blatant neglect of their charges.[7]

The feeling that he'd been dumped by his father both wounded David and hardened him. In his autobiography, David suggests that Florence, too, occasionally reflected her husband's discontent at his lacklustre attitude to school. Mercifully, probably after vocal petitioning, his residence at Hillcrest was brief and followed by periods at other prep schools – all experiences he singularly hated. At St Georges, he befriended Guy Gibson, who would later find fame as the leader of the Dambusters' pilots. Gibson, David recounted, was as a brave youngster unfailingly supportive of the more vulnerable students and quite fearless when standing up to bullies.

Difficult as it must have been to be shunted about, cricket, football and the endless adventures of a Boy Scout camping expeditions provided unforgettable pleasures. One summer scouting expedition in the Sussex countryside remained etched on his memory:

> For about an hour at midday, we thawed out and sat in the sun and said to each other: 'This is the life'. Then we got terribly, terribly damp and terribly cold again. And we stayed like that till midday the following day. Yes, and after the first fortnight, we got rather tired of a diet of sausages, bread and jam, baked beans, cupcakes, liquorice all-sorts, wine gums, and a splendid mixture of cocoa and sugar, sucked on a damp finger.[8]

As he grew, David's greatest source of exhilaration – with the exception of the lido and penny arcades – could be found at the Pleasure Gardens, where endless concert parties, dramas and musical recitals delighted audiences year-round. Piggybacking on Michael's shoulders, the pair often dashed off to this wondrous place to watch Murray King and his pantomime tumbling through *Blue Bell in Fairyland*, *Peter Pan* and *Cinderella*. A tall man with a craggy face and a booming voice, King showed astonishing skill clowning around in feminine apparel, sparkling hair nets and opera bonnets. Not long after, David was dishing out entertainment himself when he secured sixth place (behind his brother Paul) at the Grand Hotel fancy dress ball, impressing onlookers with a dazzling plum pudding costume, designed by Florence.

But it was at the Pleasure Gardens he became truly bitten by the acting bug after catching a matinee performance of Arnold Ridley's thriller *The Ghost Train*. 'I couldn't believe anything could be so wonderful,' the laughs, the characters, the sets, the plot – every moment was pure bliss. Spurred by his new passion, David leapt into his first theatrical performance playing Tweedledee, alongside his brother Peter's Tweedledum in the wood-panelled ballroom of the Grand Hotel, where Florence – encouraging the artistic side in her offspring – sat backstage organising costumes. Even though the Tomlinson brothers enjoyed dressing up and larking about at home, doing it in public before the critical eyes of the world was especially thrilling. In David's own words, he became 'a frightful show-off', and his flair for drama was apparent from an early age. Soon after, he memorised all the lines from *Alice in Wonderland* for a performance at the Holy Trinity Church. 'On each occasion,' reported *Folkestone, Hythe, Sandgate & Cheriton Herald*, 'there was a large audience, which was enchanted by the delightful entertainment.' Clarence witnessed the performance and, typically, offered no praise. His next date involved prancing around a makeshift stage at the Town Hall in a concert in aid of the Sunshine Homes for Blind Babies. 'Miss Ena Boughton as Laile, and Master David Tomlinson as her brother, Graham, and all the children, down to the tiniest tot, did very well indeed,' the local theatre critic reported approvingly.

Although photographs from these performances are lost to history, one surviving childhood snap depicts David in a rigid stage pose attired as what looks like Little Lord Fauntleroy in high socks and half-mast trousers. Glaring at his leading lady, his imagination was fired up by these dramatic simulations of a grown-up world.

Throughout his early childhood, David was below average at his school lessons and barely excelled, preferring instead to save his efforts for more worthwhile causes like devouring the latest talkies at the Playhouse Cinema on Guildhall Street, where the manager 'got so used to this solitary boy turning up that he let me in for nothing'. But his idea of heaven was at the Savoy and Odeon, or at the gleaming Central on the High Street, where, for sixpence, he could sprawl out in the front row of the upper circle and escape from home life, where, during his weekend visits, Clarence remained emotionally unavailable and occasionally spiteful.

'My father still thought little of me and told me that I was hopeless and would never drive a car,' David lamented. For the record, it was a miracle that Clarence was able to hold on to his own licence. A cursory glance through the regional press reveals that in 1912, he was booked for exceeding the 20mph speed limit on the Finchley Road – his fifth conviction for the same offence. A few years earlier, in June 1910, he was involved in a fatal collision with a bicycle in Epsom. The cyclist, an 18-year-old gardener called Frederick Tanker, died from the injuries received. The *West Sussex Gazette* noted the car was owned by a 'Mr Seaton, Connaught House, Marble Arch, and was driven by Clarence Samuel Tomlinson, Gray's Inn Place'. When giving evidence, the father of the deceased said he and his son were cycling to Croydon when, at the corner of Longdown Road and College Road, they heard a motor horn and saw a car approach. The *Croydon Advertiser and East Surrey Reporter* carried a full report on Saturday, 4 June 1910:

> The witness turned his front wheel and fell off his bicycle but he did not see what became of his son. The corner there was a very bad one. Hugh Holden, a London solicitor, who was in the car, said the deceased appeared to lose his head and wobbled, came towards the car, struck it, was on the bonnet for a second or so and then fell off and the wheel went over him.[9] The car, he said, was going very slowly – eight or ten miles hour, or less. A juror expressed the opinion that this was too fast in the narrow road in question. Clarence Samuel Tomlinson, a solicitor, who was driving the car, said his speed was eight to ten miles an hour and he sounded his horn repeatedly. When he got to the corner two cyclists emerged. One of them got off and the other seemed to stop pedalling and wobbled into the car. The deceased was put in the back of the car and driven a quarter of a mile. Then the petrol gave out, which showed that the car was going slowly and he was taken on to the hospital in a milk cart. The medical evidence was to the effect that death was due to tetanus, arising from infection of an extensive scalp wound. Anti-toxin was used without avail. The jury returned a verdict of accidental death.[10]

It seems that Florence and the rest of the family were aware of Clarence's catalogue of motoring misdemeanours, which would continue into his nineties when he was finally made to give up his licence after a further series of accidents.

In early 1931, as aviators Charles and Anne Lindbergh flew their plane *Tingmissartoq* to China and the Soviet leader Joseph Stalin called for rapid industrialization, 13-year-old David Tomlinson arrived at Tonbridge School for Boys, an establishment founded in 1553 to offer 'wholesome discipline' and make pupils 'hold themselves and walk with a good carriage of body'. Over the years, the school turned out literary luminaries such as E.M. Forster, Frederick Forsyth and great sportsmen, including England and British Lions rugby union lock forward David Marques and cricketer Colin Cowdrey. From the outside, Tonbridge looked pastoral, but behind its stone walls it was every bit an institution, with carbolic disinfected floors, strict rules and regular bells calling a halt to lessons every thirty minutes. Thankfully for David, compared to other schools such as the infamous Repton in Derbyshire – famed for its fagging and brutality – Tonbridge was pretty liberal.

While Clarence harboured hopes his son would get some real-life training, as he had done; David was installed in School House and prayed for the experience to end quickly. He confessed:

> I never passed an exam in my life. The only exams I ever passed were when I was in the service in the war. I couldn't do arithmetic; I was only vaguely interested in English, hated Latin and all that sort of thing – I loathed school, loathed it.[11]

It wasn't all a horror show, of course. With an endless supply of stodgy food and daily exercise, David sprouted upward, stretching to a full 6 foot before his fourteenth birthday. Tonbridge also, like so many English public schools, prided itself on the quality of its sporting curriculum and possessed one of the best cricket grounds in Britain, known as 'The Head,' a lush green lawn laid out in 1838. Tonbridge chronicler Barry Orchard recounted meeting a visitor gazing lovingly at The Head. 'I have lived all over the world,' she gushed, with a tear in her eye, 'but this is the most beautiful spot on earth.' Although not mentioned for his cricketing achievements, *The Tonbridgian* magazine shows David thrashed fellow student H.D. Peal at squash 9-4, 9-6,

6-9, 9-7 during a match on Saturday, 23 March 1935. Other than that, the school archivist notes, David appears to have sleepwalked through school, 'Unfortunately, he doesn't seem to have made a great impression in the school magazine either.'

As well as developing an abiding interest in cars and racing, there was another area where Master Tomlinson showed promise: English. His fluency in the language, both written and spoken, was faultless. He enjoyed books – especially tomes on world history and figures such as Abraham Lincoln – and was a gifted public speaker, despite retaining a faint stammer. There were happy memories of his enduring friendship with classmate Ronald Howard, son of the famed actor Leslie, affection- ately known to all as 'Wink' – a dashing young man, softly-spoken and confident, with a strong build and handsome face. He wore his blond hair combed back and short like a military cadet, but there are snaps where a wavy fringe gave him a distinctly theatrical look. The friend- ship blossomed quickly. 'We both had an aversion to getting knowledge,' Ronald remembered modestly, despite going on to excel at Jesus College, Cambridge. 'David used to tell how I was bottom of the class and he was next to bottom.' It was at Tonbridge where the pair became teenagers; there they enjoyed their first glass of beer, and together they tackled – with varying degrees of success – the mystery of girls.

Just prior to David's enrolment at Tonbridge, the Wall Street Crash brought about the Great Depression, which, somehow, seems to have bypassed the Tomlinsons. As millions of people were pitchforked into poverty, Clarence continued to reap a good living by dealing mostly with divorce cases – a practice he jokingly referred to as 'the lushy graft', a play on words meaning the 'lush grass'. This good fortune was attributed to the First World War, which prompted an increase in the marriage rate from 1915. Thereafter and throughout the 1920s, there was a striking growth in separations; the number of divorces obtained in 1920 was nearly double that of the previous year. The rising tide of divorces continued throughout the decade, keeping Clarence busy.

As his schooling neared completion, David did a bit of outdoor clerk- ing for his father, which involved sitting behind a barrister in court. Not long after, when he reached 18, Clarence had decided not only on his son's career, but artfully managed to arrange 'proper employment' with Shell and British Petroleum at Shell-Mex House near the Savoy Theatre in London. 'I never even had an interview,' David remembered. 'Nor any interest in being initiated into the mysteries of bookkeeping.'

The vast grey stone Shell Mex House occupied the site of the former Hotel Cecil where the Royal Air Force was born in 1918. When completed in 1932, it formed London's largest office complex with 1,692 windows and 22 miles of corridor. 'Only in the huge restaurant – which has a superb stainless steel kitchen alongside – will there be a break from the clean yet somewhat graceless severity of this monster building,' a leading architecture critic scowled on inspecting the structure.

Unsurprisingly, stuck in a third-floor office with heavy gloss paint on the walls and drab grey tiles on the floor, David's mind was barely up to the task of mundane petroleum-based chores, and his heart was elsewhere. Good friends and colleagues offset both his incompetence and incapability. 'I was illiterate. And couldn't add up then – and still can't. If you're lucky, though, you can always get someone to add up for you!'

Evenings spent in a threadbare bedsit at the top of some dimly lit stairs near Charing Cross station weren't much better. Night after night, by the dying light of the grill fire, he lay in bed pondering his plight, kept awake by blaring tannoys and the whistles of steam engines.

2

CALL OF THE STAGE

For reasons that always remained unfathomable to his parents, David quit his dreary job at Shell in late 1935. 'More than anything,' he recounted, 'I wanted to go on the stage, but my bad stammer was a fairly severe handicap. I asked my father whether, assuming that I could cure my stammer, would I be mad to try my luck.'[1]

'I have heard of many things,' said Clarence slowly, enveloping himself in a cloud of smoke as he often did to conceal his feelings. 'But this beats them all. Use your brains, man. You're going to be an actor? You can't even speak.'[2] Then, without another word, he glided out the room, and the case was closed. Needless to say, Florence also considered acting a risky endeavour and insisted the budding thespian persevere with a proper profession.

David Jr says of David and Clarence's mutual incomprehension, 'Theirs was pretty much always a love-hate relationship. Each thought the other totally mad.'

Despite the lack of parental endorsement, David ploughed on with dreams of stage stardom. 'I wanted to be an actor because it seemed quite a pleasant and romantic way of earning a living without having to work very hard. But I had no idea about how to set about getting into the theatre,' he reminisced.[3]

'It was a profession that required no qualification of any kind. I never really wanted to be anything else. It is a very attractive way of spending one's life.' The stammer, he later maintained, was 'cured by tenacity'.[4]

With money short and few prospects, he unsuccessfully haunted the West End badgering theatrical agents, producers and directors around Charing Cross, Shaftesbury Avenue and Leicester Square, while rent, and subscriptions to *The Era*, *The Stage* and the Thursday edition of the *Daily Telegraph* (which carried a theatre page) ate into his meagre savings. When not pursuing his artistic ambitions, the Holborn Empire provided some relief, where Max Miller cracked jokes from beneath a trilby hat. For David, it was the most enjoyable type of comedy. 'Max sometimes parodied the popular songs of the moment, which was a constant source of amusement. He was the funniest man I had ever seen. I was amazed by his ability to hold the audience in his pocket. He was a riot and women loved him.'[5]

Miller, a florid, beer-swigging veteran of the First World War, had earned his fame through a long apprenticeship and was described as the Cheeky Chappie, a nickname that stuck. One popular routine saw him leaning conspiratorially toward the gallery, pulling out two little pocketbooks – his red book and his blue book – and urging the audience to decide which to use. There would be a pause, loud cries from the audience and, inevitably, the 'blue book' with its saucy jokes always won. 'I went along to a nudist camp,' ran a favourite gag. 'When the nudes sat down it was like a round of applause.'

In later life, David and Miller – who eventually retired to the south coast – became firm friends. 'Every moment spent with him was golden. What could be more satisfying than to make people laugh?' David later observed, adding he didn't think comedians and comedy actors were given fair recognition. 'Unless you play classic roles you're not remembered. In 100 years' time, the names Olivier and Gielgud will be there, but not Rex Harrison's, because he is appreciated for his comedy, not his acting.'[6]

In addition to lapping up Holborn Empire turns, the aspiring young actor remained attached to the cinema, where sound was still a new toy. Fred Astaire, Greta Garbo and Clark Gable were young icons, and the Warner brothers were beginning to churn out popular films about gangsters and cowboys. 'I loved Gary Cooper – the genuine American hero. He showed everyone how to make it look easy.'[7] Action pictures were far more preferable than musicals and British films, 'Jean Arthur was my absolute favourite actress, and all American films were wonderful.'[8]

Although they never met, six decades later in retirement, David still considered Arthur his film icon. 'When I first caught a glimpse of her, I was enchanted ... she had elegance and humour.'[9] The Pittsburgh-born actress had rocked to fame on Broadway in the 1920s before finding global stardom in Hollywood, where she became known as the quintessential comedic leading lady. However, the turning point in her film career came when Frank Capra chose her to star in *Mr Deeds Goes to Town*. Her relative obscurity in later life came partly from her avoiding interviews and refusing to become a part of any kind of studio-generated publicity, a rare trait in Tinseltown, which David would later share.

After two months of knocking on doors without a nibble, David's giddying sense of control over his life was overtaken by the prospect of a humiliating return to Folkestone. 'My funds were sinking as quickly as my spirits. I could not go home and I would not admit defeat.'[10]

Finally, his genteel poverty ended when he wandered unheralded into a new career:

> One sunny morning – quite broke – I walked along Whitehall and joined the regular army. I discovered for the first time in my life just how quickly human beings can travel without leaving the ground … the foreign legion would have been a holiday camp compared to life in the Grenadier Guards.[11]

The Grenadier Guards, an elite British Army infantry regiment, can trace its prestigious lineage back to 1656 when it was raised in Bruges to protect the exiled Charles II. They became world-famous for their red tunics and bearskins, and can often be seen guarding the Royal residences.

Unsurprisingly, David's entry into the army confirmed Clarence's belief that his son's acting ambitions would come to no good.

At Caterham Barracks, Regimental Sergeant Major Bill Langridge fixed a demonic eye on his new recruits, buckling them down into a tortuous life of drilling, spit and polish. The tall, statuesque soldier with a beaky nose and roaring voice taught his charges to do everything with bayonets except sit on them. That first week, David, brow pouring sweat, traipsed around the parade ground until his new boots produced blisters on the heels. He learnt to use the weapons of war, polished and polished yet again various articles and appurtenances of clothing; made his own bed, swept and scrubbed. 'It tested human stamina to the very limit! Suddenly I had to fend for myself, all quite new to me, of course.'[12]

When the Grenadiers marched into Buckingham Palace courtyard they were personal protectors of King George V, who unbeknown to the

British public, was on his deathbed, and would soon be succeeded by Edward VIII, who was busily cavorting with Wallis Simpson, a married American socialite.

Although many aspects of military life were difficult – far more difficult than civilian life – David accepted his fate with abject resignation, cheered by sporting opportunities that provided some small consolation. Speaking years later, Bill Langridge said his young charge didn't easily fit into the social mould of a soldier and his saviour was laughter and cheek, 'He was a bit of a comedian, even in the barrack-room,' with an impulse to mimic the gaits, traits and mannerisms of his fellow soldiers.[13] In his memoirs, David gave a mottled account of army life, which brought him a variety of new experiences:

> I spent six months at a recruit depot at Caterham, where to say the discipline was rigid would be like saying the Equator is quite warm or that the monsoon season brings light showers to the tropics. The discipline in the Guards was spelt not only with a capital D but a capital everything else as well and usually set in italics. It was all spit, polish and drill. An order was an order. Nobody argued or even vaguely demurred. I was then posted to Wellington Barracks and what we did there was drill – and drill – and drill, apart from two weeks a year at Pirbright firing range. We were on guard duty at Buckingham Palace, St James's, and the Magazine in Hyde Park and also at the Bank of England; each man got a new shilling when we were guarding the bank. When we weren't marching we were polishing. But I am grateful to the Guards for one thing. They taught me how to polish shoes. I am an expert at it.

After sixteen months of spit and polish, David's stamina wavered. Clarence duly stumped up the £35 to return the King's Shilling and grudgingly suggested his son buckle down and resume work at Shell. 'It was just a question of whether the army broke my heart or I broke the army's,' David later mused. 'Who won? The army won at a canter.'[14]

Years later, David's fourth son Henry remembered hearing a story about Clarence 'walking past Dad, who was stationed on guard outside St James's Palace. And Dad said, from the corner of his mouth, "You've got to get me out of this!" But whether it's true or not, it's a good story!'

The stiff sea breezes cleared David's head on his return to the coast, where an unpaid job with the Folkestone Repertory provided the chance to play small parts and write scripts. 'I think I have a good eye and a good ear,' he said of those early years. 'That's a good deal of what acting is – listening and observation'.[15] His first credit came in *Outward Bound*, garnering enthusiasm from the *Folkestone Herald*, which described David as 'a constant source of surprise and wonderment ... his easy confidence, nonchalant cynicism and expressive gestures conveyed everything necessary for the part, and he won a richly deserved triumph.'

Soon after, fortune smiled with a job in a touring troupe, secured after answering an advertisement in *The Stage*. 'Or at least that was the idea,' David lamented. His enthusiasm dampened when it turned out to be a 'little fit-up company' playing mining towns in Scotland. 'I got the job right away. It was a rag-time little outfit. My salary was 30 shillings a week, plus a share, but the share was problematical.'[16]

It also became evident that drama was low on the list of management priorities. 'We never seemed to rehearse,' David laughed, as he painted a fanciful portrait of a bad experience. 'I don't remember ever rehearsing anything. The manager would say: "We're doing *Charlie's Aunt*, tonight." And that was it.'[17]

Unsurprisingly, the engagement turned sour:

> You know the sort of bad dream of making an entrance and not knowing the lines well; this was the actor's nightmare come true. I really didn't have the faintest idea of what was going on. We really did literally make it up as we went along.

The group toured provincial stages, learning to perform before a rough and often drunk audience. Then, late one rainy evening, David explained, the manager 'did what you often hear of managers doing, but somehow one never imagines experiencing it oneself, he skipped with the cash and left us stranded.'[18] Abandoned in Dalkeith, south-east of Edinburgh, with five other cast members, David 'did some rather smart detective work and found out where the perisher had gone'.[19] After enlisting the aid of a policeman, who heard his story, the two marched off to confront the wage-packet thief. The policeman promised to stand and listen, although he couldn't interfere as it was a civil matter. A few minutes later, the encounter with the rogue impresario instigated a row loud enough to be heard in the next street. 'The policeman's presence did the trick and I went back to the company proudly clutching our week's money. I've never been made quite such a fuss of since.'[20]

Out on the street again, David ended up sharing digs with a group of American medical students in Edinburgh. 'I had to take a job to get enough money to get back to London,' he explained, but thankfully managed to land a job as a 'Pioneer Salesman engaged to expand the distribution of a well-advertised product'.[21]

In reality, he worked door-to-door selling vacuum cleaners. Edinburgh is beautiful during the summer months, but in winter it's a forbidding place, with gusts that blow in straight from Russia, or so the locals claim. David had to clamber through snowdrifts and navigate icy pavements to reach his customers:

I was a fresh-faced English boy stinking with idealism. The Scottish housewives couldn't understand me and I couldn't understand them. The door would open and I'd say my party piece – you know, this was their great day and here, at last, was something for nothing – etc.[22]

However, such fast-talking door-to-door pitches had little effect:

I'm proud to say I didn't sell a Hoover, and in view of the fact that my customers were ladies whose husbands were lucky to be earning £3 10s a week, I thought it was a very good thing I didn't.[23]

Returning home to Folkestone, David obliterated Scotland from his memory on winning an apprenticeship with the Arthur Brough Players at the Leas Pavilion, an opportunity he 'seized with a nose-to-the-grindstone' attitude. If the army and the Scottish debacle had taught him anything, it was the gift of application, self-scrutiny and doggedness. While seasoning his craft, Brough had his young charge loading and unloading props and scenery, learning about scripting, design, sound, lighting and costumes. 'I worked hard,' David confessed. 'But, I used to sit there, like all actors do, thinking that's good, that's bad, he's terrible, I could do it better than that – why don't they give it to me to do, I would do it cheaper too.'[24] Working on a shoestring budget, Brough – who found fame decades later playing Mr Grainger in the sitcom *Are You Being Served?* – opened in Folkestone in

1929 performing *The Dover Road*, where he later introduced 'tea matinees'. The venue – famed for its warm beer, uneven stage and orchestra that baulked at the idea of playing modern tunes – became a local institution. Brough remembered a hardscrabble existence:

> Whatever our ups and downs, our greatest problem remained the finding of plays. Excluding new ones, which we must of necessity limit, we have to find about 40 a season, with only about six of the latest West End successes likely to be available. Inevitably we have to go back to the older ones, which the audience expects to be just as good as the new. The greatest enemy of the repertory manager is complacency. Whatever else you do, you must never relax.[25]

Like others after him, David opined that, although a pleasant chap and decent employer, Brough had more personality than talent. By contrast, he reserved strong praise for his actress wife Elizabeth Addyman – who thought the idea of acting was built on observation and imagination. On 5 October 1936 – the day 200 hunger marchers in Jarrow began their march to London – David made his first professional appearance on stage in J.M. Barrie's *Quality Street*, a comedy in four acts. He didn't speak; his brother Peter giggled in the audience and the family weren't impressed. 'But as far as I was concerned,' said David, 'it was a beginning'.

Over the years, many well-known personalities trod the boards of the Leas Pavilion with Brough's repertory troupe. Alastair Sim played a butler in *The Sport of Kings*, while Eric Portman appeared in *The Importance of Being Earnest* and, like David, Cyril Luckham cut his teeth there as a student. Barbara Leake joined as a juvenile during the first season; and Noel Howlett, Michael Gough, Roma Beaumont, Charles Lloyd Pack, along with countless others, added to their experience there over the coming decades.

During these apprenticeship years, there was time for other pursuits including flying, a hobby David picked up from his brother Peter, who had passed his pilot's test and been awarded an RAF commission. David zoomed skywards to discover a whole new passion, scraping together every spare farthing to pay for instructional flights in an Avro Tutor with Flying Officer David W. Llewelyn, a crazily fearless pilot famed for flying from London to Cape Town in 1935. He made the return flight in a record time of just six and a half days, beating Amy Johnson's time by eighteen hours. Lessons began at

Lympne aerodrome, a flat strip of grassland in the face of a gusty and cold wind. Llewelyn occupied the rear cockpit of the plane, and in spite of the violent winds, the pair made countless trouble-free flights, thus beginning David's love affair with biplanes. 'Winds and poor visibility didn't deter us,' he later boasted, confessing he only became nervous during his first spin towards the ground at terrific speed. He remembered wondering, as the cold rain lashed his face and the wind tore at his flapping jacket, if anything could be more wonderful.

Around the time of the Munich Crisis, when Britain, France and Italy granted Czechoslovak land to Germany, fellow actor Dennis Price gave David a foot up the theatrical ladder by fixing him an understudy role in *The Merchant of Venice* during Gielgud's epoch-making season at the Queen's Theatre. Price was in the same production, where his flair for cynical comedy found full scope – that cynicism, mixed with the full eye roll, was later deployed beautifully with a starring role as Louis Mazzini in *Kind Hearts and Coronets*.

Having bid farewell to Folkestone, David took lodgings in Hammersmith and recalled after the first run-through at the Queen's that there wasn't much to rehearse, given the extent of his part was to judder across the stage a few times in a gold-sashed robe. 'I understudied Alec Guinness's Lorenzo,' he recounted, stating his West End debut was effected with surprisingly little formality:

> I was paid £3 a week to watch Gielgud and Peggy Ashcroft performing wonderfully. Of course, I felt I could have played Lorenzo better than Alec Guinness. It is hard to believe now that at the time I thought he was decidedly wooden.[26]

As it happened, David only had a single line in the play, in which he delivered this seemingly simple message: 'Gentlemen, my master Antonio is at his house and desires to speak with you both.' Although just fifteen words, he managed to flub it on almost every performance, prompting Gielgud to lurk night after night in the wings with an uncomfortable grimace, mouthing, 'For fuck's sake Tomlinson, dear boy, try and get it right tonight.'

Ashcroft, the petite, sultry-eyed actress, took on the role of Portia, alongside Gielgud's wearily bitter Shylock, which he performed 'with the touch of greatness', according to the *Daily Herald*'s Herbert Farjean. 'It was the finest thing he had done since his Old Vic days.'

By any chalk, this was an exciting time to be in the theatre. Gielgud – who was at the height of his acting prowess – both directed and starred in the production. However, in contrast to Farjean's remarks, a deeply irritated Gielgud later tossed out a few savage comments on the state of that production. 'I tried to make Shylock a squalid little guttersnipe,' he noted, saying he abandoned a high-pitched, squeaky dialect, much to the disdain of some critics:

> Of course, it was the time of Hitler, which did not help matters. I would have satisfied more people if I had created a haughty Irvingesque character rather than a cringing Fagin-figure – though Olivier told me he liked me in it better than almost anything else I did in Shakespeare.

As an understudy, the play's fine-tuned mechanics and dialogue became engraved in David's memory for the rest of his life, and provided a note-perfect party-piece in the form of a rousing Gielgud impression. It was a performance he afforded to Ian McKellen on the *Wogan* show decades later:

> McKellen: What did you play?
> Tomlinson: Well, not much, but Gielgud played Shylock. I could do a quick burst of Gielgud.
> McKellen: Can you? Oh, quick.
> Tomlinson: If you prick us do we not bleed. And if you wrong us, shall we not revenge the villainy? That's good – the villainy.

Interestingly, David revealed that his life might have been different and taken a more serious dramatic path:

> Tomlinson: I was enjoying myself at Northampton Rep, before you were born. And of all things, Tyrone Guthrie came down and said: 'If you would like to come and see me in London, please do so.' And of course, I got a commercial job, and I never went near him. So I might have been you now, dear.
> McKellen: Yes, well, it is odd, those little turnings that you take or don't take.
> Tomlinson: I went for the money instead, you see?
> Wogan: Do you regret that?
> Tomlinson: Not at all, not at all.

Decades later, as a National Theatre Player, David's second son, Jamie, remembered being asked to do a Shakespeare sonnet:

> I phoned Dad. He immediately recited two or three over the phone, making them sound like normal English. I did not realise the years spent in rep and on tour and the endless work he must have put in to becoming … a very good actor indeed.[27]

After bidding farewell to Gielgud, David was offered a contract with the Northampton Repertory during the summer of 1938. Although the salary of £3 a week was below average, the prestige of the unit more than compensated. 'I lied my way into repertory, pretending I was enormously experienced,' he confessed.[28] 'They would say, "What have you done, where have you been?"' to which he responded by rattling off the names of theatre companies he had never been near, so, as he said, 'One conned ones way in.'[29]

Sifting through a weathered box of newspaper archives, a cutting reveals David's arrival in Northampton was enough for the local *Mercury* to dispatch a reporter. A photograph from that day shows an attractive, well-dressed young man with a profile good enough for a young romantic lead. Under the headline 'Mr Tomlinson's wide experience,' the paper noted two other new recruits, Taymar Saville and Judy Bacon, joined on the same day. 'David Tomlinson is tall, dark and youthful-looking,' was the gist of the write-up.

Amanda Howson from the Royal & Derngate Theatre, which runs the same venue nowadays, recalled matinee idol Errol Flynn was with the company before embarking on his American adventure. 'Life in the Rep kept everyone very busy,' she says. 'A hectic schedule saw the same company performing one play in the evening while rehearsing the next week's play during the daytime – and all while learning lines for the play coming up the week after that.'

Indeed, for the paying audience, seeing such a wide variety of plays in repertory was a distinctly stimulating experience and proved revelatory for David, as he stretched muscles he didn't know he had.

He was as versatile as he was subtle, spending three years playing love cheats, cashiers, dead bodies, reporters, lawyers, businessmen and policemen, as well as the crooks, and was especially delighted to receive an enthusiastic response to comedy performances. 'I was very surprised when audiences laughed at me. Really.' *George and Margaret*, the story of a day in the lives of a modern family in London, sat among his most memorable touring plays. This light-hearted piece of nonsense was well-trod ground: just as everything seems calm and tranquil, the family is thrown into chaos by the suddenly announced arrival of their old friends George and Margaret for dinner that evening. The unbearably snobby mother demands all family members attend, despite the protests of her children. As the tale unfolds, the anticipated arrival eventually provides a catalyst for various members of the family to resolve their personal crisis. The play ambles along in loose fashion, ending without George and Margaret ever having appeared on stage.

Critics described the production as a diverting cross-section of middle-class family life so popular in the theatre at the time. 'It was this play that started the vogue,' the *Newcastle Evening Chronicle* opined:

Last night's Bank Holiday audience enjoyed every kind of laugh from the quiet chuckle to the all-in. Geoffrey Clarke does a very subtle piece of acting as the father of the Garth-Banders, and Ethel Hope Johnstone as his wife gives an excellent character study. Hector Ross, formerly at Jesmond Playhouse, makes a welcome return to Newcastle in the part of Claude, the moral brother, played with a fine sense of humour. His more normal brother is spiritedly played by Ian Jarvis, while Margaret Cooper is delightful as the coltish modern daughter, David Tomlinson is the young pianist whom she loves, and Judy Bacon and Barbara Bruce are a couple of maids – ancient and modern.

In due course, the production turned up in Exeter, where it became a news event after the local critic enthused about the 'splendidly tip-top cast'. The hoopla surrounding the first performance led to 'good houses and hearty laughter and applause, such comedy-drama as this is ever-increasing favour with playgoers'.

David learned quickly that the sense of tradition and collective achievement was what made old-style resident repertory work so valuable. It was in places like Exeter where he began to appreciate the simple life of a wandering actor, lodging in shabby theatrical boarding houses piped with lukewarm water, ill-lit landings and lumpy beds:

I absolutely adored touring. It seemed to be such a lovely way to spend one's life, travelling around the country and being paid for it. I even liked the threadbare dressing-rooms in the grand old theatres of the grand old industrial towns, which in themselves I found fascinating.[30]

On one occasion, an old landlady told him of the kindness of her previous guest. 'Do you know,' she gushed, 'that man went out on Saturday night, met a sailor who had nowhere to stay and let him share his bed.'

'Lovely gesture,' David replied, without batting an eyelash, hoping no one ever shattered her illusions, as 'no one is better for losing them'. [31]

While some actors liked to drift in and out of public houses or visit the bookies, the free time enabled David to admire the view here and there, or explore musty antique shops, where he gained an appetite for the Georgian period, 1750–1830, and Regency furniture and fittings. He picked up a profound knowledge of the subject and slowly began amassing an impressive collection, which was stored at his parents home in Folkestone.

Meanwhile, news concerning the escalating fragile peace in Europe continued to emanate from the press. First and foremost in everyone's mind was the looming presence of Adolf Hitler, a subject David discussed at length during luncheons with Clarence, who, by this point, was becoming less remote. In fact, he lavished high praise on David's performance of John Royd in *Quiet Wedding*, a production that featured Sarah Churchill, the second daughter of Winston.

'Miss Churchill has a difficult part as Janet Royd, but she succeeds in investing it with fine lights and shade,' was the opinion of *The Stage*, which noted in the same review that David 'enacts the bridegroom in a light-hearted and amusing way'.

Offstage, as well as on, Churchill was a sort of symbol of the theatre of her era, with clipped British speech, flamboyant evening dresses, gaudy jewellery, and seemingly in awe of no one. 'She had mesmerizing assurance and was marvellously stubborn but womanly,' a critic observed.

In his memoirs, David recounted staying at the same Leeds hotel as Churchill, where, given the fantastic menu on offer, he ate and drank like a sailor on leave. Desperate to meet Winston Churchill's daughter, Clarence motored up one evening from London to join the pair for dinner. 'She charmed him. Of course, just being who she was would have been enough for Clarence but she was also the ideal dinner companion.'

Although being every inch a lady, Churchill maintained her dignity despite suffering torment from her philandering husband Vic Oliver, an Austrian comedian seventeen years her senior who she had married in 1936, much to her father's disgust. 'After the show she always rang Vic,' David remembered, 'and as often as not it resulted in tears as the phone was sometimes answered by a female voice.'

In the coming years, she divorced Oliver, had affairs, dropped and gained weight and was pushed through treatment for alcohol addiction. In her descending spiral, she was taken into police custody for making a scene in the street on several occasions and spent a short spell on remand in Holloway Prison, bringing her career to its knees. David recounted that a chance encounter in Ireland decades later proved an unhappy experience: 'I felt a clout on my back. It was Sarah, withered, haggard and blind drunk. Her person and her dignity were in shreds and she was asked to leave the hotel.'[32]

3

Dark Clouds

The fragile peace in Europe unravelled at breakneck speed during the summer of 1939. Even without rationing and blackouts, public concern was exacerbated by the rapid growth of the army and air force, which had seen 2 million people join up. Finally, when Hitler ordered his troops into Poland on 1 September, David knew which way the wind was blowing. During a rare family conference on the issue, Clarence – a man still traumatised by his own war scars – became a reassuring wellspring of hope. 'I often recall my father's words,' David said, "It will only last a couple of month's old boy!"'[1]

For thousands of actors and entertainers, normal life stopped abruptly when the government closed theatres and then, when Nazi air raids failed to materialise, reopened them.[2] With this good fortune, David appeared at the Opera House, Leicester, on 21 September with *George and Margaret*, before reprising his role in *Quiet Wedding*, a performance greeted with thunderous applause at the Royal Court Theatre in Liverpool. 'Mr Tomlinson,' noted *The Stage*, portrayed a 'very human and likeable bridegroom' while, the *Daily Post* described him as 'forthright, honest and not too appreciative of psychological subtleties'.

With the onset of war, the coldest winter for forty-five years descended on Britain as troops from the British Expeditionary Force landed in France to shore up its defences. While many thespians seemed loath to touch the issue of war work, some begrudgingly enlisted in the Entertainment National Service Association – or ENSA – a new unit producing 'all-star concert parties' and troop shows. Basil Dean, a prickly theatrical producer, controlled ENSA's portfolio of actors, comics and musicians. To begin with, he packed them off in touring concert parties to factories and military installations. Eventually, as their fame grew, a distinguished roster of stars including Evelyn Laye, Arthur Askey, Vic Oliver and Billy Bennett clamoured to do their bit before audiences in uniform. There were other entertainers, too. George Formby packed up his ukulele to rap out 'Imagine Me in the Maginot Line' and 'When I'm Cleaning Windows' in a tent jammed with tired and homesick troops in France. The formula usually consisted of a stand-up comic, a singer, a few pretty girls, a large dollop of sentiment and crowds of grateful troops savouring the respite from war work. However much flak they received from the audience, ENSA certainly couldn't be accused of not trying. In some cases, Dean's efforts were so dogged that he laid on morale-building 'all-in wrestling' evenings, and countless ropey stage productions ranging from Shakespeare to Dickens.

Instead of joining ENSA, David's first patriotic duties were fulfilled in the Butcher's Film Service production of *Garrison Follies*, a bawdy comedy set around a fictional RAF aerodrome where airmen attempted to stage their own ENSA-type concert party. The film, all but lost for decades, starred Barry Lupino and H.F. Maltby, the latter known for his association with Will Hay. It was shot at the 'extremely grubby' Nettleford studios at Walton-on-Thames, a barn-like structure sitting under thick layers of dust.

Although an exciting experience, David considered Butcher's the 'lowest of low,' given it focused on cheap two-reelers hindered by appalling scripts, many unchanged or bastardised from their stage originals. Output was mostly 'slam-bang populist' aimed at working-class audiences in Wales, the Midlands, the North and Scotland. 'It was the most austere studio in Britain, if not the entire world,' David noted. 'Butcher's,' another employee opined, 'was a dump with a sort of leisurely charm – the films were a very parochial kind.'[3] In Hollywood, such outfits were dubbed poverty-row studios, which remained outsiders even when they succeeded.

But the best evidence of Butcher's success could be seen in cinemas across Britain, where a constant need to meet the public's appetite cheaply ensured the company flourished. 'I heard of one producer,' broadcaster Roy Plomley once recalled, 'who made travelogues by photographing picture postcards, provided musical background by playing the organ himself, and spoke his own commentary.'

As it happened, David's experience on *Garrison Follies* proved priceless as he discovered, unlike in the theatre, making movies was no uninterrupted flow and required endless patience. He learned camera technique, emoting on cue, filming split scenes photographed from different angles, continuity, stop and go signals, and dealing with the constant background disturbances on-set, which can infuriate actors. David kept tight-lipped about frustrations over Maclean Rogers' direction, which, he reckoned, kept *Garrison Follies* within the realm of mediocrity. Rather, to everyone's surprise, Rogers caused non-too-subtle sniggers by keeping his assistant busy replenishing Guinness supplies throughout shooting. But any anxieties about the film faded when a cluster of reviews proved largely positive: 'This is a cheerful, tuneful, light-hearted spectacle guaranteed to cure the worst dose of blues,' the *Monthly Film Bulletin* proclaimed. 'Barry Lupino is excellent as Alf Shufflebottom, the resourceful plumber.'

No doubt quietly buoyed by his film experience, David returned north to the Theatre Royal in Leeds for a twice-nightly stint with The Court Players in Max Catto's vividly imagined thriller *They Walk Alone* alongside Peggy Ramsay, who in later life represented Alan Ayckbourn and J.B. Priestley, and famously discovered playwright Joe Orton. Garbed in a black pinafore, Ramsay portrayed a homicidal sex-maniac maidservant, which the *Yorkshire Post* thought created 'undiluted melodrama,' erupting into a 'firm crescendo of fright'.[4] The only criticism, if it was, came with the assertion that 'although a trifle over-sophisticated in his demeanour,' David was 'a good juvenile lead'. Engagements continued at a furious pace, and by the time the company arrived in Wales for another outing of *Quiet Wedding* in late spring, the troupe was working close to exhaustion.

As this was going on, German troops were oiling their guns in preparation for an invasion of Denmark and Norway, while the Luftwaffe brought the war closer to home by raiding British naval positions at Scapa Flow. Although no pacifist or internationalist, David, like so many others, resisted going into the service as long as possible by entertaining a population looking to escape, if only briefly, from the bleak realities of the day. 'Of course,' he admitted, 'I knew it couldn't last forever,' but his distaste for military regulations, spit-and-polish, rigid company commanders and lack of money was still raw.

In any case, there were other battles being fought on home soil. A week before the Germans overran Belgium and Holland; David found himself in court facing Charles Henry Forsythe, the managing director of Unit Productions. The case – which showed that even in war, the mundanities of everyday life continued – concerned an incident from the previous December, when he was booted out of *Shoot the Works*, a review starring comedian Joey Porter and contortionist Doris Hall. According to court papers, all hell broke loose when David took the opportunity of putting in his two-pennyworth by advising a female co-worker to kick-up a fuss when she was forced to change costumes without a curtain for privacy. 'If I were you,' he whispered to the red-faced actress, 'I shouldn't go on unless screens are used.' As fate would have it, the producer's secretary overheard the remark, leading to his dismissal.

For David, the episode was an unjust humiliation and without blinking, Clarence rushed forward with his colleague C.E. Rochford to bring the case to Westminster County Court. 'The secretary was apparently annoyed by the attitude of Mr Tomlinson with reference to the incident about the young girl, and openly called him Lord Haw-Haw,' a court reporter noted in a dispatch splashed over the pages of the *Daily Mirror*, *Manchester Evening News* and *Birmingham Mail*.

In his defence, Forsythe claimed 'complaints had been made that he (David) was running about with the girls of the show'. He asserted 'as to the supposed nude, Mr Tomlinson was supposed to be in his dressing room waiting for his call, and not on the stage. I told him that he had no business there and that he had no right to speak to the girl.'

In his ruling, the judge awarded David £12, the equivalent of two weeks' salary in lieu of notice. Although the incident – and his father's part in it – was never mentioned again, it showed another twist in their extraordinary relationship. Throughout his son's nascent career, Clarence continued to live and work in London during the week, while Florence endured a lonely existence at the family home in Folkestone.

It was around this time – which in view of later events is important to mention – something disconcerting started to bother the Tomlinson brothers. As their occasional attempts to make contact with Clarence at the Junior Carlton Club often proved unsuccessful, it was decided an investigation, of sorts, should be launched. Discussing the issue over drinks, the brothers agreed something was amiss. Was their father harbouring skeletons in his closet? Why was he never at his club? Should they embark on ferreting out clues? It was clear, however, with the looming prospect of a German invasion, probing the Clarence mystery would have to wait. In any case, Peter was busy piloting Spitfires and working as aide-de-camp and personal pilot to Arthur 'Bomber' Harris, the man who refined the science of saturation bombing, while Paul was posted north to prepare for RAF operations. David, meanwhile, continued to tour around Britain, where normal days, even in civilian life, were rare. On several occasions, he displayed indomitable resilience as German incendiaries and splinters rained down on London. One time, according to family legend, he was walking with a girlfriend when the sirens began wailing.

'Quick, quick … lay down David!' the terrified girlfriend screamed.

'Not in this suit!' he shouted back, refusing to duck for cover.

All the more remarkable, says David's son Jamie, was an incident he witnessed years later at the family apartment at Chelsea Cloisters on Sloane Avenue. 'Dad was sitting talking to a stage director and there was a bomb warning outside,' he recounted. 'The stage director immediately lay on the floor under the table hands over ears face down. "Christ Roger! What the hell are you doing?" Dad said, having not budged an inch.'

As the aerial attacks increased during 1940, it was evident that David's theatrical career would be suspended for the duration. All throughout the summer above the West End, Londoners could gaze up and see RAF pilots fighting Nazi planes. On the ground, the smell of cordite, the sound of glass being swept up and choking dust cloaked every inch of the city. Surprisingly, and much to the delight of the theatrical profession, the pressure of the Nazi bombardments induced people to be frenetically social, a phenomena that ensured entertainment venues were always packed. The singer Vera Lynn, who was starring in a review with David's pal Max Miller at the Holborn Empire, remembered there was a 'boom in the whole cheer-up business. There was a feeling that if Hitler was going to drop a bomb on you he might as well catch you having a laugh in the stalls as hiding under the stairs.'

Since the beginning of the war, regulations dictated that theatre programmes include air raid instructions, while actors kept their gas masks and helmets close at hand, pegged on hooks in the wings.

Before packing up his greasepaint, David had time to join the cast at the Prince of Wales, Birmingham, in *The Police Are Anxious*, a drama of family life that played to full houses. He assumed the role of Harry Grahame alongside the portly Frank Cellier – best known to audiences for playing Sheriff

Watson in Alfred Hitchcock's *The 39 Steps*. 'Not only did he help me with my performance, but he also took me to his house in St John's Wood,' David remembered, when the play moved to Streatham. 'We would have supper there and talk far into the night. Perhaps at this stage, I was looking for a father figure and he filled the bill nicely.'[5]

A dashing young actor named John Le Mesurier, who was destined to become a lifelong friend, played Richard Monroe, while gaunt-faced Ernest Thesiger, a character actor of consummate skill famed for his performance as Doctor Septimus Pretorius in *Bride of Frankenstein*, portrayed Phillip Marslow. Reviews were excellent: 'Dorothy Black and David Tomlinson are putting up outstanding performances in supporting roles,' the *Evening Despatch* enthused.

David spent the last weeks of 1940 touring devastated cities and other hard-hit towns in a piece of fluff called *Once a Crook* before the curtain finally rang down in Nottingham. 'The RAF got me just before Christmas, and it was a bloody cold one too.'

4

FOr KING aND COUNTrY

And so, after surveying a diary full of crossed-out engagements for November 1940, David Tomlinson enlisted in the RAF but was far from satisfied. He complained to anyone that would listen that the Air Ministry had behaved abominably in not sending him for pilot training like his brothers. 'I had set my sights on becoming an operational pilot,' he sighed wearily, 'but the request was ignored at every turn.'

Instead, at the age of 23, he was marched into the Chain Home radar station at Newchurch near Folkestone to locate enemy bombers. As the war widened and unfolded, the importance of the RAF radar units increased accordingly. 'I was not at all pleased at not being made operational at the time,' David lamented, 'as I was vaguely ready for heroism but can't pretend that I didn't enjoy a warm and safe job, although one could never see an end to the war.'[1]

Working with a dozen other men, evenings were spent tracking aircraft on a device beaming radio waves far beyond the shores of Britain unaffected by fog, darkness, or cold. Routines could change suddenly with a chance sighting of a German plane, or, worst of all, the shadow of a squadron headed inbound. For the most part, life at Newchurch – located on one of the oldest parts of the Romney Marsh – was generally healthy. There was a steam-heated shower block, sports pitch, Naafi and three sufficient meals served daily. Although the job could be riveting, of greater interest to David was the sudden glut of propaganda films that would provide gratifying interruptions from military life. Improbable as it may seem, given the pressing demands of war, Maclean Rogers – the Guinness-swigging director at Butcher's – secured David a tiny role in the Royal Army Ordnance Corps film *Name, Rank and Number* designed to illustrate the methods used by Germans to extract information from prisoners of war. In all, David's scenes consumed little more than five minutes' screen time and it's doubtful – even given time for malfunctions and false starts – that the entire production took much longer.

To modern eyes, the film seems farcical, but in 1941 the government considered it of national importance and over 200 prints were distributed at home and in the United States, where it was recirculated by the US War Department. Even out in the far-off backwaters of Ceylon, David's brother Michael was astonished to catch it playing at the camp cinema.

Not long after, David's loyalty to king and country was on view when, suited in RAF dress uniform, he joined well-wishers at Ronald Howard's wedding to Patricia Horsman. Sandy-haired 'Wink', by then a sub-lieutenant in the navy, had sprouted into a dashing 6ft doppelganger of his father, Leslie and, like David, longed for operational service (which later arrived when he served as a gunnery officer on HMS *Belfast*, from where the first shot of the D–Day invasion was fired).

Although still inwardly seething about remaining on RAF ground operations, 1941 brought David to an all-time high professionally. He reprised his part of John Royd in a film version of *Quiet Wedding*, a celebration of a simple, middle-class marriage ceremony, without a single reference to the war in it. Starring Margaret Lockwood, it utilised every element of British comedy from the fussy mother, the helpless father, doddery vicar, pompous magistrate and ubiquitous village police officer. The film became a symbol of home and hearth and the values that the British were fighting for; an impressive achievement given filming was compounded by Luftwaffe raids, which left the company bombed out of the studio on five different occasions. 'There were bombs dropping all over the place,' Lockwood remembered. 'We never stopped falling flat on our faces or rushing off to the shelter.'[2] And in the middle of this, Lockwood had to play a light comedy scene with 71-year-old A.E. Matthews. 'He took the whole thing in his stride and used to come wandering back onto the set saying, "Come along, let's get acting again."'[3]

Though artfully managed throughout, director Anthony Asquith – a likable, eloquent, fair-haired chap – who took to wearing a Home Guard uniform and helmet during filming – considered moving production to Gainsborough Studios at Shepherd's Bush, where a vast basement morphed into a provisional bomb shelter. Despite his peculiarities, David thought Asquith worked differently to other directors; using a gentle, emphatic and feminine approach:

> He was the most unassuming of men. He nibbled his lips shyly before speaking with a slight stammer. He curled himself up under the camera as a scene was being shot in an attempt to make himself invisible. He was always eager to apologise for non-existent faults.[4]

David's assessment wasn't uncommon – Asquith must have had a certain *je ne sais quoi* to rise to such a legendary status and was never short of assignments. Much to everyone's relief, *Quiet Wedding* was a moneymaker as well as artistic success. Critics hailed it as 'a tonic for the times,' with the *Monthly Film Bulletin* leading the chorus of praise:

> Advantage has rightly been taken of war-time conditions to gather more actors and actresses generally acknowledged to be great artists than would have been financially possible in peacetime, and to that number has been added a sprinkling of lesser-known players who, from their performance in this film, will soon join the ranks of their more famous colleagues. The photography, sound recording, and decor leave nothing for the fault-finder, and the producer has welded his material into something worthwhile. But over and above material and individual is the inspired direction of Anthony Asquith. No subtlety of glance, movement or dialogue has been missed, no possible highlight omitted.

What's remarkable about *Quiet Wedding* was its appeal overseas. 'Comical' and 'charming' were the two best adjectives Canada's *Globe and Mail* critic Roly Young found to describe it:

> I don't want to build you up to the idea that there is any of the Abbott and Costello type of comedy in this picture and cause you disappointment by giving you a wrong impression. I do think, though, that most of you will come away from *Quiet Wedding* feeling that you've had a swell time and a lot of fun.

Down the coast in New York, where the film was distributed by Universal, critic Nelson B. Bell called it 'box office dynamite'. With so much attention lavished on the production, David – now firmly established as an actor with promise – whisked Clarence, Florence and Paul to the world premiere at the Plaza in London, where they rubbed shoulders with Viscount Scarsdale, the Earl and Countess of Jersey and marquee diva Margaret Lockwood, who turned up in outsized jewellery and well-padded shoulders over which draped a dazzling head-to-toe fur.

Spurred by the successful returns of *Quiet Wedding*, Walter C. Mycroft, the former head of production at Elstree, offered David four days' shooting on the farce *My Wife's Family* with Charles Clapham, John Warwick and Patricia Roc. The main plot spins around a naval officer hoping to spend a relaxing shore leave with his wife, but their plans were disrupted by the arrival of the mother-in-law. To make matters worse, further complications come with the discovery of a baby in the summer house. Although this familiar yarn enjoyed some good-humoured chuckles, the jokes were tired. 'The direction is straightforward but unimaginative, and the photography and settings are satisfactory,' the *Monthly Film Bulletin* noted.

While the film advanced David's acting profile, back at Newchurch all efforts to be accepted for pilot training continued without success. His dismay was dimmed, somewhat, by an offer to feature in Leslie Howard's highly imaginative *Pimpernel Smith*, the story of a modern Scarlet Pimpernel, alongside Frances Sullivan, Mary Morris, Hugh MacDermott and Raymond Huntley. 'It was too good to be true and one of my happiest movie experiences,' David reflected.[5] As the plot developed, it became clear that Howard had created more than a pot-boiler. The film presented an especially rich and succinct slice of anti-Nazi propaganda that – in Howard's own words – was about Christian ethics and the conflict of two philosophies – 'the Nazi philosophy of oppression and the other philosophy for which we are fighting'.

When filming commenced at Denham Studios, David was charged with playing a student in a tale of a rather vague and retiring British professor (Howard) outwitting the Gestapo by whisking anti-Nazis out of pre-war Germany before you could scream 'Heil Hitler'. Structurally, his escapes were planned with the old Pimpernel ingenuity – a scarecrow standing in the middle of the concentration camp – Howard in disguise; a bogus official at Goebbels's Ministry of Propaganda – Howard in disguise. The picture was full of fine scenes, helped by Francis Sullivan, playing Von Graum, a beefy Gestapo official, who kept the plot moving at speed.

'I thought it was a rather good film actually, but I was very interested in Leslie,' David said proudly, describing Howard as being good-humoured and without affection. 'He was a beautiful actor, a very clever actor. He had marvellous secret romantic quality the sort of thing they don't go for so much today. You knew he was really the hero and he would fight to the last and do it in a gentle way.'[6]

David Jr says that, until his dying day, his father idolised Leslie Howard, sometimes almost to Howard's son Wink's irritation:

> No doubt Wink also recalled eccentricities in his father's character that passed non-family by. DT remembered Leslie from his schooldays standing on the touchline watching Wink playing rugby. To act with his idol was the opportunity which he would have imagined in his dreams. That it should have happened such a short time before he was killed made it even more poignant.

Naturally, as with *Quiet Wedding*, the war itself did nothing to improve the film-making process as frequent air raid warnings, ack-ack fire and distant explosions sent everyone scampering for shelter. With a stiff upper lip, Howard told journalist Carey Longmire during filming:

> I wouldn't want to be anywhere now but England. When an air-raid warning sounds, no matter if we are within seconds of finishing a scene, we must stop work immediately. That's an absolute must because they shut the power off and we have no more light. Everybody is supposed to go to the shelters. It's surprising though how little delay there is.[7]

Co-star Mary Morris never forgot dashing to Denham's underground corridors, which had been converted into shelters with accommodation for 800 people. On one occasion, her intimate scene with Howard was interrupted twenty-two times by aircraft noise, a fact that probably pleased the leading man.

'I think it no secret that Leslie Howard was a womaniser,' David confided to his memoirs, noting that Morris was the object of his attentions, 'although it was fairly well known that her affiliations were to members of her own gender. Leslie seemed to regard that as a challenge to be overcome. She, a very sweet woman, rebuffed him gently.'[8]

When released, *Pimpernel Smith* magnificently outperformed Howard's wildest dreams and left David in no doubt his star was rising. The influential *Motion Picture Herald*, the American film industry trade paper, noted the 'cast, from British standards, is a distinguished one', while the *Liverpool Evening Express* thought it would:

> warm your heart and make you glad you are on freedom's side. If you have read your Scarlet Pimpernel you will get the lowdown on this new picture, which has the merits of modernity, topicality, and deuced fine acting of a cleverly written story.[9]

As well as capturing the public imagination, it later transpired that *Pimpernel Smith* had a remarkable real-life impact by inspiring Swedish diplomat Raoul Wallenberg to mount his daring rescue operation in Budapest, which saved 90,000 Jews from Nazi concentration camps. The film was one of the earliest movies to openly discuss German labour, concentration and death camps.

Less well known is that Winston Churchill personally selected the movie, among a small handful of other films, to be shown in the wardroom onboard the battleship HMS *Prince of Wales* during his treacherous journey across the Atlantic for a top-secret conference with American President Franklin D. Roosevelt, a meeting that culminated in the Atlantic Charter, which set out a vision for the post-war world.

When *Pimpernel Smith* slammed into the West End at a gala premiere, David – his dark hair slicked back with Brylcreem – was snapped by the *Tatler* sharing champagne and a private joke with John Mills and Margaret Lockwood. But before the euphoria had dimmed, his heart sank when news arrived that Peter had crashed in Holland while on an RAF mission – an event which hit the Tomlinson family like an electric shock. 'It was a fearful blow,' David remembered. Peter's high-level reconnaissance mission over Hamburg had taken a great deal of pluck as he navigated hostile skies to secure valuable photographs. 'He was flying an unarmed Spitfire in order to reach maximum height but they were prone to engine failure,' David wrote later.[10]

When Clarence heard the news, he stood rigid, paralysed in shock. The scene remained crystal clear in David's memory for the rest of his life. Eventually, the family found some emotional contentment when it transpired Peter was alive and in German captivity, an ordeal borne with extraordinary fortitude.[11]

Although a crushing blow, Peter's fate did not dull David's euphoria with a posting to the Commonwealth Air Training Plan – the main overseas organisation for training pilots. His selection, though belated, was tribute to his intelligence, physique and enthusiasm – lack of courage, it seems, was never a Tomlinson problem.

Clarence and Florence bid a hasty farewell to their son before he left for Liverpool. From there – with a heavy kitbag on his shoulders – David climbed aboard the majestic Royal Mail Ship *Andes* at the Princes Landing Stage at Liverpool to embark on gruelling eight-day voyage to Canada; he would not see his family for another year. 'I left Liverpool via Manchester to go by pleasure cruiser (!) to Canada for flying training,' David later joked. 'It rolled like hell, not being built for the North Atlantic!'[12]

If enemy aircraft, or worse submarines, were spotted – a klaxon honked and bells sounded on deck, and every gun post was manned within minutes:

We had no uniforms yet, so we were in civilian clothes and outnumbered on board by captured Luftwaffe aircrew in uniform, impressively smart and on their way to internment. We were a somewhat desultory bunch in contrast to the Germans, who exercised on one of the caged decks and looked more ready for war than any of us.

Although many vessels on the same route were ruthlessly stalked by U-boats and torpedoed, the *Andes* remained unmolested and survived long enough to become the last ship to escape Singapore before it fell to the Japanese.

After docking at a dispersal base at Moncton, New Brunswick, David curled up for three days on a train clacking across the barren landscape – passing Quebec, Montreal and Ottawa – toward Saskatchewan and the RAF's 34 EFTS (Elementary Flight Training School) at Assiniboia. 'If you had removed the cars from Assiniboia's main street and replaced them with horses,' David observed, 'you could have shot Gary Cooper in a cowboy film.' But on the bright side, 'Assiniboia was also quite un-rationed and the drug store was, therefore, a great attraction.'[13]

The airstrip at 34 EFTS in the Western prairie was protected by a 10ft barbed wire fence, dotted with arc lamps, and a sentry posted at the main gate. Whatever the weather – which was usually an extremely bitter 'dry cold' – pilots mustered for elementary training after breakfast. 'Throttle back, flaps down … and hold on …' became the order of the day, but icy air often meant cadets were strictly limited to just sixty minutes of flying. David's previous aviation experience did not make success inevitable and, much to his horror, he crash-landed a training aircraft in a farmer's field and hurt his shoulder on his very first flight, an accident caused by a faulty fuel line, not pilot error. In fact, rather than blotting his copybook, David was praised for managing to save the plane by ditching in a snowdrift. In addition to practical training, energy was devoted to learning navigation, flight plotting and meteorology. 'I did my elementary flying training in a Fairchild Cornell, a Canadian-built version of the USAAF PT-19 and PT-26 primary trainers, and not unlike a Miles Magister to look at except it had closed cockpits,' he recounted in an article for the RAF Museum at Hendon.

While theory and book work kept the young pilots studying at all hours God sent, Trevor Best, one of the liveliest members of the unit, recalled teaming up with David to stage the occasional dramatic production or concert in the mess hall. 'In Canada, we were all British together, those in training and those being trained,' David noted. 'I didn't see as much of the country as I would have liked at first because I had to work very hard at the theoretical part of the flying training.' [14]

More courses followed at RAF School No. 41 SFTS (Service Flight Training School) in Weyburn, 160km west, where fellow trainee David Ince (later DFC) recalled David's past had caught up with him and he was being urged to leave the RAF and return to acting. 'He could, they said, make a greater contribution to the war effort by playing in patriotic films, and yet he desperately wanted to fly on ops.'

Ince – who later took the British distance record for gliding with a flight from Suffolk to Land's End – remembered arguing that, as an actor, David's service flying would be invaluable. 'And so it proved to be, for his portrayals of aircrew in later wartime releases were quite masterly'.

From his bunk in Weyburn, David wrote long letters home detailing his exploits and received many in return. There was concern for Florence in Folkestone, which had been bombarded from German positions 21 miles away on the French coast, leaving hundreds dead. The town was also subjected to deadly 'tip and run' raids by Luftwaffe pilots. The drumbeat of bad tidings continued when Paul was grounded after his Beaufighter engine failed during take-off at RAF Wellingore – the same runway where John Gillespie Magee Jr, author of the poem 'High Flight', took off on his final mission. Though disappointed, Paul was installed in Peter's old job of assistant to Arthur Harris at Bomber Command – a post that, remarkably, Michael, David's eldest brother, also briefly held. 'He was PA to Harris and as an intelligence officer to bomber squadrons, mainly Lancasters,' David wrote years later. 'This was his greatest regret because he longed to have served as a pilot like his three brothers. He had flying experience before the war but failed the medical because of poor eyesight.'[15] After the war it emerged, however, that Michael often surreptitiously included himself on bomber raids over Germany. 'An amazing thing to do as it was strictly illegal for an intelligence officer to do and he only admitted it to me reluctantly.'[16]

Just before Singapore fell, Michael was posted to the lush forests of Ceylon, which provided the canvas for his acclaimed 1976 book *The Most Dangerous Moment*, a polished and studious study of Japan's military adventures in Burma, Thailand, the Dutch East Indies, Malaya and Singapore. In later years, his wartime reminiscences were frequent, says David's fourth son, Henry. 'Uncle Michael would say when you've seen 18-year-old men climb into airplanes never to come back – and burnt alive – you tend to get hardened.'

Over in Canada, before his passing out parade, David was asked to submit preferences for the unit he would like to join. Understandably, like every other new pilot, he was chomping at the bit to see action over Germany and chose Bomber Command, or, failing that, 'any other operational posting'. In the meantime, he was put in charge of twenty-seven sergeant pilots. 'It would have been reward enough for my six months of diligence to get my "wings" but there was more. We were chosen to do a goodwill tour of Canada' to promote understanding between the two countries with whistle-stop visits to Toronto, Winnipeg and Montreal. 'Canada was beautiful and my time at Assiniboia, Saskatchewan and also in Weyburn was wonderfully enjoyable,' he reflected.[17]

With the goodwill tour over, a stroke of good fortune afforded a spell of leave in New York, where David stayed in a bedsit at Sutton Place, not far from where the UN now sits on Manhattan's East Side. 'New York was delightful and vibrant; it had its own brand of all-American optimism.' David recalled locals were thrilled to meet a genuine RAF pilot walking among them. 'They slapped my back, shook my hand and were just delightful.'[18]

On arrival in the 'Big Apple,' he virtually skipped along East 57th Street past Carnegie Hall and on to the Broadway district to see Ralph Bellamy's performance in *Tomorrow the World*, a topical drama about a fanatical Hitler Youth recruit. After pounding the streets – where nothing seemed remotely warlike – he caught a performance of Helen Hayes starring in *Harriet*, about the life of Harriet Beecher Stowe, the author of *Uncle Tom's Cabin*, at Henry Miller's Theatre. Other draws included the Silver Grill near Times Square (a popular refuge for British actors, offering cheap dinners and dancing) and the newly opened 'army canteens' serving cut-priced meals to servicemen. While the city completely captivated David; it was a chance encounter with a woman on a stairwell that turned his heart upside down.

Her name was Mary Seaton-Lindsay, and she was stunning. David never forgot the first time they met, when, while dashing up the stairs to his apartment, they literally fell over each other – but it was a magical experience. She was the 'most beautiful woman I had ever seen,' he said. Mary, a 34-year-old Seattle-born widow, with raven hair, almond eyes and an intriguing smile, worked at the British Ministry of War Transportation office on Broadway. She was the daughter of L. Seton Lindsay, a vice president of the New York Life Insurance Company, who resided at a plush apartment at 410 Park Avenue.

As it turned out, Mary was quite the high-toned Renaissance woman; she could paint, sculpt and was a popular hostess. With each encounter, the tension between them grew. She spilled her heart out about her marriage to Major Guy Hiddingh in 1934 and how they had lived in England but moved to New York with her two boys – Michael, 8, and John, 6 – when the war broke out. She explained how her world collapsed when Hiddingh was killed in action in Libya while serving with the 14th/20th King's Hussars in November 1941. 'We became completely in love and taken with each other,' David gushed. 'Although she was quiet and gentle, she drew everyone to her, becoming the focus of any gathering.'[19]

The days passed warm and sultry, and a brief engagement was followed by a wedding at the ivy-covered All Angels' Episcopal Church on the Upper West Side on 29 September. Mary's dress was light silk; her hair worn in a mass of curls drawn flowing down the back of her head.

Sheffield-born vicar Ralph Sanders Meadowcroft officiated, with L.C.W. Figg, the British Consul, and Nancy Hill-Lindsay acting as witnesses. A small bridal party was headed by financier and textile industrialist Malcolm G. Chace, a close family friend who arranged a reception at the swanky Passy Restaurant on 63rd Street, where they shared roast beef and several decanters of red wine.

With the Atlantic closed to civilian traffic, there weren't any Tomlinson family members at the ceremony, but David managed to get word to Clarence, Florence and his brothers.

The morning after the night before found the young couple at a tower apartment with storybook views of Central Park. 'It was just too good to be true,' David thought as he read details of their union in the *New York Herald Tribune*: 'Announcement was made of the marriage of Mrs Guy Hiddingh, of 156 East Seventy-Ninth Street, to Mr David Tomlinson, a pilot in the Royal Air Force':

The former Miss Mary Lindsay is the daughter of Mr Seton Lindsay, of New York. Her first husband, Major Guy Hiddingh, British Army, was killed in action. They had two sons. The couple have gone to Canada on their wedding trip.

5

GOODBYE AMERICA

The next day they cut across the city to Grand Central Station to depart for a blissful fortnight of long walks and bracing dips in the wilderness of the upstate countryside. 'I was the luckiest fellow in the world,' David remembered, as they excitedly mapped out a future life together.[1]

However, back in New York, before the honeymoon glow had even faded, the RAF ordered David's immediate recall. 'We were going back to war. Mary was soon to follow me, once we had overcome the red tape ... which was to prove more binding than we anticipated.'[2]

Over the intervening days, his recall prompted a frantic appeal to the United Kingdom Air Liaison Mission for permission to take Mary and the kids in tow – but the shipping of troops and cargo through the U-boat-infested Atlantic took precedence over civilian movements. Despite groping their way through reams of red tape, authorities said gloomily that the family must wait and be patient. Two weeks would pass, however, before David shared a farewell kiss with Mary before sailing into the setting sun aboard the *Aquitania*, leaving his new family in America. If he had known that he had closed the door on another chapter of his life, the parting might have been unbearable.

David's arrival in Britain was as depressing as the atmosphere that hung over it. His excitement at the prospect of piloting bombers or fighters were dashed with a posting for further training at No. 8 EFTS, Woodley, the airfield where Douglas Bader had lost both legs during a flying stunt a decade earlier. David's second son, Jamie, recalled:

I was always told by Dad that when he returned to the UK that he and a group of pilots looked at a notice board to see where they were going to be posted. It was a long list of names that had fighter or bomber next to each name. I never heard him say he had a preference for fighters or bombers. The way he drove cars when we were young would indicate fighters. He drove very fast and very capably. He was astonished to get to his name and see 'instructor'. So, somewhere the powers that be had made that decision. Was it because they wanted him for movies? He was slightly older and that might have had a bearing … An instructor of 25 with 18 and 19 year olds!

After Woodley, David hunkered down at an EFTS at Booker in Buckinghamshire, an airfield overwhelmed by a kaleidoscope of changing faces learning to navigate the perilous bombing routes over Germany. He found himself teaching troops how to use gliders for landings during the badly miscalculated Operation Market Garden in Arnhem. 'We gave them only three hours' solo training,' he later wrote of the men in his charge. 'They could never be sure where they were going to land and no one put a lot of faith in their chances.'[3] In fact, more than 17,000 men were killed, wounded or went missing during Operation Market Garden, one of the darkest campaigns of the war.

Separated from Mary by the width of the Atlantic, David felt the tide of war lapping around his feet throughout the autumn of 1943. Almost daily, he wrote her passionate letters of undying love, to which she responded with similar sentiments. 'Mainly I was concerned with the arrangements for bringing Mary to England when that dreamlike summer in New York turned into a winter nightmare. Tremendous obstacles stood in the way of my wife joining me.'[4]

As the days passed, the 'Tomlinson file' stayed open and grew thicker until eventually, after months of toing and froing, Mary was confident her new life in London was not far off and took the children out of school. It seemed the necessary paperwork was finally being drawn up. Even better, it was even possible the family could be in Britain to celebrate Christmas with the Tomlinsons.

Then, to her surprise and relief, she was issued a passport by the US State Department but stunned to discover the children were refused travel documents and would have to remain in the United States and wait out the war.

It's not known whether she made contact with David at this point, but it's doubtful given her acute agitation.

Just after midday on 1 December, Mary – with the children in tow – checked into the Henry Hudson Hotel on West 57th Street, giving her address to the receptionist as 230 Bay Shore Avenue, the home of her brother, Owen. The family then took the lift to their fifteenth-floor room. The next morning – her eyes haunted and puffed with sleeplessness – Mary ended her life and those of the children – in a manner everyone struggled to explain. Police records detail how, dressed in a nightgown, she rose from bed, unlatched the window and plunged to her death at 8.05 a.m. She did not leave behind her sons, holding John to her body and Michael by the hand. It was all over in seconds. All three struck atop a one-storey extension near 9th Avenue and were killed instantly.

A local tailor named Morris Greenbaum found the bodies after hearing two crashes on the roof of his shop, which shattered the skylight. Attempting to piece together the tragedy, Detective Edward Houlihan of the West 54th Street precinct, pointed out that Mary had been distraught over being unable to join David with the children in England, concluding she actually dropped Michael from the window and then plunged with John in her arms, but there were no eyewitnesses. Given the sensational nature of the murder-suicide, details were splashed on the front page of all the evening newspapers (including the fact the boys were found wearing pyjamas). At the time of her death, Mary had US$30 in her purse and the police found an overnight bag containing toilet articles and children's clothing; no note was found in the room. The bodies were identified by Owen, Mary's brother. Even back then, bad news travelled fast, and a transatlantic *Reuters* cable ensured the suicide – but without the finer details included in the US press – appeared in the 3 December editions of the *Daily Herald* and *Western Mail's* 'To Put It Briefly' section:

> Mrs Mary Tomlinson (34), wife of Flying Officer David Tomlinson, now in England with the R.A.F., plunged to death with her two sons, aged six and eight, from the 15th floor of the Henry Hudson Hotel on West 58th Street, Manhattan, yesterday.

In a kind of small mercy, David was informed of the tragedy by his father before the news broke. Rubbing his eyes, Clarence's voice quavered for a second before he unburdened himself. It was a blood-freezing moment for David, who ran his hand despairingly over his forehead, as his mind whirled frantically. 'The end was as unreal as the romance,' he remembered.[5] While every suicide is a mystery, Mary left many people wondering why such a decent, kind, beautiful, young woman would do such a thing. Ever nearer to despair, Florence suffered what was undoubtedly a nervous breakdown and spent several months convalescing in hospital.

Remarkably, the turbulent events in New York did not prevent David from returning to duties, where his fellow servicemen became a tonic of the first water. Writer James Kettle, the author of *The Life I Lead*, a play about David's life, said that in a society brought up in the outward suppression of emotions, 'David was not someone who wore his damage on his sleeve. It was unbelievably tragic, but he had emotional stamina. He was very much a Churchillian "keep buggering on" type of gentleman.'

David seemed to take heart from a later revelation that Mary had struggled with depression and neurosis throughout her adult life. However, the divulgence that her leap was not her first attempt at suicide left him in shock. Friends later testified how she could alternate from being bright and cheerful, then depressed and morose.

'Somehow,' David noted solemnly, 'that still did not answer my questions. On her grave was placed a statue of a Madonna and child which she had sculpted. I have never been able to bring myself to visit it.'[6]

The subject of Mary remained a closed topic for decades. 'The only way we found out about his first wife was when my brother David had to take his marriage certificate to a post office to make a photocopy, then looked at the document and saw "widower",' Henry says. 'And that's when he realised my dad had been married before.'

Later in life, David offered Henry some profound advice, which he recalls word for word:

I remember my Dad saying to me there will be times in life that something will happen and you cannot imagine that you'll ever recover. He said that humans have this incredible ability to take shock and trauma and it's almost like they analyse it and dissect it and bit by bit you come through it. And I think he was trying to tell me, 'believe me, I know about trauma'.

6

a way to the stars

Nobody knows what the war cost David Tomlinson emotionally, but he had done a lot of living when D-Day arrived on 6 June 1944. As 155,000 troops supported by 13,000 aircraft headed for France, Flight Lieutenant Tomlinson was busily teaching his 'ab initio aspirants to fly' at Booker, while at the same time busily plotting his return to Civvy street. 'I have to state that in all my service, never ever, did I hear a shot fired in anger,' he remarked as the curtain slowly began to fall on the Second World War.[1]

While still in uniform, film work arrived on Terence Rattigan's *Journey Together*, a full-length feature produced by the Royal Air Force cinema unit with David cast as 'Cadet Smith', supporting Jack Watling and Richard Attenborough's portrayals of 'John' and 'David' – two airmen ambitious to become pilots. It was a theme with deep resonance for David. At first glance, the movie appears to be a documentary but swiftly develops into an engaging feature. The highlight for the entire cast was that Edward G. Robinson, famed for his tough, sinister appearance in *Little Caesar*, was signed to play a flying instructor. Robinson was like no actor that David had ever met. Born Emanuel Goldenberg, he was raised in Romania but fled persecution with his family to the United States. After mastering English; he dropped out of legal studies and won a scholarship to the American Academy of Dramatic Art, breaking into legitimate theatre and talking pictures soon after.

'He was a lovely man, brilliant actor – top class – right on the top line,' David thought. 'What an extraordinary actor he was. Tiny, big backside, fat tummy, not handsome – but he had an attraction about him that was riveting.'[2]

Just before shooting commenced, Robinson had become something of a wartime icon after accompanying a gaggle of war correspondents across the Channel to become the first Hollywood star to entertain in France after D-Day, and the old boy adored it. Like with *Pimpernel Smith*, the unfussy style of *Journey Together*, directed by newcomer John Boulting, proved so popular that several movie theatres ran a repeat programme. *The Observer* wrote, '*Journey Together* is very good; observant, touching, reticent, witty, perceptively directed, gaily written, charmingly acted, and altogether right in fact and feeling.'

Flush with funds from *Journey Together*, David was able to start a new life from scratch. He sealed the rental of a handsome Victorian apartment on a lively stretch of Upper Brook Street near Claridge's and secured the services of interior decorator Paula Lawrence. 'Obviously,' he noted, given the austerity situation, some ideas were modified but 'luckily you didn't need coupons for period Regency and Victorian furniture.' Actor Bryan Forbes never forgot staying there in the late 1940s after finding himself without a roof over his head. 'David Tomlinson came generously to the rescue and offered me bed and board in his luxurious flat in Upper Brook Street. He was an impressive character altogether ... drove the last of the classic Jaguars. He took one look at my wardrobe and pronounced judgement. "Don't bother to give those suits away. Burn them!".'[3]

From dawn to dusk, the Brook Street area offered a vibrant nightlife filled with singers, artists, writers and a colourful band of locals. The local art dealer Freddy Mayor, a cigar-puffing bon viveur with a passion for the races, became a close friend. David's reverence for Mayor and his gallery on Cork Street was nearly boundless. During an eventful career, Mayor championed Francis Bacon, Alexander Calder, Paul Klee and Henry Moore. 'He was the most respected and honest art dealer with a marvellous eye,' David said, recounting how Mayor introduced him to impressionism and managed to sell him a landscape by the avant-garde master Pierre Bonnard, which, after some persuasion, he later sold back to Mayor for ten times the price. 'It was a beautiful picture.'

Meanwhile, as the Allies busily drove the Germans back from the beaches of Normandy into Germany, David landed a plum part in another Terence Rattigan patriotic drama *The Way to the Stars*, directed by his old friend

Anthony Asquith. With a stellar cast including Michael Redgrave, John Mills and Trevor Howard, it became one of the finest wartime achievements of the cinema, doing for the RAF what *In Which We Serve* did for the navy and *The Way Ahead* for the army. For the most part, filming took place at Denham, given that the high temple of British production at Pinewood had been requisitioned to store food rations. Although Denham and Pinewood were about 2 miles apart with little but woodland and wheat fields between them, David preferred Denham, which was wilder with a trout river running through it. In contrast, Pinewood boasted a squash court, perfumed garden, indoor swimming pool and a well-stocked bar, which was filled with a tinkling of glasses after lunch.[4]

The Way to the Stars opened with a series of memorably framed shots at an abandoned RAF station. The camera panned over deserted runways and empty barrack rooms highlighting disregarded souvenirs of departed airmen. 'It was different in 1940,' the narrator explained, opening the story of how young fliers survived their ordeal in the Battle of Britain by attitude alone. The plot required David to don RAF flying fatigues – in which he cut something of a stellar figure, standing at 1.8m tall with dark eyes, fair skin and brushed back hair. 'It never ceases to be a profound shock to see oneself on the screen,' he mused. 'But there are times when you think: "That is not bad." But I have seldom found an actor who likes to see himself on the screen. I have never liked myself on the screen at all.'[5] That said, actor Lawrence Douglas remembered David being especially finicky about his appearance in later years:

> In his dressing room he used to have a little glass paraffin jar which lit up with a little blue flame. He kept corks on his dressing table and he would darken them down in the smoke and the flame then dab it onto the back of his head – so that was his technique for looking good on stage!

Accustomed to carrying a gas mask and tin helmet, David was fully prepared when filming was interrupted by 'doodle-bug' flying bombs. Standing on his front lawn, John Mills watched open-mouthed as one spluttered overhead before exploding on the backlot. 'Close call, but, thankfully, nobody was hurt.' Mills, whose name usually meant good box office, thought *The Way to the Stars* Asquith's best film and was equally impressed with the musical score by William Walton and poems by John Pudney. Although Trevor Howard's breakthrough performance was the greater attraction – and on which much of his renown rests – David appeared in several important scenes and provided a humorous turn mimicking American accents.

The Way to the Stars proved a satisfying experience at its first public exhibition before RAF top brass, including Air Chief-Marshal Sir Sholto Douglas, Bomber Harris and the Secretary for Air, Harold Macmillan, who later became Prime Minister. 'No film could be less consciously heroic or more effectively moving,' the cinema critic of the *Birmingham Daily Post* opined. '*The Way to the Stars* is one of the outstanding pictures of the past year.' *The Scotsman* thought the film provided a valuable service for British-American understanding by frankly admitting superficial differences and uncovering common ground in the essentials. 'It demonstrates again Britain's supremacy in the fiction-cum-realist genre. It is, in short, a good film, warm, human, and sincere.'

7

THE rANK SET

When it finally arrived, the war ended with a whimper, not a bang. Remarkably, given all that Britain had suffered under the terror of German bombs, normal life resumed swiftly – the lights were back on in corner shops, the lines were longer at demob offices and the steady hum of construction returned to the background noise. Repairing destroyed houses, factories, shops and churches led to one of the biggest reconstruction efforts the world had known, after the endless Nazi destruction inflicted on London, Birmingham, Portsmouth, Plymouth, Coventry and Hull.

The Tomlinsons, too, were adapting to this new reality. Although the family had never lost hope of seeing Peter again, his return home after four years behind the barbed wire of German prison camps seemed like a miracle. Arthur Harris personally took charge of his recuperation. 'Peter,' Harris said, 'anything of mine is yours – up to half my kingdom.' It transpired that since 1942, the Red Cross had given only fragmentary details of Peter's incarceration, so when it was later revealed that he had served time in four camps the Tomlinsons were left aghast. At one point, he was engaged on digging the so-called 'Douglas Bader tunnel', which German guards discovered, resulting in Bader being moved on to Stalag Luft III and Peter, along with two others, packed off to the notoriously strict Oflag XC at Lübeck. 'Peter was less complimentary about Douglas Bader,' says David Jr. 'Bader made no bones to all prisoners that it was their duty to escape. Bader was himself admired by his captors, though he poked much fun at them. Goering made a trip to the camp just to meet him, but Peter felt that everyone else got punished for Bader's misdeeds.'

Just as the terrible wound of Mary's suicide seemed to be healing, David's agony at seeing Peter proved overwhelming. He spoke of how, after dragging himself on foot through a treacherous landscape on a forced march to Flensburg, advancing Allied troops set him free. 'He was thin as a rake after four years in camps.' After recovering from the effects of malnutrition, Peter had one final adventure in Germany, as military historian Air Commodore Henry Probert discovered:

> Harris had been told soon after the war that Zhukov (Stalin's army chief) would like to meet him, whereupon (Peter) Tomlinson accompanied his master in his personal Dakota to Zhukov's Headquarters, presumably near Potsdam, though Tomlinson could not remember. Tomlinson did recall the warmth of the welcome and the generous liquid hospitality but not what was actually said; since they had not taken their own interpreter they had to rely on Zhukov's. But the rapport between the two men was totally apparent, said Tomlinson.

After demob, Peter bid farewell to London and joined Arthur Harris in Cape Town to help establish the South African Marine Corporation, which operated charter ships to the US, Canada, and Britain. At the same time, Michael continued life in Ceylon, finding work on tea plantations, while Paul took up a post in the United States. Their decision to quit Blighty was hardly surprising given the strong economic medicine administered by the new Labour government, culminated with sweeping nationalisations and the strengthening of the welfare state. Many returning troops noted a decline in living standards – author Tennessee Williams went further, complaining England was about the most 'unpleasant, uncomfortable and expensive place in the world'.

Only David remained in Britain and set about gaining a foothold in the film industry, which, remarkably, was not among the casualties of the new age of austerity and make-do-and-mend mentality. In fact, studio bosses were optimistic that a new phase in British cinema would emerge, for which there were two main reasons. Hollywood scooped up over £17 million from British cinemas annually, a problem discussed endlessly in the House of Commons, where calls to limit American imports and aid the local film industry gained traction. A second, more important issue, resulted in Hollywood directors being accused of having never heard a shot fired in anger, leading to the soft-soaping of storylines. A London critic contended:

> In their hothouse existence they seem to have lost touch with real life. Too many American films involving soldiers, and their complex relationships with the world they left, have been utterly spoiled by false sentimentality, ballyhoo, nationalism and undiluted propaganda.

Naturally, this led the way for more home-grown entertainment to which audiences could relate, thus providing British actors with new opportunities. On returning to civilian life, David was immediately engaged to play an intelligence officer in Launder and Gilliat's production of *I See a Dark Stranger*, the tale of a violently anti-British Irish girl starring Deborah Kerr and Trevor Howard.

Although not among Launder and Gilliat's most skilful works, it was brushed off by critics as having too many loose ends, events without motivation and crises skimmed with a glib phrase. 'It is the cinematic equivalent of Irish blarney which inspires most of the film,' the *Monthly Film Bulletin* noted. It wasn't all bad though; David gave a good, forthright performance as a solid, responsible military man, while Raymond Huntley's characterisation as an enemy master spy was notable, as was David Ward's equally sinister performance as his Nazi cohort.

A warming relationship with the Rank Organisation led to the role of an amiable 'boffin' in Peter Ustinov's first major assignment, *School for Secrets*, again alongside Raymond Huntley, Richard Attenborough, Pamela Matthews, John Laurie and Ernest Jay. Ustinov, who considered life to be much more of a marathon than a sprint, was an army private when commissioned by Rank to polish the script. 'I did all my research in private's uniform at RAF stations,' he remembered, 'often getting rooms which were reserved for visiting air marshals.'

When completed, Ustinov gathered an irresistible collection of English types, including the newly knighted Ralph Richardson – then in the middle stages of his prestigious theatrical career. Publicity material posed the question: 'What happens when five scientists, differing in character, mode of living and outlook, have to live and work together for six long years?' A young Kenneth More, working as an extra for £10 a day, told the story of how Ustinov, 'prowled around in an old grey pullover,' with ruffled hair. 'I thought him a very odd young man.'[1]

By contrast, David thought Ustinov knew his lenses, lights, comedy and tempo: 'He was a marvellously clever man and a wonderful raconteur and a very good actor, very clever.'[2] But even better was working with Richardson – who was quick to offer sympathy about Mary's suicide. 'It was a dream come true,' David commented admiringly.

A natural actor, Sir Ralph played an 'unconfirmed bachelor-scientist' working with a team of 'back-room boys' exploring the mysteries of radar experimentation. In later years, Ustinov often span the yarn of how Richardson turned up on set 'half Falstaff and half himself bellowing his delight at being alive', but because of a wonky denture, 'whistling like a kettle on certain sibilants'. Not that the public noticed; the final print shows Richardson, in true Shakespearian fashion, lingering on vowels and carefully enunciating every syllable. David drove into the project with gusto. The thrust of the piece was to convey the importance of civilian scientists during the war, with the emotional highpoint featuring David, as the youngest boffin, crashing in an RAF bomber while testing an experimental radar system. Pamela Matthews, who beautifully played his heartbroken wife, was informed of the incident by another egghead type, Dr McVitie, portrayed by John Laurie:

McVitie: What is the worst thing that could possibly happen to you?
Pamela: You've come to tell me that my husband is dead.
McVitie: Yes. He crashed in an aeroplane testing something new. He went instantly, couldn't have felt a thing.

Notices were favourable. A glowing review in the *Sketch* noted: 'With the exception of Ralph Richardson, none of the players are top-rank stars. They are there not for the sake of their names on the theatre canopy, but to do a job of acting, and they do it magnificently.'

Like so many former servicemen adjusting to civilian life, David kept a close ear on the Nuremberg trials broadcast daily over the BBC, which climaxed with ten of Hitler's henchmen being executed – a just sentence for the agony inflicted by the Nazis on his brother Peter. Meanwhile, almost every weekend, he trooped off with friends to Lympne airfield for his fix of flying adrenaline, and later that summer showed up in *Fame is the Spur*, a Boulting Brothers feature, alongside Michael Redgrave as a socialist with evaporating values. With several pages of zesty dialogue, David shone as Lord Liskead, an extremely well-mannered but dithering Tory campaigning for a long-held family seat: 'I ask to serve you, as my father served you … as my grandfather served you and errr … as his father served you, for him.'

There was rich historical resonance in the film, which saw Stage 5 at Denham given over to an expensive Yorkshire market square set, alongside a reproduction of 10 Downing Street built for a scene where Suffragettes chain themselves to the railings. The Boultings even sought personal advice from Lady Pethick Lawrence – wife of the Secretary of State for India – one of the original Suffragettes, while John McNair, the General Secretary of the Independent Labour Party, was drafted to play a street orator when Roy Boulting sought a 'real voice' rather than an actor.

David's role as Liskard was secured by his own ability to conduct business affairs without the help of an agent or theatrical representation. Using the well-worn motto: 'Do they want you and can they pay?' he navigated negotiations in 1947 with the Rank Organisation, Britain's leading film producer, which boasted an impressive roster of players, including John Mills, Eric Portman, Will Hay and Margaret Lockwood.

Established in 1933 by J. Arthur Rank, a little-known figure outside flour-milling and Methodist circles, the company became the biggest force in cinema and the owner of Pinewood and Denham Studios, with interests in every branch of the business – including the manufacture of cinema seats. In just six years, Rank's spreading empire took over the Gaumont and Odeon circuits, which, between them, collected a third of box-office receipts. However, in comparison to Hollywood hotshots like Sam Goldwyn, Jack L. Warner and Louis B. Mayer, J. Arthur Rank was positively dull. Producer Michael Balcon remembered Rank as being uncomfortable with small talk, but the most tolerant of men. 'He is a teetotaller, but when entertaining he will drink ginger ale and lime because it looks like a real drink and guests don't find it uncomfortable.'

David's contract was sealed in the anteroom of J. Arthur Rank's office on South Street in Mayfair with David Henley, the man in charge of new talent and the famous glamour 'charm school' where young starlets were coached in the art of walking, laughing and diction. Before the war,

Henley had served as general secretary of Equity and as an agent representing Vivien Leigh and Robert Donat. Within the course of tea and biscuits, David signed on as a contract player. 'Any uncertainties were put to rest, it was a good contract,' David noted with satisfaction. The agreement was reviewable at any time and stipulated he would be paid weekly by Rank, with his salary rising annually; but his services could be sub-let to other studios, if required. To go from irregular paydays to a fixed weekly salary in one jump was, for Clarence, at least, a tangible sign of progress. It also offered, in comparison to the average repertory job, a lot of money.[3]

No sooner had the ink dried on the contract than Rank set about committing David's talents to celluloid. A new, but not entirely pleasant experience came with the endless publicity stunts doled out by PR guru Theo Cowan, a plumy-voiced former Royal Artillery colonel who was once described by *The Stage* as 'the greatest show business publicist of his generation'. All performers at Rank, no matter who they were or what their purpose, were subjected to the publicity department. Known as 'Beau Nosh' given his enormous appetite, Cowan generated the ballyhoo of positive headlines by sending stars out to promote films at dancehalls, cinemas and holiday camps. One of his most discussed triumphs came when he escorted a group of stars, including Jack Hawkins, John Gregson and James Robertson Justice, to the Venice Film Festival, where, with typical skill, he cajoled reporters into publishing a flurry of 'exclusives'. His *pièce de résistance* was accomplished with the help of the Royal Navy's Mediterranean Fleet combined with Diana Dors startling Venetians by waddling into a press conference wearing a tight mink bikini – every major newspaper carried the story.

In many ways, Cowan acted as a mentor and introduced David to his tailor Gieves & Hawkes on Savile Row and shirtmaker Turnbull & Asser in Jermyn Street as he cultivated a sense of style; elegant, smart and casual at the same time.

For a short time, David's interest in flying became the focus for his 'image' as an adventurous type, but with a sense of fun. One such Cowan-inspired stunt involved David taking actress Valerie Hobson – who later married John Profumo, the government minister who became the subject of a sensational sex scandal – for a pleasure flight in a Tiger Moth for the *Picture Post* feature 'Valerie Hobson Learns to Fly'. Such assignments were a rare joy, given tearing through the skies remained David's favourite pastime. 'You are all alone up in the sky, nothing but you and the world,' he beamed after clocking up 1,400 flying hours, an astonishing number.

Work, meantime, hurtled on at a relentless pace with a modest part as Lancelot Handel Crowther, the 'epitome of the snobbish playboy' in the *Master of Bankdam*, a film set amid the tumult of a Victorian mill-owning family. The film was the handiwork of Walter Forde, who directed David, alongside Tom Walls, Dennis Price, Anne Crawford, Jimmy Hanley and Nicholas Parsons. Looking robust at age 64, Walls was best known for presenting and co-starring in the Aldwych farces in the 1920s, but David noted, 'By then, Tom was near the end of his life. I liked him – that was interesting. I had several talks with him.'[4]

Nicholas Parsons, who was himself carving a career in cinema, claimed he was first offered David's role of Crowther but took a smaller part as Edgar Holeyhouse due to other commitments. The film opened to luke-warm reviews. Otis L. Guernsey Jr, writing in the *New York Herald Tribune*, observed while 'not quite as weighty as most films of its type', incidents were 'uncluttered in Walter Forde's direction, and they come along at a pretty good rate'. John Ross in the *Daily Worker* noted that, at a time when all eyes were on the local film industry, the *Master of Bankdam* 'possessed all those characteristics which have marked the best British pictures – sincerity and warmth, plenty of salty, north-country humour, authenticity of back-ground, fine acting and a worthwhile story'.

Away from the studio, David found plenty of time for fun, with the lure of London nightlife with its big-band ballrooms and cocktail bars remaining a magnet for theatrical types. Popular haunts included Pigalle at Piccadilly with its razzle-dazzle dancers and Quaglino's in Jermyn Street for late-night cabaret or Ciro's in Orange Street, a top spot for dining and dancing. His private life never did offer much fodder for gossip, until he became involved with Thora Hallgrimsson, a lively 18-year-old Icelandic student and the eldest daughter of Hallgrimur Fr Hallgrimsson, the chair-man of Shell in Iceland. Exactly where and when they met remains a mystery, but she was 'better-looking than any Scandinavian you ever saw,' David told a reporter, not without some pride.[5] He said Thora spoke English with an 'attractive foreign accent', and could often be seen gad-ding about town with friends from showbiz circles.[6]

As their romance blossomed, David marched into the kooky mermaid *Miranda*, which was being rushed through production to beat the American feature *Mr Peabody and the Mermaid* to the screen. 'I was not originally cast in the film but after three weeks of shooting, the first version was scrapped and re-cast,' David noted, saying he found it amusing that the film became a cult classic.[7] 'I was given the part of Charles the enamoured chauffeur. It was a good part and the first time the critics began referring to my "sadly heroic face".'

For comic freshness, 22-year-old Glynis Johns starred as the mermaid hooking Griffith Jones, a doctor, during a fishing holiday in Cornwall and forcing him to take her back to London. Johns looked ravishing and showed herself to be a willing comedienne. Standing at just 1.63 metres, she had been a professional since the age of 12 and never stopped learning, looking for new ways to make it interesting. The theatre, she said, was the only normality she ever knew:

> My father taught me to listen to what the other actors are saying. I wanted to lead what I thought of as a 'normal' existence, but I soon found I wasn't as normal away from the theatre as in it. Acting … acting is my highest form of intelligence, the time when I use the best part of my brain.

Although she looks petite on screen, David recalled being frightened to death that he would sprain his back lugging her about. Every morning, the crew grappled to squeeze Johns into the mermaid tail after a good deal of pulling, pushing and tugging. 'She had to be carried to parts of the set where shooting was to take place, wearing an ingenious mermaid tail made by the Dunlop Rubber Company, which, by the way, weighed a bloody ton.'

The tail was commissioned by producer Betty E. Box, who was embarking on her own journey towards becoming one of the leading lights in cinema. 'She was very driven, especially at that time,' her late husband Peter Rogers recalled. '*Miranda*, I think, was important in that it gave her a very successful start in comedy production, which, like me, I suppose, she loved.'

In fact, Box always believed a film's basic intention was to entertain. 'I don't think film is a medium for social statement,' she once said. 'Its raison d'être is to entertain. I don't think the mass audience is interested in films of social significance.'[8]

The shooting schedule – at least as far as David was concerned – became increasingly hurried as each day went by. Given the race against time, *Miranda* kept Box busy as her writers pecked furiously at typewriters making revisions, even as shooting was underway. During a visit to the Shepherd's Bush studios, journalist Bill Strutton witnessed a chaotic but high-spirited production where:

> all sorts of queer props were arriving by convoy. Production men ticked off the list such strange items as: One giant starfish, two tons of beach pebbles, three hundred carp, four truckloads of seaweed from Bognor Regis, two crates of fossils, one truck of assorted seashells, and so on.[9]

The film opened on schedule and most of the critics cheered *Miranda's* ingenuity. The *Essex Newsman* gave a big thumbs up for this 'excellent antidote' to the Berlin Crisis, the first undisguised battle of the Cold War. *Cosmopolitan* went further, affording special praise to David's performance as the butler/chauffeur going happily under the spell of *Miranda's* 'open feminine assault', while *Tatler* was impressed with his 'true sense of the serio-ridiculous', Even John Ross, the *Daily Worker's* notoriously nit-picky reviewer, said the only people who could stand up to *Miranda's* charming eccentricities were David, as the butler/chauffeur, and Margaret Rutherford, clumping about as the nurse. 'The others are little more than cardboard figures.' The film became an instant box office draw, leading David on a string of ballyhooed promotional events, including a visit to Ramsgate to hand out prizes at the Miranda Girl bathing competition, where female contestants dressed up as mermaids. 'There's something fishy going on here,' David cracked to reporters during a photocall. 'Fishy … get it?'

Life, by now, was being lived at a fevered pace – with days spent at the studios and evenings with Thora. The pressure of having to turn out four films a year as a contract player was, he said, like being at cinema school. Coming hard on the heels of *Miranda*, David found himself cast as Jimmy Marshall in *Broken Journey*, a low-tech nail-biter about the crash of an American plane in the Alps, notable for its visual splendour. Working from a script prepared by Robert Westerby, David played one of thirteen people marooned on a glacier with little hope of rescue – where a shortage of food and warmth provided the main source of anguish.

Originally titled *Rescue!*, then *We Want to Live!*, the story involved the talents of quick-witted Margot Grahame, Raymond Huntley (still one of the busiest personalities on the British screen), Guy Rolfe, Derek Bond and Andrew Crawford. As it happened, filming turned out to be a testy affair marred by blistering heat untamed by primitive air conditioning. 'The cast had to continue to act wrapped up in woollen scarves and heavy coats buttoned right up to their chins,' director Ken Annakin lamented. One of the most promising British directors at the time, Annakin's life story was as exciting as any script. He had started work in an income tax office but quit to travel to New Zealand, Australia, Hawaii and America. On his return to London, he briefly worked in publicity, joined the RAF, then entered the film industry when he left the service.

Annakin's commitment to his film – and adherance to a strict shooting schedule – was outstripped only by his remarkable perseverance to finish under budget. His exhaustive account makes plain *Broken Journey* was no easy task. It took forty-five days to shoot with twelve actors squeezed into a blazing hot mock fuselage of a Dakota aircraft, where Francis Sullivan – who David had starred with in *Pimpernel Smith* – suffered a mild heart attack. 'But that may have been induced by his bloody fidgety performance,' a studio wit joked at the time.

Behind the scenes, the production was notable for a young Dirk Bogarde – a latter 'the idol of the Odeons' – unsuccessfully testing for the part of passenger being transported in an iron lung. But even without Dirk, the plot was redeemed by a sterling cast and reviews were generally good. 'The characters are strongly drawn, and the atmosphere created by the despairing group is tense and moving,' one critic noted. 'The beautiful snow scenes were actually filmed on location 10,000 feet up on a Mont Blanc glacier.'

As life at Rank settled down into something resembling normality, David's career was perking along nicely. He received acclaim for his supporting work in *My Brother's Keeper*, the tale of two escaped prisoners making a break for freedom, starring Jack Warner as a hardened criminal and a youthful-looking George Cole as an impressionable teenager awaiting trial for a crime he hadn't committed. David provided comic relief as Ronnie Waring, a newly wedded crime reporter chasing the story with his fiancée, played by Yvonne Owen. Nine days of filming in Buckinghamshire, Oxfordshire and Ashbridge Park kept the cast bouncing from foot to foot in the cold but the entire production was completed under budget and on time. *My Brother's Keeper* was released to generally positive reviews, with the *Sunday Post* describing 'another of these escape-cum-hunt films, but it has a lot of good points. Naturally, a great deal

depends on Jack Warner, and he certainly takes the honours for acting.'
For its part, the *Church Times* observed, 'David Tomlinson adequately supplies the inevitable reporter to cover the story. The title implies a moral;
is it the responsibility of society for criminals or of the old lag for the
raw youth?'

Back in London, David continued to squire Thora around town, romanc-
ing her vigorously with candlelit dinners and as much attention as he could
lavish. It seems the relationship progressed along these lines until the onset
of spring when, for some reason – possibly David's intention of proposing –
her father attempted to tear knots in the affair. Although details are sketchy,
he successfully demanded she return home, a development that prompted
David to fly out to Iceland in hot pursuit. 'We're not engaged … yet,' he
told the *Daily Herald*, as he fast-talked his way to the airport. But not all was
well in Reykjavik, as Hallgrimsson family opposition ensured there was no
magazine-story happy ending.[10]

Bizarrely, this final split resulted in a strange twist of fate when, some
years later, Thora married George Lincoln Rockwell, the self-styled
leader and founder of the American Nazi Party. Rockwell later described
meeting Thora while serving with the US military in Iceland, a year or so
after her split with David. She was 'tall, blonde, aristocratic in looks and
bearing, she had the face of an angel and the figure of a French model,'
he boasted. With all the fanfare of a state event, the pair tied the knot
at the Reykjavik National Cathedral, where Thora's uncle, the Bishop
of Iceland, officiated. God only knows what David would have made of
their honeymoon, which, in true fascist style, was spent near the ruins of
Hitler's villa at the Obersalzberg. 'We stayed near the home of the Fuhrer
in the fairy-tale setting of the Bavarian Alps,' Rockwell proudly noted
in his 1961 autobiography, *This Time the World*, written six years before
his assassination.

On touching down in Britain, David's private life hardly held still.
Women were still in his thrall. No sooner had he airily brushed off his
Icelandic fancy, than he embarked on a brief, yet exciting affair with actress
Dinah Sheridan, whose most famous work in *Genevieve* was yet to come.
For several months, she remained one of David's more assiduous escorts
and was constantly spoken of as a potential wife. She was a good pal,
good listener and fellow actor with whom he could identify easily. 'There
was certainly a time when Dinah was close to the Tomlinsons generally,'

says David Jr. 'My grandmother liked her and my youngest uncle, Paul, was good friends with her and her third husband Jack Merivale.' The romance was brief though, and a few years later Sheridan married John Davis, Rank's waspish top executive, who trapped her into a loveless union that left her in a state of emotional flux. At Rank, Davis ruled supreme, running the company, as *The Times* once observed, as a personal fiefdom: 'He was loathed as much as he was admired and was notorious for the way he bossed around the Rank Organisation's contract film stars and starlets and for the cold-blooded manner in which he axed executives.'

David Jr says:

On any showing Davis sounds to have been a very cruel husband to Dinah and their divorce in the early 1960s attracted quite a lot of publicity and certainly lined the lawyers' pockets,' 'In fact the case went to the Court of Appeal, where one of the judges was Lord Justice (Rodger) Winn, brother of Godfrey, who had actually tried a case at the Old Bailey in the early 1960s where DT had served on the jury: contemporary memories record that he was pretty appalled at [Sir John Davis'] treatment of Dinah.

The brief Tomlinson–Sheridan affair is interesting, given that director Ken Annakin later suggested that David was elevated to John Davis's 'hate list' – and although he doesn't say why, it was more than likely due to his jealousy given David's previous association with Dinah.

As memories of the war began to fade, British actors felt reasonably certain that the future was bright when the Chancellor shook up the film industry by slapping heavy duties on imported American films.

In response, after grappling with huge losses, Hollywood scrambled to keep pace by enforcing an embargo on their movies entering the UK, which, until the levy, had filled about 80 per cent of cinema programmes. Initially, the Cinematograph Exhibitors' Association asserted the absence of American films would cause no great hardship. 'On the contrary,' they said, 'much may be gained. For example, greater opportunities for the British film industry, and a nation-wide screening of good Continental films.'[11] With the sudden elimination of their main competition, Rank led a resuscitation effort by rolling out an investment programme in November 1947 to make forty-seven original scripted films over the following year.

But the sudden burst of patriotic bustle did not last long as the government revoked duties on Hollywood flicks, unleashing a flood of American releases, including *Miracle on 34th Street*, *Welcome Stranger* and *Till the Clouds Roll By*. As a result, Rank pulled the plug on dozens of projects as the company entered a tailspin and began haemorrhaging money. And as if that wasn't bad enough, audiences made a beeline to rival cinema chains showing new Hollywood imports, along with the backlog that had gathered dust during the embargo. On cue, John Davis stepped forward to slash actor salaries and cut back on sumptuous productions. Davis almost ceased to develop film projects, loath to spend any money on movies that weren't guaranteed to offer a healthy return. From here on in, making modest films with a sure return became de-facto company policy; a move his opponents asserted was cruel, short-sighted and worsened the plight of the film business. 'He was a statistician, an accountant and he observed films as people observed sausages,' film executive Sir Denis Forman caustically observed, adding that originality, risk taking and breakthroughs were absolutely unknown to Davis.

Remarkably, David took all of the disruption in stride when he embarked on seven weeks of shooting of *Easy Money*, a movie that was cheaply made and looked it. The film – a quartet of separate dramas – tells the story of people finding fortune on the football pools. He performed in the first episode as part of the Stafford family presided over by the larger than life Jack Warner as the father, alongside Petula Clark, Yvonne Owen and Marjorie Fielding. More work with Warner followed, playing the awkward Harold Hinchley, a smallish role, but a great character part in *Here Come the Huggetts* and *Vote for Huggett*, both pictures that further established the young director Ken Annakin and teenage songstress Petula Clark.

Although hated by highbrow critics, the Huggetts provided wildly popular feel-good entertainment. The films were an ode to small-town camaraderie headed by humble factory worker Joe Huggett, played by the unflappable Warner, and his wife Ethel, portrayed beautifully by Kathleen Harrison, an actress David greatly admired. 'I loved that woman,' he wrote years later. 'She was not a cockney, but actually from Lancashire!'[12] Much of the humour derived from a host of Rank players including Susan Shaw, Flora Robson, Jimmy Hanley and that vivacious teenager, Diana Dors.

Although generally uneventful, the Huggetts films gave an endearing portrait of working-class life: sometimes up, sometimes down, but always chirpily moving steadily along.

Despite never camouflaging his dislike of public relations tours, David joined a micro-budgeted promotion for the Huggetts by shuttling up to Derby to speak at the Odeon Cinema and the Hippodrome, where he was presented with a Crown Derby ashtray. From there, it was up north to Lancashire for a reception of mill workers in Bolton, followed by a personal appearance at local cinemas. Occasionally on such jaunts, there were invitations to speak with young thespians. During a trip to the Midlands, he made fun of his own public image and professed to be unsure why he had become an actor. 'I think that actors in the theatre invariably are as good on the films,' he told members of the Nottingham Playhouse, 'but I think that a film actor who has no such experience will very often come to grief in the theatre.'[13] He was thoughtful for a moment before going on: 'I am not saying there is no difference in the technique, though many will disagree with me. The important thing you need is talent, and the acid test is whether you are credible in the character you are playing.'[14] Such promotional tours were useful and, although David hadn't matched the exposure of many other Rank players, he was beginning to be noticed. Regional newspaper critics started to single him out for special praise, with the entertainments editor of the *Sunderland Echo* keeping an especially keen eye out:

For some considerable time, I have been perplexed by the erratic appearances of a young English film actor whose vacancy of expression has never been bettered and whose hesitancy of manner has caused a great deal of amusement. Was he that rare creature, a young man with a unique dramatic sense of comedy or was he the proverbial cinema flash in the pan? I feel without any hesitation that David Tomlinson has undeniably won himself a place amongst the finest of our younger actors. I have rarely been so amused by an individual performance as I was by his chauffeur in *Miranda* and it was not the slapstick comedy which produces laughs and is then forgotten, it was the quiet comedy style which we remember with joy because every time it is recalled it gives us fresh amusement.

Whilst in the Midlands, David took the opportunity to make a tour of his past. He went to Northampton and visited the Royal Theatre, where he'd debuted in front of an audience a decade earlier, then stopped off in Manchester where wartime memories of *Quiet Wedding* and Sarah Churchill came flooding back. As his star continued to rise, David returned to Denham to rub shoulders with the glamorous Jean Kent, Albert Lieven and Rona Anderson in *Sleeping Car to Trieste*, a weaker echo of *Rome Express* about a ragtag group of passengers on the Orient Express caught up in a cat and mouse game for possession of a stolen diary. It was the one movie that German actor Albert Lieven made under contract to Rank, and a highpoint in a career of ups, downs and long periods of inactivity. His Germanic looks and accent epitomised the film noir genre that was popular at the end of the 1940s, and utilised by producers looking for an occasional departure from the standard fare. As such, director John Paddy Carstairs followed the sure-fire touch-and-go formula of random clues, sinister spies, shots in the dark, thick-accented foreigners and, for comic measure, David performing his shtick as a dunderhead called Tom Bishop, a whisky-guzzling wise cracker.

However, not all was well on *Sleeping Car to Trieste*. On top of script disagreements were the clashes of temperament. 'I was playing a super-spy of some kind,' Jean Kent complained through gritted teeth. 'But who was I spying for?' As well as confusing plots, the actress expressed impatience with Carstairs: 'You never knew where you were with him.' In a single day, Kent managed to alienate the producer, director and the entire makeup department. As if that wasn't bad enough, her costume — a woollen dress with cape, and a mink coat over an evening frock — left her furious. 'I had silly clothes. I wanted to be very French in plain black and a little beret but I had to wear these silly "new look" clothes.'[15]

While the director did whatever it took to keep Kent out of diva mode, shooting was kinder to Rona Anderson (later Mrs Gordon Jackson), who had never appeared before a motion picture camera. 'I did enjoy doing it. It was a film full of nice little cameo performances. Paddy Carstairs had a good way of relaxing you and I think he had a very good way with actors generally,' she remembered, adding that Carstairs had spotted her in *Bunty Pulls the Strings* with the Glasgow Citizens' Theatre and hired her on the spot.[16]

The brightest moments, according to the *Yorkshire Post*, came from 'charming newcomer Rona Anderson and David Tomlinson is rapidly becoming one of our best light comedians, in his element here as a hearty dog whose efforts to get his pals out of trouble generally land them further in'. A characteristically sour review came from the *Manchester Guardian*, which accused Carstairs of gathering a 'number of pleasant, polite actors and actresses, putting them on a train and hoping that something exciting would come of it. He was wrong. It doesn't.' The *Observer* also failed to appreciate the plot: 'Its corridors chock-a-block with profusely sweating spies and suave policemen, *Sleeping Car to Trieste* puffs wearily along a well-worn track in the wake of *Rome Express* and *Stamboul Train*.'

After *Sleeping Car to Trieste*, David joined the run-of-the-mill romp *Love in Waiting*, which awarded the young star his first top billing. Although a relatively small role for a lead, he breezed through scenes as a befuddled restaurant manager battling the attentions of waitresses while fending off black-market racketeers. Seen today, the film is diverting and probably led to the *Daily Mirror* selecting him among six 'little-known players' who, it prophesised, would be leading film stars the following year. 'None of these six may be of that giant stature,' the paper explained, 'but they are getting their chance. There are four girls and two men. The men are older because they gave good years to war.' Unsurprisingly, Diana Dors, the provocative blonde 17-year-old, led the ladies. As for David, then 28 years old, the *Mirror* reported: 'He doesn't want to be a star. Now he is moving up and looks like being the outstanding romantic lead comedy actor of 1949.'

This kind of prediction was music to the ears of Theo Cowan, who occasionally came out from behind his desk to accompany David to the BBC Television Service, the era's newest novelty. He appeared more than once on *Play the Game*, an early quiz show made on the cheap, where a decorative scoreboard provided the only ornamentation on the otherwise bare-bones set. Back then, TV was exclusively operated by the BBC, which maintained a studio at the Alexandra Palace, directly underneath its sole transmitter covering the London area, meaning Florence and friends over in Folkestone were unable to tune in. But, if there was any remaining doubt about his newly attained status, it was eliminated with a 'star spot' on *Picture Parade*, a popular BBC movie programme. 'From among the actors and actresses that have sprung into greater prominence this year,' noted the *Radio Times*, 'David Tomlinson tells listeners something about his career.'

Back at Pinewood, David buckled down to work on *Warning to Wantons*, a piece of fluff about a sweet-faced young woman escaping her strict convent school and entering high society. The film spins the yarn of David standing for Parliament as a Conservative and failing, then standing again as a Socialist, only to be beaten by his butler who gets in as a Tory. David despised the production, which was notable for pioneering the 'Independent Frame' method. This was bankrolled by Rank to cut production costs using a back projection and background plates to minimise set construction expenses, eliminating location shoots and cutting down the number of days artistes worked. Dubbed 'prefabricated films' by journalists, the scheme saw entire movies produced under a single roof. In short, the idea was to shoot background footage only: the ocean breaking over rocks, the front at Blackpool, a crowded Piccadilly Circus, or Newmarket during the races. The footage was then projected from behind on to a transparent cinema screen set up on the studio floor. In the case of *Warning for Wantons*, an important sequence where Anne Vernon 'apparently walks' through the vast cloisters of a Portuguese convent and pauses in close-up by one of the innumerable pillars was used to demonstrate the process. Only one solitary pillar was built in the studio, the rest were shot on location six months earlier. When completed, *Warning to Wantons*, which would have cost £200,000 and taken six months to produce, was made in half the time and at half the cost. In reality, though, the technique, during its brief lifetime (it was abandoned in 1950), cheapened the look of many good films and was detested by crews, unions and artists alike.

Although wildly pilloried, the *Church Times* noted that if *Warning to Wantons* were cut to half its length it might prove good entertainment. 'As it is, only one thing makes it worth seeing – David Tomlinson continues to be David Tomlinson.' The *West London Observer* thought the bright spot in the film was a 'good performance from David Tomlinson, who has been playing small parts long enough to deserve a break'.

That break arrived when Betty E. Box engaged him for role in *Marry Me* alongside Derek Bond, Susan Shaw and Carol Marsh. However, the initial euphoria soon turned sour when news arrived that it would be the very last picture to be filmed at Shepherd's Bush after Rank abruptly eliminated the jobs of hundreds of employees during production – highlighting another symptom of the industry's failing health. The drama at Shepherd's Bush marked a turning point in British cinema that had seen Rank bleed over £6 million since 1945 and rack up an overdraft of £16.2 million, in part because of its huge size and the many companies under its umbrella.

The first intimation of serious trouble arrived just before shooting commenced when Rank dismissed 600 technicians at Denham and Pinewood, with threats to further pare back its staff of 34,000. 'No amount of optimism can now disguise the fact that Britain's film industry is on the downward slope and is no longer in a position to haul itself up again by its own bootstraps,' the *Manchester Evening News* asserted in a front-page commentary about the unglamorous economics of cinema. 'There is little doubt that a large number of British films are first class, but there are two principal snags: there are not enough of them and not enough box-office receipts going to the producers,' a reference to high entertainment taxes and 'middlemen' scooping up large slices from cinema receipts.

Having experienced Rank's dysfunction at first hand, David put out feelers about a return to the stage, 'should the right offer present itself' – his underlying rationale was obvious. Meanwhile, over at Pinewood, work began on *Helter Skelter*, a nutty yarn about a group of friends trying to cure a young woman of hiccups, featuring Carol Marsh and Mervyn Johns. Director Ralph Thomas considered it a typical 'Sydney Box Friday night picture':

> You were quite likely to finish shooting on Friday, plan to go into the cutting rooms on Monday to look over your stuff and get your cut ready, then go for a drink, and you'd be given another script and be told, 'The sets are standing and you start on Monday – this is the cast!' It wasn't necessarily good and we didn't get a lot of money, but it was regular.[17]

One such 'Friday night picture' came courtesy of Paddy Carstairs, who had directed *Sleeping Car to Trieste* and invited David to feature in *The Chiltern Hundreds*, in which he played Viscount Pym, a man who changed fiancées as quickly as his political views. Lana Morris and Helen Backlin gave marvellously funny performances as the rivals for his affections, whilst A.E. Matthews recreated his stage role as Lord Later, and Cecil Parker took the part of Beecham, the butler. 'A charming little bit of nonsense,' David noted approvingly[18], as did Bosley Crowther in *The New*

York Times, who thought the charms of the picture came with several stinging sideswipes at the plutocrats, peers and parasites, and kids class distinctions and traditions in a pleasantly good-natured way. He praised A.E. Matthews' 'addle-brained old codger,' and David's portrayal as a thoroughly light-weight young lord.

Not long after, during a publicity jag for *Helter Skelter*, Ian Dalrymple invited David to burrow into the role of an RAF prisoner-of-war alongside Leo Genn and Anthony Steel in Eric Williams' *The Wooden Horse*, a celebration of courage and endeavour. Wartime Germany had become a popular setting for motion picture plots and this feature took David to Luneburg Heath, near Hamburg, for the tale of an audacious PoW escape using a vaulting horse to conceal a secret tunnel. Produced by Dalrymple's Wessex Films, one of the autonomous companies grouped within Rank's Independent Producers initiative, *The Wooden Horse* is still talked about today as it sparked a new cycle of post-war epics, including *The Colditz Story*, *Albert R.N.* and *The Great Escape*. Dalrymple and director Jack Lee purchased the film rights after out-bidding John Mills, who was also keen to make it. 'I expect John would have been very good in it also,' Lee remarked, 'probably better than Leo Genn, who was very stolid as an actor.'[19] That said, David, Genn and Steel – making his screen breakthrough – played out their roles with a gentle insistence on their superiority, while the Germans were shown as baffled and irritable rather than menacing. Though everybody in the film got to perform a turn, Genn was the undeniable star, as a stern-faced, determined British officer, whilst David turned in a subtle but commanding performance as Phil Rowe, a member of the escaping group.[20] After a series of personality clashes and technical glitches, filming dissolved into a disorganised free-for-all.

'It was the most chaotic picture I ever worked on … everybody thought it would be a disaster, but it was a great success,' David laughed, insisting the older it got, the better it held up. 'It proved naysayers wrong.'[21]

Behind the scenes tensions worsened when Steel turned up the temperature after discovering Genn was 'getting paid thousands', while he was earning just £15 a week. 'It made me pretty mad,' he confessed later. Naturally, this caused some chilly exchanges, as other cast members retreated discreetly beyond earshot. However, under the circumstances, there was some opportunity for mischief. Bryan Forbes, who played Paul in the movie, remembered Genn transporting his Rolls-Royce to Germany for the duration of the shoot 'and somebody thoughtfully filled the petrol tank with sugar, which rendered it something less than the best car in the world'.

Despite the obvious challenges, Jack Lee, a man known for his genial charm, managed to hold the production together, even though he botched the shooting schedules. Lee described Steel as a physical type, 'a young chap who could do certain things, though he didn't have much acting to do in this'. Occasionally to relieve the boredom, David joined the crew for nights out in Hamburg courtesy of the British Occupation Forces, which operated a whirl of bars, clubs and a plush officers' mess adorned with Oriental rugs, mahogany bar and dark-wood panelling at the former Atlantic Hotel, once Hitler's preferred retreat in the city. At the weekends, the candle-lit restaurant was usually given over to couples to revive the foxtrot and waltz, but was invaded by the entire Rank crew throughout the shoot.

All told, the picture racked up a budget of over £400,000, a respectable sum for 1949, and ran, after cutting, to 9,228ft of celluloid. The Hungarian-born studio boss Alexander Korda – who lived in Claridge's in great style – edited the film personally. 'The story,' David recounted, 'is that he sat in the theatre and we had about seventeen times as much film as we needed and he edited on his own because he was a very clever man.'[22] By then, Korda was at the height of his cinematic career and basking in critical acclaim for his production of The Third Man. 'The marvellous thing about Korda,' David mused, 'was he could do it all, couldn't he? He could probably act the parts as well. He wasn't just a promoter like so many of them are – he was responsible.'[23]

When released, the Sketch lauded The Wooden Horse as ringing 'true as a gold sovereign, and is wonderfully exciting'. 'There are no women to clutter up this man's business,' wrote The Daily Herald's Paul Holt, applauding the adventures in this womanless land. 'It is becoming a truism about British films that never are they so good as when they get a group of men in trouble. In his Church Times column, critic C.B. Mortlock, who often wrote as if drunk on movies, noted the film was 'filling the Rialto and the Ritz from morning to night':

There is a pleasant air of understatement running through a great deal of it, and the authentic atmosphere is skilfully established at the outset by showing the Germans as credible human beings — indeed, occasionally likeable. The film is predominantly objective and has much of the quality of a documentary. This is a film in which individual actors are subordinate to the history they enact; but there are good performances by Mr Leo Genn, Mr David Tomlinson, Mr Antony Steel and Mr Jacques Brunius.

As the year 1949 rolled to an end, David continued to toy with the idea of a return to the theatre. But before making any firm commitment, there was one last unforgettable blast with the Rank Organisation prior to his contract being permitted to expire without renewal. Although discouraged by this turn of events, his part in *So Long at the Fair* is memorable given it was the last Gainsborough costume melodrama. Dirk Bogarde, the young actor who had been rejected for a bit part in *Broken Journey* a few years earlier (the producer reckoned his head was too small and his neck too thin for films), landed the starring role after featuring in *Boys in Brown* and *The Blue Lamp*, which critics adored. Jean Simmons portrayed a spirited and headstrong young English tourist whose innately sophisticated brother Johnny Barton, played by David, disappeared from their hotel during the great 1889 Exhibition. The incident opened a baffling mystery where everyone she questioned denied ever knowing the young man. It was standard Gainsborough fair, complete with Victorian costumes and a dramatic final scene that saw David bandaged and bedridden having caught the bubonic plague.

Directed by Terence Fisher, a furious smoker, later known for his Hammer Films, the project was Betty E. Box's first at Pinewood after Shepherd's Bush was shuttered. She remembered a smooth production, except when location filming in Paris clogged up traffic on the Place de la Concorde during a horse-drawn carriage scene. To be in Paris in 1949, she said, was to be in the middle of an atmosphere of luxurious creativity. Having gained freedom from Nazi occupation just four years earlier, the city was palpably buzzing in the same way London would a decade later. David was equally enthusiastic – there was nothing about Paris he didn't like – the people, the food, and the entire French attitude towards life. The location shoot also afforded the dewy-eyed Bogarde, a former army intelligence officer, an opportunity to wander down memory lane. He had landed in France on D-Day, served throughout the European campaign and was with the advance guard of the Free French Brigade that liberated Paris in 1945. During breaks in filming, he roamed unaccompanied on a bicycle to revisit a suburb village cafe at Jouey, where, as the first Allied soldier to be welcomed, he was given a meal of strawberries and wine. David enjoyed the company of Bogarde and Simmons, who – after endless boozy nights – was often left fighting off a hangover. 'She was prone to use the odd one-syllable expletive, which DT probably considered unladylike,' says David Jr. 'But even more unforgivably she stubbed out her cigarette on the Jag's dashboard: I don't think he easily forgave her for that!'

Although a comparatively small role, *Variety* ventured to say David scored 'another personal hit,' in a part 'remembered by everybody who saw the movie'. An era ended with *So Long at the Fair*. From then on, David began operating independently, unbound by any studio contract. 'It's a strange kind of job,' David told *Film Parade*. 'It's a job that has its ups and downs. If there is a slump at present in British studios it will pass, and is only, perhaps, the result of over ambitious productions which have made British films known and admired around the world.'[24]

This new reality as a free agent didn't worry him – he could personally choose roles from the scores of scripts that ended up on his desk. Furthermore, he refused to engage a theatrical agent, preferring instead to steer his own course. This decision though – as his son Henry later divulged – occasionally manifested itself in an idiosyncratic way:

> We would suddenly hear the phone ring and he would scarper, and I would stand at the sitting-room door listening, thinking 'why is dad talking with an American accent?' And then it became clear that he had this imaginary manager/agent called Harry Gunnell, who my father said was much more interested in him than anybody else, so he was very good at doing the deals.[25]

According to David's widow, Audrey, Gunnell was inspired by the song 'Have I told you About My Harry':

> I never liked it. I never liked to advertise it in the hope that very few people knew about it. I didn't like anyone knowing about that – imitating an American on the phone. Sometimes he used to get Alice (the house-keeper) to make phone calls for him.[26] The less I knew about Harry, the better.[27]

For a short period after leaving Rank, David was represented by Laurie Evans at 'London International', a man regarded as one of the best agents in the business despite his phobia of talking to clients (except Laurence Olivier and Ralph Richardson). Then, after falling out with Evans, he approached up-and-coming talent agent Michael Whitehall, who, according to his memoirs *Shark Infested Waters*, heard DT could be difficult, 'especially when it came to money' – a fact which by then was common knowledge. Over lunch, there was a little exchange in which David asked Whitehall to personally handle his affairs, but *without* the standard 10 per cent commission.

'What's in it for me?' Whitehall enquired.

'The prestige of having me on your books,' David radiantly declared.

On one occasion, David told Cordell Marks from the *TV Times* that he was incompetent at administration and hopeless at mathematics. 'I remembered,' wrote Marks, 'that the agent for the incompetent Tomlinson is that successful agent David Tomlinson.' David brushed off the observation with a wild grin, 'sincerely and truly, even though it isn't true. What else could I do but act? If you are completely hopeless in this life, go on the stage.'[28]

David didn't enjoy being interviewed, and developed an irreverent, topical style, but knew exactly how to deliver massive overstatements that get the laughs. 'He probably wasn't as blinkered as he claims, he just enjoys sending himself up,' Cordell sighed.[29] Indeed, David delighted in pulling the legs of listeners, especially journalists.

8

THE 1950S

As rejuvenation fever swept Britain – buoyed by a strong economy and high employment – David was living a life he loved and thoughts of putting down roots and purchasing a retreat away from urban pressures filled his mind, sparking a search for a dream property. After five years in central London, the idea of living genteelly in a small village had become more appealing.

Meanwhile, in an effort to freshen up his theatre skills, 1950 saw him return to the stage for two weeks of appearances in Noel Coward's well-worn play *Design for Living* and a further fortnight in the less well-attended *The Petrified Forest* alongside André van Gyseghem at the Nottingham Playhouse, where facilities were best described as 'primitive' given there was no foyer, no bar, and lack of wing space meant actors could walk straight from the stage on to the street. In fact, on one occasion, David had to cry for help off-stage and banged on the street door. During the brief run – for which payment was generously waived – David was asked by a young drama student if his return to the theatre would be useful. 'Definitely, it is invigorating to have the opportunity of playing in the theatre as often as possible,' he exclaimed. 'Away from the theatre for a very long time it was very easy to stagnate.' Indeed, the reason for this sojourn in Nottingham was based on planning an eventual return to the West End stage, but even though 'ideas were in the offing' nothing was set in ink.

On the closing night of *The Petrified Forest*, MGM producer Hayes Goetz phoned out of the blue to offer David a part alongside Walter Pidgeon in

Calling Bulldog Drummond, an action flick about quick-fisted Scotland Yard officers on the hunt for a gang of thieves. Snappy dialogue, a sprawling cast of characters, action sequences, and narrow escapes didn't stop the *Monthly Film Bulletin* dealing it a hard hand, citing a cliché-ridden script suffering from the miscasting of leading players. 'As a schoolboy adventure story, however – for which it was no doubt intended – it is not bad at all.' David Jr said although his father's part was critical to the plot, he was happy to see the film filter down the studio drain. 'Dad was not overly complimentary about the brace of Bulldog Drummond films, though I think he quite admired Walter Pidgeon.'

As luck would have it, while *Bulldog Drummond* was still being edited, David's dream theatre role arrived with an invite to star at the Lyric alongside Robert Morley in a saucy French farce about a wife sharing her favours while wrecked on a desert island. In a period when censors worked much harder than they do today, *The Little Hut*, bankrolled by impresario Hugh 'Binkie' Beaumont's company, H.M. Tennent Ltd – known in theatrical circles as 'the Firm' – managed, somehow, to receive the official stamp of approval. 'It was far less risqué than the French version,' David explained, 'but then sex hadn't caught up with us in those days.' The three-act work had been penned by French playwright Andre Roussin for the Paris stage, with the English version adapted by Nancy Mitford, the one-time toast of the chic London social set.

In comparison to grubby film studios, David adored working at the Lyric Theatre on Shaftesbury Avenue, near Piccadilly Circus, which boasted a colourful past in the city's theatre history. It had opened in 1888 to present comic operas, and later diversified into light comedies, musicals and dramas featuring the cream of British talent. After the war, it became home to *The Winslow Boy* and *Edward, My Son* (which also featured Robert Morley).

As rehearsals began, Morley raved about Oliver Messel's exotic jungle setting with its amusing tricks and gimmicks – including palm trees and coconut cocktails. Back then, the softly spoken Morley, an actor with considerable girth, was considered one of the most versatile entertainers in the country, having ascended to the top rungs of stardom in *Treasure Island* and dozens of West End productions, some his own. Nine years older than David, Morley was largely shaped by the same forces. He was born to a major in the British Army, while his mother was raised in South Africa. And, like David, he despised school and once famously snapped on being invited to give a speech at his old school: 'The only reason for me visiting Wellington would be to raze it to the ground.' It later transpired that Morley had also spent some of his childhood in Folkestone, although their paths never crossed as children, but Morley had similar memories of the resort's genteel make-up.

'Though not at all religious, in later life Morley and DT also remembered Canon Elliott, the vicar of Folkestone's Holy Trinity Church from 1918 to 1929,' explains David Jr. 'Morley thought Elliott, who became a frequent broadcaster on the radio, a consummate showman. Attending an Elliott service at Holy Trinity was not unlike a trip to the theatre.'

Like so many other actors, Morley varied his stage career with film appearances and, prior to *The Little Hut*, had featured alongside Humphrey Bogart in *The African Queen*. 'Bogie and his wife Lauren Bacall came to see the play,' David Jr, recalls. 'Dad rather liked Bogart, who wasn't a bit like his tough guy film characters. He was well educated and also very courageous, having stood up to Senator Joe McCarthy and not been blacklisted.'

Although an enjoyable experience, David and Morley were often at loggerheads with the 'somewhat intense' *Little Hut* director Peter Brook – 'not in our view, an attractive man – and, good heavens, wasn't he young,' David caustically remarked.¹ Brisk and argumentative, 25-year-old Brook had arrived fresh from directing Laurence Olivier in *The Beggar's Opera* and John Gielgud in *Venice Preserved*. The young director confided to Mitford in whispered tones that, 'Morley's great fault was that he was so disloyal,' prompting Mitford to retort, 'I am disloyal myself.' Morley later cracked that Brook kindly took their coats when they arrived for rehearsals and helped them back on at the end of the day. 'We had to give him something to do after all,' he joked acidly.

For the entire run, the performances were as comical as the material, even though Morley tired easily and unsettled Brook with his 'bloody infuriating' ad-libbing, winking and habit of casting long-sided looks at the audience. Unsurprisingly, he became a legendary sort of figure upon whom old anecdotes were often re-hung, and rightly so, says actor Griff Rhys Jones:

> David once told me that Robert Morley used to turn up for the show and, if he had enjoyed a particularly good, but tiring, afternoon at the races, he would come on stage, sit down on his chair and not get out of

that chair just because he felt like it. Normally, he'd be acting by pouring himself a drink or looking out of the window, or whatever, but if it had been a long day, he would literally sit through the entire play without getting up from the chair![2]

Rhys Jones said that, although the yarn got better with each retelling, it was funny enough without embroidery. 'But what did make the story even funnier was David's ability to beautifully mimic Morley when telling it. He was mischievously brilliant and did a perfect high squeaky voice.'[3]

Morley's son Sheridan remembered how on another occasion, 'David came off the stage saying, "It's disgraceful, there is a couple in the stalls actually copulating during our big scene!" "Well, my darling," said Pa, "if we can't entertain them, they must do it for themselves."'

Despite his comedic quirks, Mitford considered Morley 'excessively cautious and pessimistic,' but was heartened when at the opening night party, the portly star arrived to flashing camera bulbs and a crush of back-slappers. '*The Little Hut*,' he told her, as he sat back and lit a cigar, 'would be a smash hit and run for two years.'

According to friends, this 'clairvoyant ability' to spot a thumping success had become legendary, as Sheridan Morley recounted:

> I used to stand at night in the wings at the half watching him watching the audience as they arrived. He would stand on that darkened stage, peering through the side curtain checking how many of them had come, and doing a rapid percentage to work out his takings for the night. For somebody that was totally non-mathematical, he could calculate 10 per cent of a full house at the Lyric or the odds at 13 to 5 on a winner at Windsor faster than any calculator.[4]

In the case of *The Little Hut*, Morley's financial prediction was, literally, right on the money. 'I was a little taken aback when I heard that,' David once said. 'I'm greedy you see. I'll do films in the day and theatre at night, back then, I had sufficient stamina'

While David never considered himself a perfectionist, he was extraordinarily disciplined and often hid himself in his snug little Chelsea apartment – known in the family as his 'purdah' – and not emerge until he had learned his lines. David's fourth son, Henry, says when he had a script to study, he became totally involved. 'Dad didn't like us around when he worked. He didn't like the idea of people treating a film set or a stage like it was somewhere to play; he took it all very seriously.'[5]

Binkie Beaumont's office milked *The Little Hut*'s press potential for all it was worth. If you happen to look at period newspaper theatre listings, adverts for *The Little Hut* hail it as 'The New Smash Hit!' and the 'West End Sensation of 1950–51'. Beaumont kept a well-leafed cutting in his wallet of David Lewin's first-night notice from the *Daily Express*, to be whipped out at any given opportunity. In it, Lewin applauded Morley, who 'gambols cheerfully through it all accepting his wife's lover, and chasing butterflies with the same prosperous air of self-satisfaction'. He added: 'David Tomlinson, as the lover, effectively torments himself and at one point even succeeds in saying his lines and balancing a pole on his chin at the same time.'

The huge noticeboard outside the Lyric was plastered with rave reviews. 'David Tomlinson does admirably by the humourlessly passionate lover,' wrote *Tatler*'s Anthony Cookman, while, 'Miss Joan Tetzel, playing the amoral heroine, persuades us that there is only one note in the part; and on that note of gay readiness for anything that may come she strums most effectively.' The *Sunday People's* more cautious review reported the play started as a comedy, 'goes on as a romp, and finishes as a pantomime', while J.C. Trewin in the *Observer* thought Robert Morley was like a bland seal:

> David Tomlinson has some of Naughton Wayne's ruefulness and Joan Tetzel as a blithe young woman with a past is like a constantly fizzing drink. Peter Brook, the director, juggles the whole thing delightfully against an exuberant Messel setting in tropical Technicolor.

David remembered Tetzel as being bright and charming, though quite eccentric. He often told a story how at dinner with him and Robert, she asked the waiter a succession of questions, confirming if they cooked fish in a particular way. 'Each time, regardless of how it could be done, he said "Yes Madam". She persisted and eventually got the "No" she had probably been seeking from the off, whereupon she said: "What a shame because that is the only way I really like it to be done." Robert leaned forward almost threateningly. "Don't you ever do that again!"'

Along with their irreverent wit and a mutual hatred of school, David and Morley also shared a passion as serious students of the turf and the pair began spending an increasing amount of free time together. Morley seemed to admire David's military background; he reckoned his co-star 'was never one to cheerfully take orders from officialdom' and could not suffer fools gladly.[6] The unique thing about David, Morley declared, was you always knew precisely where you stood with him because he always said exactly what he thought. David's widow Audrey thought the two chalk and cheese in many ways:

> Actually, they were both enormous personalities; otherwise they had very little in common. Robert must have been his closest friend – or he liked to think Robert was his closest friend. He was certainly influenced by him. Robert thought David was a wonderful actor and David thought Robert was a wonderful actor.[7]

According to David Jr, Morley had an unorthodox, individualistic approach to life; he was 'a self-styled communist but also an extraordinarily generous man'.

Looking back on their friendship, David recalled how 'Robert was a terrible practical joker. He was a leg puller – in an evil sort of way!'[8] An example of that evil humour made it into the pages of Morley's memoir, *A Reluctant Autobiography*:

> David, like myself, used to make films during the run of *The Little Hut*, and he came back one evening from the studio full of a bloody row he had had with the director, which ended in his walking off the set. The next morning I sent identical wires to them both, apologizing, but signed with the other's name. They approached each other with tears in their eyes and started their speeches of thanks simultaneously … then suddenly realising that each was clutching a telegram the other had not sent, they stopped abruptly and I like to think the row started up afresh.

As a consequence, David was quick to respond and invited Morley 'on a jaunt to France' in a chartered plane in way of a small treat. Enthusiasm waned when the conveyance – a vintage biplane, sitting under an ugly sky – began spluttering into life. When the nose lurched during the flight, Morley's horror – magnified by the open cockpit, whirring piston engine and foggy goggles – increased. 'Do you know the trick if she stalls?' he bellowed across the fuselage. 'There is no trick if she stalls,' David shouted back, 'the engine just stops and that's it.'

Sheridan Morley reckoned, 'Although you could insult David's acting, the one thing you could never insult was his flying,' as he told the tale of another incident:[9]

He used to fly my father over to Le Touquet for a little light gambling. During one flight, on a rather foggy Sunday morning as they passed through the clouds, Pa asked David if he knew where they were. 'No,' said David indignantly. 'I'm a pilot. I was in the war, I had radar. I had instruments and all of that. We are exactly over Paris.' Exactly at that moment the fog cleared and Pa saw Lancing College sparkling in the sunshine. 'They've moved that,' he said and David didn't speak to him for the rest of the weekend.[10]

David Jr says that tale caused a ripple because Morley wasn't the most reliable historian:

When his autobiography *A Responsible Gentleman* was serialised in 1966, DT was pretty furious with his description of the flight to Le Touquet. Within a week DT was making a surprise appearance to confront Robert in Leeds on *The Eamonn Andrews Show* in front of a bewildered array of Yorkshire and England sports personalities, including cricketers Freddie Trueman and Brian Close, and Leeds United's Jackie Charlton, but the anger was skin deep. DT confirmed to me that, 'They've moved Lancing College' was the only part of the story that was true.

After spending a few blustery days sloshing through the muddy back roads of Buckinghamshire, David's quest for a countryside retreat ended with a tip-off about an old property. Sitting near the ancient Roman road that runs from the north by Buckingham to London in the village of Mursley, he inspected Brook Cottage, a crumbling, derelict house.

A tiny dot on the map, Mursley sits near Bletchley Park, the former top-secret home of the Second World War code-breakers, with the village itself centring on a 12ft granite cross erected to the memory of locals lost during the First World War, which reads:

To the glory of God and in proud and undying memory of those men of this parish who fought and died for their country during the Great War. 1914–1918

David vividly remembered handing the cheque to buy the cottage to Adrian Beecham, the previous owner and son of the famed conductor Thomas Beecham, knowing it was money well spent. Before the ink on the title deed had dried, he was seated at a meeting of Winslow Rural District Council applying to execute alterations to make Brook Cottage habitable. Council notes show the surveyor, Mr C. Piper, observed that the property had been neglected, but from the 'public health point of view his proposals were perfectly satisfactory. The Council agreed to Mr Tomlinson's application.'

There wasn't the smallest detail that escaped David's attention. While a team of builders drifted through the door, he personally supervised the installation of genuine Regency and Georgian interiors and exteriors salvaged from across the South-East. Friends and family praised his clever, dexterous job of orchestrating renovations (a mission, he later said, was never finished). When the dust had cleared to reveal the 'new Brook cottage', Alix Palmer, a journalist at the heart of Fleet Street during its golden years, drove over to inspect the property:

It's peppered with pictures and comfortable with antiques. Embroidered among the trees is a tiny summer house, now an office, complete with telephone, more pictures and a photograph of a bespectacled podgy, little boy in knee-length pants – Tomlinson in his first school play. Standing out like a Victorian bustle on one of their 12 acres of land is the empty house of the late Sir Thomas Beecham.

Mursley's newest resident was quick to cultivate the friendship of an assortment of local characters, having no desire to be left alone, as Henry recalled:

My Dad grew to love that village. You see, he was in many ways incredibly normal. He lived an authentic life. Over time, his mates included the local cabinet maker, who he was fascinated by. He knew a lovely seamstress who lived in a worker's cottage at Woburn and the gardeners – those were really his mates, obviously, he had other actors as friends.

Jamie agrees:

He loved the real country people. The Cleavers who farmed at the bottom of Church Lane, near Brook Cottage, were lovely to Mum and Dad from the off. They brought them eggs and never charged. Dad was fascinated by the few expert trimmers who could still lay a hedge properly and would stop to talk to them.

While hammering away at his new property, an offer arrived for a small role playing a lab assistant in *The Magic Box*, a drama on the life of William Friese-Greene, designer of the earliest cine camera. The film was made as a contribution to the much-hyped Festival of Britain at Battersea Park, where nearly 40 acres of land was being dug up to be turned into 'festival gardens', a river restaurant, and a special picnic centre – costing the taxpayer £770,000.

Once finalised, producers marshalled practically every star in Britain into the film led by Robert Donat as Friese-Greene, with David playing his assistant. Maria Schell gave a tender and attractive portrait of his first wife, but the prize cameo came from Laurence Olivier playing an 'alarmed policeman'.[11]

Meanwhile, as David continued to enjoy the embrace of the critics for the continued success of *The Little Hut*, he signed with producer George Brown to play Puffin in *Hotel Sahara*, another sure sign he was on a roll. He remained cordial with director Ken Annakin after their collaboration in *Miranda*, *Vote for Huggett* and *Broken Journey*. Annakin – by now known to the cast as 'panicking Annakin' for his jittery temper – regarded *Hotel Sahara* as the type of comedy he had always wanted to make. 'It is a subject that lends itself to slight fantasy,' he told the *Daily Express* before the film went on to the floor of Pinewood on 1 January 1951.

George Brown dreamt up the plot over a pint of beer in a Fleet Street pub. It told the story of hotel in the Western Desert occupied, in turn, by soldiers from Britain, Germany and Italy. At first, a few of Brown's friends had their doubts – who would want to see a picture about the Desert Campaign now? But Brown kept pushing and secured a distribution guarantee, backing from the private sector and the National Film Finance Corporation and, most importantly, the services of Yvonne De Carlo from Hollywood. No expense was spared on Ralph Brinton's Arabian sets – including a fake sunken oasis and plasterboard hotel – which were wheeled on to the floor as sets from the *Browning Version* were knocked down. The hotel was modelled on one Ken Annakin had visited at Kuintandinia, near Rio de Janeiro.

For genre authenticity, Brown scrambled to locate four Arabian dromedaries (camels) by personally scouring circuses and zoos across Britain. Peter Ustinov, then at the height of his talents, delighted as the hotel's Middle Eastern proprietor alongside the exotic-looking Yvonne De Carlo – who, years later, found fame in *The Munsters* – playing his beleaguered fiancée.

At 6ft 1in with lush golden hair, Albert Lieven looked every bit a 'thoroughbred Nazi' as Leutnant Gunther von Heilicke, the leader of the Afrika Korps platoon, while the British contingent consisted of David, Roland Culver, Sydney Tafler and Bill Owen, the actor later known as Compo in *Last of the Summer Wine*. The film had everything it needed: a great cast, emotion, surprise, gags, great visuals and nothing superfluous to bog it down. Patrick Kirwan had written some excellent dialogue for David, whose screen character displayed an amorous fixation with De Carlo, which initially seemed promising, but was thwarted as opposing forces occupied the hotel.

However, the laughs lasted only a few days, according to Annakin, whose gossipy memoir recounted displays of temperament:

> David had the worst habits of London theatre actors. He loved to upset and upstage other actors' performances, even to the extent of stopping in the middle of a perfect take and saying he'd seen a mouse running across the set! Roland Culver was an old stage pro who could cope with all these tricks but Albert Lieven was a serious-minded actor trained in the Rhineheart School in Vienna and could not understand this often stupid and sometimes vicious byplay.

Annakin's claim is refuted by Audrey Tomlinson, who brushed it off as being the product of a fertile imagination:

This is absolutely untrue, of course. David never upstaged anyone. He helped actors; he helped them to get laughs. He wanted the best for everyone and hated actors who had not learnt their lines. He hated too many takes. He was always professional and ready to work. He knew the costs of film-making.[12]

Annakin also reserved caustic words for Yvonne De Carlo, claiming she 'needed at least seven full rehearsals. So, I discovered I had to take her aside and rehearse almost continuously during the time the cameramen took to light the scene.'

However, David and De Carlo held each other's talents in great esteem. So much so that she even named her rat-sized Chihuahua 'Puffin' after his character. There were frequent cast drinks at her suite in the Dorchester too, where she was billeted for the duration of filming. Peter Ustinov and the Canadian actress Suzanne Cloutier were regular visitors and became engaged a few months later. *Hotel Saraha* won fan approval nationwide, critics affording special praise for De Carlo as being 'more alluring than ever in her exotic veil dance'.

After a crowd-pleasing premiere, the road led back to the Lyric, where *The Little Hut* continued to boom. It was at this time that Roger Moore, a darkly handsome young actor, began cutting his teeth as understudy to David for the princely sum of £10 a week. The job, Moore later recalled, needed patience enough to sit through interminable repetitions of rehearsals and performances, memorising everything he saw. On one occasion, when David fell ill with a severe bout of flu, he was called to deputise, and Morley helped him through the under-rehearsed stage movements. 'He signalled with his eyes,' Moore laughed. 'It was marvellous of him and I have never forgotten it.'

David howled at the memory of how on another occasion, the future James Bond star provided more drama off-stage than on. Temptation, it seems, had seen him embark on a steamy affair with the 'diminutive, saucy, lusty-voiced' singer Dorothy Squires, who was a dozen years his senior. All hell broke loose when his wife, actress and ice skater Doorn Van Steyn, discovered the tryst and burst through the stage door at the Lyric to launch an all-out physical assault on her philandering husband. Gripped with horror, Moore sought urgent refuge in the backstage dressing rooms, from where David guided his young charge – by then with blood flowing from his hands – out of a side door with the parting advice that he should stay with his wife: 'He didn't listen, silly boy. He married Squires.'

Years later, Moore rendered a slightly different version of events:

> I emerged one evening from the stage door at the Lyric and there was Doorn and she bit me! She bit me on the hand. Mind you, my hand may have been raised to strike her but I let out one almighty yell, which added to the mirth of David Tomlinson and Robert Morley, who seemed to react to this backstage domestic comedy with schoolboy glee.

'Another visitor to London who came to *The Little Hut* was Errol Flynn,' says David Jr. 'According to Roger Moore, Flynn was looking to pick a bone with David, who had sent him a telegram making out that it came from a mutual girlfriend':

> Flynn caught up with her and she reasoned that DT (David) must be the culprit. Flynn had little difficulty getting past the stage doorkeeper and cut a menacing figure in the wings. However, it must have been smoothed over and they spent some time together. [13]

Exhausted by scandal, Flynn was a regular backstage visitor and had developed a thirst that would, in varying degrees, help define him for the rest of his life. 'He was a lonely man and we often dined together,' David recalled, noting his natural grace and charm. 'I never saw him remotely drunk … I liked him enormously and he was always marvellous company.' [14]

As well as driving the Hollywood icon to meet Florence at Wellfield Road in Folkestone (she lay speechless at his surprise appearance), David revealed that Laurence Olivier had once confided to him that Flynn, if he had wanted, could have been 'the greatest classical star in the theatre'.

'My father found him good company and strangely vulnerable,' says David Jr. 'Flynn had never really got over his prosecution in 1943 for sex allegations involving two 17-year-olds. Though the jury had cleared him, it had undermined his self-confidence and he was drinking himself into an early grave.'

By the end of 1951, David had conquered the West End, appeared in the Royal Command Performance at London's great vaudeville house, and cornered the film market for befuddled characters, despite an emerging threat from a recently demobbed actor named Ian Carmichael, who was cutting his teeth in a revival of *Wild Violets* – the two became firm friends. There is a story from an anonymous, but well-placed source, that it became a running joke that David often rejected roles where he smelt the whiff of failure, only to later discover that the producers then turned to Carmichael. 'It is absolutely true. If David had the good sense to turn down a part, they would send it to Ian.' On one occasion, David drove over to see Ian in a play in Oxford. 'Don't, don't tell me David! You're going to say that you turned this play down!' Carmichael exclaimed.

As *The Little Hut* continued to attract punters, David joined the cast of Alan Melville's *Castle in the Air*, a low-rent comedy about an impoverished aristocrat desperate to sell his crumbling castle before it is requisitioned by the Coal Board. Edward Dryhurst, an old pal from the *Master of Bankdam* produced, while Henry Cass, fresh from working with an unknown actress called Audrey Hepburn in *Young Wives' Tale*, directed. Filmed entirely at Elstree, David poured it on thick as the self-effacing Earl of Locharne alongside Margaret Rutherford playing a dotty historian at her pithiest when musing on marriage. 'I want a man in my life,' she barks, 'but not in my house.'

Their scenes together are the backbone of the film, and highlight the happy off-screen relationship David shared with Rutherford, who was also close to Robert Morley, an actor she thought 'gifted with wit as very few people are'. Born in Balham in 1892, Rutherford had taught piano, dramatic art and elocution before leaping into the world of theatre. At the age of 33, she embarked on the grind of repertory before finding fame playing characters with a touch of eccentricity. (She always detested the label that she was eccentric but admitted hanging hot water bottles under her tweed cape for winter travels and asking engine drivers to fill them up.)

The film is studded with comic moments from Barbara Kelly, then the wife of actor Bernard Braden, as a buxom American lady eager to buy the castle, while Brian Oulton excels as a thin-skinned manager from the National Coal Board. Patricia Dainton, who had made her name in *The Dancing Years*, drifts in as a beautiful family ghost. Even though the screenplay has flashes of topical wit and great visuals, the notorious critic Milton Shulman described it a mausoleum of weary and abused gags:

Apparently working on the theory that no one has ever gone broke by under-estimating the intelligence of British cinema audiences, *Castle in the Air* proudly points up each faded witticism with everything but a fanfare of trumpets. It hails and signposts each expected laugh as obviously as if it had been a subtitled joke.[15]

David came to dislike Shulman and by the 1970s was prone to say he needed 'a colonic irrigation to rid himself of all those undigested plays' he'd had to review. In actuality, *Castle in the Air* was hardly the mess Shulman claimed. Howard Thompson in the *New York Times* noted David 'who heretofore has been guilty of a post-Eton starchiness, uncorks a sly resonance as the amiable, badgered hero'.[16]

Meanwhile, love – of a sort – was in the air when David announced his engagement to 25-year-old Jill Clifford-Turner, a perfectly coiffed beauty with a café au lait complexion and smouldering libido. Clifford had worked in the Venezuelan Embassy and a builder's office before her first screen chance came playing the 'second air hostess' in *No Highway* alongside Glynis Johns, James Stewart and Jack Hawkins. By then, she had lopped off the 'Turner', and as a close friend and companion of Jean Simmons – part of movie aristocracy – she managed to win a handful of tiny roles playing vixens, wounded victims and good-time girls. With a glass in hand, Florence toasted the couple, while the union was also championed by Robert Morley.

Soon after, the future Mrs Tomlinsons charm's were shown off to the press in the near-empty Lyric Theatre bar, where David, dressed in a conservative black suit, and Jill, sporting a white turtleneck sweater, posed for the *Daily Herald*. 'The tall young comedy actor with the attractively crumpled face has announced his engagement to dark-haired Jill Clifford, who was discovered by Jean Simmons.' Details of the bridal dress, 'ballet length and in the season's most popular shade of cream caramel' were revealed in the tabloids, while readers learned Jill adored 'sophisticated black' and her 'practical trousseau' included several evening, cocktail and afternoon gowns.

There was a snag, however. The relationship soon dimmed when film director John Paddy Carstairs, known for his wandering eye, invited Audrey Freeman, a 21-year-old actress, to lunch. 'He was very correct and brought his wife too,' Audrey noted approvingly. Carstairs had spotted the young dancer in Emile Littler's *Zip Goes a Million* at the Palace Theatre, shortly before she moved to *Love from Judy* at the Savile Theatre on Shaftesbury Avenue, the big musical hit of the moment. 'Audrey is vivacious, versatile and hopes to become another Ginger Rogers,' reported the *Sketch*, describing her as a girl with a bright future.

During that fateful lunch, Carstairs revealed he was directing David Tomlinson at Pinewood in *Made in Heaven*, a comical romp by William Douglas-Home, the eldest brother of future Prime Minister Alec Douglas-Home. Jamie, David's second son, recalled:

Mum said she loved David Tomlinson. Mrs Carstairs said she didn't! Mum much later found out that Dad did not rate Carstairs and had almost certainly not hidden his feelings … and had probably, at some point, been rude to Mrs Carstairs!

So, Carstairs invited Mum to watch some of the filming at Pinewood and she was introduced to Dad and Petula Clark. In the afternoon, Mum was leaving Pinewood to go to work at the Palace Theatre that evening. Dad asked where she was going and probably as much out of spite to Carstairs – given her very good looks – offered her a lift. Mum went back to London in Dad's chauffeur-driven car. The relationship began quickly but Mum had to put up with Dad being somewhat undecided.

'Jill was a very pretty girl, very photogenic,' says Audrey, 'but she was lazy. She really wasn't prepared to work in any sort of way, even though she knew a lot of people in the film business.'[17]

Furthermore, Audrey hadn't anticipated that her attraction to David would be so magnetic:

He definitely had charisma. I was truly smitten. He had immense sex appeal. He didn't know it and laughed when women were suggestive. I thought it terribly funny. I think comedians do have it you know – people that make you laugh are very attractive. He was unusual wasn't he? I do see why he was appealing – he was different, so different. He wasn't like anybody else, I don't think.[18]

Despite his somewhat compromised position as Clifford's suitor, David Jr recalled hearing about an outrageous get-together:

> Mum told me a story about our Dad later taking her and Jill to lunch. It was perfectly civilised, but pretty clear that he was comparing them and he came down firmly in favour of Audrey. There was nearly eleven years between David and Jill, but even more between him and Audrey.

Jamie adds:

> Thankfully for us, Dad said something about not being prepared to sleep with a bag of bones (Clifford). So thanks to Carstairs and the bag of bones and Mum's incredible good looks and being so special, we boys are here today! Clifford had a flat near Sloane Square and was known as 'Silly Jilly'.

Six weeks after they were engaged, in spite of his mother's woeful warnings, David disengaged Jill 'by mutual consent' and his friendship with Audrey blossomed into romance. Years later, to Audrey's astonishment, Florence – in a prim tone of voice – blurted out that she could never forgive David for not marrying a woman of *her* choice. 'Not very nice to say that to your daughter-in-law,' laughs Jamie. 'But that's what she said.'

As for Jill, she resumed her gadabout life, jetting off with actresses Isobel Dean, Zona Marshall and Lana Morris to Buenos Aires to attend the Argentine Film Festival. Years later, Jill was named as the 'other woman' in the high-profile divorce case of Major Charles William Anthony Graham Greenish, an officer serving in the Life Guards. Meanwhile, actress June Whitfield, who shared a dressing room with Audrey during the run of *Love from Judy*, observed the romance between David and Audrey develop. 'There was great excitement,' she remembered, especially when David 'called in from time to time'. [19]

As all this was all going on, on-camera life continued with *Made in Heaven* – a schmaltzy story, ironically, about a couple who enter a contest to prove their relationship is blissfully happy, but for whom things go wrong when they employ a sexy Hungarian maid (played by Sonja Ziemann, a strikingly beautiful German stage and screen actress).

David took star billing as Basil Topham, alongside a prim and proper Petula Clark, who, at just 19 years old, glowed with a bun of blonde hair and marbling brown eyes. 'I was old enough to be her father,' David joked when cast as her husband. 'Petula was a charming, sweet, clever, talented girl.'[20] A minor flap ensued when, in a sudden move, filming was switched to Technicolor. 'We were told the picture was to be in colour, meaning all my dresses had to be made again,' Clark explained.[21] As this was happening, John Paddy Carstairs was in Hamburg testing Sonja Ziemann, who won the part 'because she had 'the gay sparkle' the maid's role required.

Production was cheered by David's old pal A.E. Matthews playing Grandpa Hillary Topham, a finicky pensioner armed with an ear trumpet and bad temper. 'I remember nobody ever knew how old he was,' David laughed. 'I think he must have been around 150, even then!'[22] Known as the 'Grand Old Man' of theatre, Matthews, or 'Matty', had enjoyed his greatest success on stage, but was remembered as an irrepressible raconteur and deliverer of devastating put-downs. He once told the yarn of smelling smoke at his cottage, only to discover a fire in the sitting room. 'It demolished my armchair, except for the castors,' he explained. 'I rang up the insurance people – they were delighted to hear from me because they thought I was dead.'[23] On another occasion, during a show business lunch, the guest speaker droned on 'with not the glimmering of an end in sight'. With a heightened air of dramatic tension, Matthews stood up. 'Pardon me,' he groaned as he veered into self-parody, 'but I'm very old and will probably die soon, so would you mind getting a move on?'[24]

However, even the presence of Matty couldn't stop *Made in Heaven* opening to a crush of indifferent reviews. The critic of the *Picturegoer* was rather tactful, but his message was clear:

It is just cream-puff comedy – and the least bit stale cream puff at that. The main thing though is not to analyse but to swallow it whole and enjoy it. It's well-tried and not always especially true British comedy, but the film has a happy air about it.

In a departure from the norm, the year ended with David rehearsing at the BBC's Broadcasting House, a strange locale for him. It seems the BBC had made periodic attempts to entice him to feature in radio dramas, but to no avail. However, with some arm twisting from Jack Warner, David joined the cast of *Trial and Error*, the primetime Christmas Eve offering on the BBC Home Service, alongside Michael Shepley and Thora Hird. The story took listeners from a toy shop squabble over being short-changed to a light-hearted finish in court, and according to the BBC, had 'all the ingredients of a good Christmas comedy'.

9

THAT FUNNY CHAP

Just after *Made in Heaven* went on general release, David joined the ranks of illustrious castaways on radio's *Desert Island Discs*, a programme in which a well-known person is asked, 'If you were to be cast away alone on a desert island, which eight gramophone records would you choose to have with you.' At 11 a.m. on 5 February 1953, David was escorted into studio 3E at the BBC's Broadcasting House to record his only appearance as the 174th guest. Roy Plomley, the venerable but dogged host, preferred highly scripted joshing about as opposed to the semi-serious interview format used nowadays. Although no recording survives, a script does – complete with annotations pencilled in by David and Plomley – showing a seemingly leisurely exercise filled with warmth and wit. David explained how he could thoroughly enjoy symphony concerts, a good old-fashioned knees-up and a bit of boogie-woogie. He picked out classical compositions from Puccini and Verdi – as well as works by Gertrude Lawrence, Joan Hammond and 'Whispering' Jack Smith. His favourite record was 'La Chanson des Rues' sung by Jean Sablon. 'He's the only singer of light songs that I've never tired of hearing. And this particular record is to me quite perfect. It's simple, gentle, and restful, and I find it utterly charming'.

Asked about his opera selection, David admitted:

I think I'd have enjoyed them more, if I'd known a bit more about what was going on. Like all serious music, opera obviously needs to be studied a little to be fully appreciated, and I'm afraid I haven't studied very hard.

I'd like to be able to pretend that my taste in music is rather more high-brow than it actually is, and I've been sorely tempted to include some rather classy stuff in this programme for fear of being thought a complete clod. But the truth is that I like my gramophone light and simple and above all restful, so more often than not I put on something very, very light and on the whole, very, very low brow.

However, he explained, there was nothing low brow about his request for a recording of Sir Laurence Olivier speaking the third act soliloquy from Hamlet:

I'm a devoted fan of two great actors – and it's been a bit of a job to decide whose voice I'm going to take. The two actors are Gielgud and Olivier. The question was decided when I found that Gielgud hasn't recorded anything from what I found to be his most exciting role, and incidentally one of the most memorable evenings I ever spent in the theatre. I refer to *The Lady's Not for Burning*, whereas Laurence Olivier has recorded some speeches from his masterly film *Hamlet*.

To conclude, Eddie Gray's juggling equipment was chosen as his luxury. 'To prevent getting bored, I could come back from my island and shake them at the Palladium.'[1]

In the months that followed, David picked up supplementary income as a member of Radio Luxembourg's Saturday evening game show *What's My Line*, alongside panellists Barbara Kelly, Lady Barnett and the deep rich voice of David Nixon, who all attempted to guess the occupation of a guest. Long before the advent of commercial TV, Luxembourg had become the most important radio outlet for advertising and the emerging genre of soap operas, game shows and pop music. By chance, BBC producer Leslie Bridgmont – on the make for new talent – heard the show and secured David for a starring role in a new 'tailor-made' BBC Home Service situation comedy *A Life of Bliss*, where he became familiar to millions as the sepulchral voice of David Bliss, an absent-minded bachelor stumbling from one calamity to another with the help of Nora Swinburne, Esmond Knight and animal impersonator Percy Edwards. Although David seldom spoke about the series, he expressed frustration with the slipshod delivery of scripts by Godfrey Harrison, which were often still being written on the day of recording. 'He was not only late with scripts,' BBC producer Edward Taylor later recounted, 'he was very very late' – and sometimes Bridgmont had to rewrite the rewrites.

Despite the hiccups, record summer ratings led the Home Service controller, Andrew Stewart, to congratulate the variety department on thinking it up. 'If we can do this in August, I think we can do better in the autumn and winter.' Radio critics were full of praise too: 'It is silly-clever, not silly-stupid,' wrote the reviewer of the *Manchester Guardian*. 'The tone is light, the pace is fast. The cast is a nice change from the world of grating accents and dim facetiousness of most episodic BBC features.'

There was just one catch. Bridgmont remembered how the project nearly came unstuck just as a second series seemed imminent:

Tomlinson was playing in *The Little Hut* at the time, and when the show ended its London run, six weeks after we started, he was under contract to go on tour with it, which made it impossible for him to do the Sunday recordings.[2]

Ordinarily, the loss of a star would have been the end of it:

Either it had to be taken off or we had to change horses in mid-stream. We realised that to find another David Bliss was not going to be an easy task; but fortune smiled, and we hit on the absolutely right person in George Cole.[3]

Rank had given Cole a five-film contract but dropped him after two pictures; television and radio, it seems, was his natural media. Even with a change of star, Godfrey Harrison's erratic writing methods continued to tax the patience of all involved. Unbowed, he regularly finished scripts while the cast were on stage recording the first few pages, with the baffled audience often shuffling out before the end of the recording, complaining in muted whispers. Remarkably, the series continued to notch up high ratings, transferring to television in 1956. In the future, David would occasionally appear on airwaves of the BBC, but he would never star in a situation comedy again.

In mid June, just as the coronation celebrations honouring the new Queen Elizabeth II were in full swing, Audrey discovered the subject of

Clarence could release mixed feelings when prodded. 'When I met David he was just starting an investigation, trying to make out where his father was,' Audrey explained.[4] Given that Clarence could still never be contacted at his London Club, there were many shrewd observations on the issue. 'I know he was doing as much as he could to find out about him. His father cast a long shadow.'[5]

Meanwhile, the formula roles kept coming and as their romance blossomed, David and Audrey appeared together in the flimsy comedy *Is Your Honeymoon Really Necessary?* at Nettlefold Studios, Walton-on-Thames – the scene of his Butcher's film debut a decade earlier. The rehearsals, Audrey said, were totally trouble-free but the finished product had the dubious distinction of being, arguably, David's worst film.

Based on a stage play adapted by Talbot Rothwell, who later found fame writing the *Carry On* films, the action took place within a hotel room, where Bonar Colleano found himself on honeymoon with not one wife, but two. To save film and time, the plot was shot mostly full-frame, without many close-ups and with as few takes as possible, preferably just one. Diana Dors strutted around as the platinum blonde Candy, the cause of all the trouble, while David kept a stiff upper lip as Frank Betterton, a much-harassed lawyer unwillingly involved in the debacle. Audrey, who had several scenes, mostly with Sid James, played Lucy, the maid.

In true bawdy fashion, director Maurice Elvey invented shots where Dors seductively leaned forward, backward and with the occasional pause to bend over. According to David Jr, his father was not overly complimentary about the film: 'Though it was memorable because my Mum was in it and they were keeping their romance a secret.'

Is Your Honeymoon Really Necessary? performed remarkably well at the box office. The *Monthly Film Bulletin* unashamedly cooed at Diana Dors 'exuding 100 per cent sex', while the *Daily Worker* gave an earthier review, complaining that Bonar Colleano 'savagely inhaled' about 300 cigarettes in beds, on beds, and even under beds:

> I had the impression that he needed them to steady his nerves every time
> he realised what he had got mixed up in. For some obscure reason the
> director has insisted on Bonar standing on his head with his back to the
> audience for long periods, which tends to cramp his dramatic style. After
> so many beds, I found myself yawning loudly and snuggling down in my

seat. David Tomlinson is convulsive as a rabbit-faced Wodehouse moron. He has a moment of truth when he exclaims: 'I can't see anything funny in all this.' How right he is.

Outside the studio, while London soaked through a cold, wet spring, David made a momentous decision. After, no doubt, privately rehearsing the scene, he mustered up the courage to propose to Audrey and in early May the couple married in a modest ceremony at Ealing Registry Office. Guests included best man Bill Meldon, who was an international oarsman and a police detective sergeant. 'Bill may well have been the only British police officer to row for team GB: in all likelihood DT met him during the 1948 London Olympic Games,' says David Jr. Also at the registry office were interior designer Paula Lawrence, who remained a lifelong friend, Mary Lynn, a theatrical costumier and Alice Mantle, David's flat-keeper.

Under the banner, 'Audrey weds in secret,' the *Daily Mirror* carried a photo of the 'singing and dancing college girl' on its back page, noting: 'Audrey is playing in the musical *Love from Judy* at the Savile Theatre in Shaftesbury Avenue. Just 400 yards down the road, David is starring in London's longest run-play *The Little Hut* at the Lyric.'

In almost no time, the couple moved into Brook Cottage, where the people of Mursley – the tiny picture-postcard parish of a couple of hundred souls – made them welcome, as Audrey recalled:

> It was certainly a new life for both of us away from the city. I found it a little difficult at first as I was trained for a career, not to run a house in the country, but David wouldn't have minded me continuing – actually, there was nothing he could do about it, it was up to me, but I couldn't do two things.

As it was, the newlyweds filled their marriage with affection, music, dinner parties with sportsmen and actors and celebrations at every new success.

Audrey recalled it was also around the time of moving into Brook Cottage that David's disconcerting feelings about his father resurfaced, saying there were some tantalising references to the ongoing mystery. '[David] really did as much as he could to find out about him. It was obvious something wasn't quite right, but he still wasn't sure,' she said, adding that, yet again, the subject was 'put on the back burner'.

For all its sweep, *The Little Hut* bowed out of the West End in late 1953. By the time the curtain fell, it was the seventh longest-running play in the history of the London theatre and one of the last plays to be seen by King George VI before he died. In the meantime, with more opportunity to enjoy the pastoral charm of Mursley, the couple threw themselves into local life by first presiding dutifully at the local Conservative Association Christmas jumble sale, where a reporter from the *Buckingham Advertiser and Free Press* was duly dispatched to cover the event:

> David Tomlinson's wife, Audrey Freeman, the actress, who was besieged by autograph hunters, picked the winning ticket for a superb cockerel given by Mr Charles North and won by Mr Bull, the Branch Treasurer.

Many in the village held tight to their traditions, so the Tomlinsons were delighted to help organise Mursley's thirteenth-century fair by persuading television star Bruce Seton to cut the ribbon. The event saw children dance around a maypole in period costume and, for a special dose of spice, a deer was roasted and venison served. By April the following year, after a 'labour which seemed to go on forever', the Tomlinsons celebrated the birth of their first child. The enormity of the event was overwhelming for David. 'What a great help I was,' he reminisced, recalling how he followed an ambulance carrying Audrey to the Royal Bucks Hospital with tears streaming from his eyes:

> I really thought she was going to die. Instead she produced an incredible eight-and-one half pound boy, David Redvers – named after her father. It was April 6th, 1954, CST's 71st birthday, and at the age of nearly thirty-seven I was a proud parent.[6]

While everything had been done to prepare for the new arrival – decorators had fashioned a nursery and a nanny was hired – it was the purchase of a new practical family car that led David to a rare flash of temper and some unwelcome publicity. Being a man who was never one to take injustices with calm equanimity, he was left outraged by an incident at a motor dealer on King Street, Hammersmith, when he arrived in his old Jaguar to pick up a new Ford Zodiac. Details revealed in West London County Court showed how the situation boiled over quickly. George

Hall, the manager of the dealership, told Judge Sir Gerald Hargreaves: 'I did not know who he (David) was. He seemed very annoyed because we had not put a red carpet down for him.' But it was not the lack of a carpet, but a difference of opinion over the worth of David's Jaguar that began the kerfuffle.

When David ordered the Zodiac, he was offered £525 for his Jaguar in part-exchange. Three months passed before the Zodiac was ready. Garage employee Arthur King said:

> At first he refused to hand me the keys of the Jaguar to make a second test. He said his time was very precious and that he did not want to be messed about. Finally, he let me try the Jaguar, and I discovered that the clutch was wrong, the engine rattled badly, and so did the bearings.

Insisting the car needed repair work, King drove down the price of the part exchange to £425 on the Jaguar, but after some lively haggling, increased that offer to £475. However, David was not easily placated. 'Mr Tomlinson made a rude remark about car dealers, but he made out a cheque for £431 for the balance due, and in a rage tore up one he had written for £381'. Hall added: 'The next day, Mr Tomlinson wrote to say that he had stopped his cheque for £431. He enclosed one for £381, as the correct amount due.' So the firm sued to recover the balance of £50.'

When questioned, David insisted the Jaguar was 'perfect', telling the judge he was 'astonished' when Mr King said he could not allow him the original sum of £525 on the Jaguar. 'When I handed the cheque to him, I said I had written it subject to taking legal advice.' When asked why he left the showroom in a rage, he said: 'I felt I had been cheated.' Much to David's dismay, the car firm won its claim. As an added sting in the tail, the showroom owner told reporters: 'I am prepared to give the £50 to any nominated charity. I only brought the suit on a matter of principle.'

Such outbursts from David were no surprise, says Jamie: 'Dad had no safety mechanism. He said exactly what he thought. He was also utterly fearless.' In fact, as a child, Jamie witnessed his father being threatened a couple of times:

> They expected the film character and got the real person. Life was a serious business off the set. He was unable to hide what he thought if he did

not like something or did not rate somebody. He could be charming. On his best behaviour he was wonderful. He was terribly funny if he wanted to be. He was shy but could be very shy and unsure of himself. He could behave appallingly. Normal people wanting to say something have that wonderful safety mechanism. They think … I don't think I should say that.

As Audrey adapted to motherhood, David went on to star in one of his best-loved works alongside Michael Shepley, Kathleen Harrison and Betty Paul in the West End production of *All for Mary*, a hotel-attic-bedroom farce by Harold Brooke and Kay Bannerman. David took to the job with relish, saying he thought the story had all the comic wit of a 'copper-bottomed hit'. In the script of *All for Mary*, Clive (Shepley) and Humphrey (David) are on holiday in a luxury hotel in the Swiss Alps, where they find themselves rival admirers of Mary, the innkeeper's daughter. But before long, both are struck down by chicken pox. The central character – not by design perhaps, but certainly in fact – is the adorable old fusspot Nannie Cartwright (Harrison), with her finger raised in perpetual admonition at the naughty behaviour of her grown-up former charge. David confessed to being among her legions of fans, 'Kath is superb, both on stage and off.'[7]

Tatler applauded one of the 'gayest evenings in the theatre for a long time', while *The People* hailed the show for providing the 'biggest laughs of the season', heaping special praise on the 'slightly batty' Harrison, 'a nurse who couldn't forget she had once been a nanny'. The show ran for nine months at the Duke of York's, followed by a twelve-week tour of the provinces. David Jr recalled:

Later, when I was growing up, I remember my Dad telling one rather irreverent story about Kathleen getting a bit of flatulence during a performance and trying to muffle the noise by scraping her heel on the stage; presumably she wasn't entirely successful as Dad was able to tell the story!

In later life, Ian McKellen, widely regarded as one of greatest stage and screen actors, revealed to David during a live television interview, that *All for Mary* had been the first play he ever saw in the West End. 'I was right up there at the top of the Gods in The Duke of York's. And I looked down, I only ever saw the top of your head, but you were terribly good!'

After a gruelling regional tour, David's spirits were heartened with the offer of a starring role as 'Humpy' Miller in the film adaptation of *All for Mary* alongside the devilishly handsome Nigel Patrick, who played Captain Clive Norton. Like David, Patrick had rebelled against his parents when it came to career choices. He once told how his peppery father demanded he train as a chartered accountant but 'the delightful old gentleman for whom I worked thought that I was not cut out for accountancy. He thought I would be far happier following a dramatic career,' which led to repertory in Birmingham and Northampton.

Although humour that works onstage doesn't always translate to film, *All for Mary* proved a winner for Kathleen Harrison, who joined the cast along with Australian actor Leo McKern, playing Gaston Nikopopoulos, a none-too-bright guest, and singer Jill Day as Mary. Despite being heard on radio and records as the lead singer for Geraldo's Orchestra, Day came with no acting experience. 'She is quite remarkable,' David sighed happily to the *Daily Express*. 'You know I thought it might be difficult at first – girl with no experience. But Jill has great composure. She's not worried by anything.'

All of the cast had their moments, but McKern's pompous spikiness as Nikopopoulos, was only outshone by Harrison, who proved she could still steal a scene without breaking a sweat.

At this point in time David could have rested on his laurels. However, as the curtain fell on 1955, Harry Alan Towers – an 'Arthur Daley'-type producer noted for some productions of dubious taste – twisted his arm to star with Valerie Miller in 'The No Man', a half-hour TV episode for the syndicated series *Theatre Royal*, broadcast on ATV in London and in the USA in the *Lilli Palmer Theatre* series. David's character was the juicy role in the show in which he played a mild-mannered chap pushed around by everyone except a female colleague (Miller), who was determined to make a man of him. Despite working on a shoestring, Towers attracted big-name performers such as Orson Welles, John Gielgud, Michael Redgrave and Christopher Lee for his TV specials, which he then offloaded into syndication to stations in Britain, the USA, South Africa and Australia.

At the same time, David branched out into the children's field when he recorded an LP of A.A. Milne's best-loved songs and verses for Conquest Records that Christmas. His meticulous attention to detail was seen in his approach to this project, which was hailed as one of the finest children's discs ever made and is still raved about by personalities, including Gyles Brandreth:

> I seem to remember that Christopher Robin Milne, whom I knew and who had mixed feelings about his father's nursery poem, rather admired it, too. Tomlinson was a master craftsman – with a brilliant light touch – and nothing illustrates it better than those recordings: one of the delights of my childhood.[8]

The record featured the full-sized Westminster Concert Orchestra conducted by Cyril Ornadel, the London Palladium's musical director. 'This is a simple, gentle, bedtime recording, beautifully spoken and sung by David Tomlinson, well-known British film actor and comedian,' the sleeve description noted. 'A father himself, Tomlinson has the rare ability to talk intimately to small children on their own level without appearing patronising.'

In fact – still dizzied by his own fatherly experiences – David mentions David Jr on the recording, which became one of the World Record Club's 'exclusive series', scooping the *London Evening News* special award in the children's class of 1956. The record won him a wide overseas audience, good notices and a great deal of personal satisfaction.

Funnily enough, David Jr recounts that David was seldom available to read a story, though it happened occasionally:

> Our childhood memories were mostly pretty happy, but when Dad was in the theatre he obviously wasn't around at bedtime. I do once remember him coming into my bedroom very late at night as he often would drive home from the theatre and, without realising that I was awake, tucking in the bedclothes and I think he probably did that a lot, though usually we'd be asleep.

10

COMING OF AGE

David returned to the screen in 1956 for what would be one of the most fulfilling years of his life. First up was a role in *Three Men in a Boat*, based on Jerome K. Jerome's 1889 novel and co-starring the weather-beaten Jimmy Edwards – a former RAF pilot, who, like David, had trained in Canada during the war. After the conflict, Edwards cut his teeth at London's Windmill Theatre, the famous Soho training ground for aspiring comics. But it was in the BBC radio series *Take it from Here* that he eventually gained widespread fame. *Three Men in a Boat* is a rousing, colourful historical farce, beautifully scripted by Hubert Gregg, a sensitive man with a great feel for comedic material. The story provides the basis for a pleasant Victorian boating holiday, with predictable consequences. Directed by Ken Annakin, the story tells how three young boater-hatted men in stiff collars decide to take a holiday on the river, partly for amusement, and partly to escape the women in their lives. Their misadventures led to some rowdy comedy, shot amid lush English scenes from the Henley Regatta and the giant maze at Hampton Court. As the film got rolling, A.E. Matthews returned in a side-splitting cricket scene along with a delicious sequence from a mongrel dog, Montmorency, who accompanied the tourists during their adventures. During filming, at a lock somewhere near Cliveden, David was informed that, after another tortuous labour, Audrey had given birth to their second son James Adam, known in the family as Jamie.

The adjustment to married life had been more difficult for Audrey than David. She confessed:

It was only when Jamie was born that I began to settle down. I was trained for a career, not to run a house … I couldn't leave my children before breakfast in the morning and not see them until after they'd gone to bed. That just wasn't an option.

Meanwhile, shooting continued on *Three Men in a Boat* along the Thames – where the weather was, to put it politely, changeable – as David recalled:

Actually, it was the worst summer recorded in England's history. It rained more that summer than any other time since the Romans … and they filmed it on the River Thames. Have you ever swum in the River Thames? It's like the North Pole. We did an awful lot of sitting around.[1]

In spite of having to keep an anxious eye on the skies above, 'Larry Harvey, Jimmy Edwards and I sat in a little boat and all we could do was knock-it-back and try and keep warm. Then suddenly the sun would come out and they would say "get in the water".' David recalled most days the weather started nicely but by lunchtime was blowing a Force 7 gale:

I remember a wonderful, lovely moment when the sun was shining and everybody was pleased. They got a camera on a pontoon on the river. They got a crowd of 1,000 and a lot of boats. The assistant director was saying, 'Ladies and gentlemen would you please be so kind as to get into the boats and row out towards us.' Well, they got in the boats and of course three hours later they collected them all (downstream) because the one thing they hadn't heard about, the powers that be, were the strong currents of the river![2]

After sipping their last snifter of brandy, they embarked on another tricky scene during a storm that saw the waves turn into great hills. David and Jimmy – hamming it up grandiloquently – bailed out the water splashing over the side of the punt. At moments like these, David admitted to a hankering for the simple pleasures of a studio-based comedy where 'toilets, warmth and proper food were taken for granted'. But in the end, all turned out well. The realistic colour exteriors impressed critic Bosley Crowther, who lapped up what he described as a British Keystone comedy set in the Edwardian age. 'If you're looking for a pleasant summer picture, this should be your dish of (iced) tea.' The *Times of India* shrewdly observed a broad farce, which was not 'quite as rollicking as some of Mr Annakin's previous comedies,' while reviewer Patrick Raymond thought the film returned viewers to a sweeter, more innocent age. 'Jimmy Edwards as Harris and David Tomlinson as Jay were perfect in their roles.'

Meanwhile, David toyed with several ideas. The one that intrigued him most came from producer George Minter, who called with an offer to star in *Carry on Admiral*, adapted from the 1947 farce *Off the Record*. As a film-maker, Minter had brought several successful pictures to the screen, including *Scrooge* and *The Pickwick Papers*, before establishing his own production company. The essence of the story follows the misadventures of a parliamentary press secretary and a navy officer unwittingly exchanging identities after a boozy night out. Val Guest, a calm and sanguine man, wrote a screenplay overflowing with naval gags and also directed. He possessed enormous skill in telling a good story, and came with a wealth of experience having worked at Gainsborough scripting Hitchcock's *The Lady Vanishes* and Will Hay's *Oh, Mr Porter!* Unsurprisingly, he packed the screenplay with situations involving torpedoes, people falling in and out of the water, embarrassing moments with pretty girls and all the ingredients of British farce. The film was also visually impressive, having been shot in 'SpectaScope', a short-lived British attempt to emulate Hollywood's 'CinemaScope'.

Once production commenced, David deployed for a seven-week shoot in Plymouth, Chatham and aboard HMS *Defender*, where some of his funniest scenes were shot with hundreds of ratings and the band of the Royal Marines. In terms of pure spectacle though, the *Defender*, a Daring-class destroyer, stole the show having distinguished herself in the Mediterranean during the war. Thanks to Minter, she enjoyed one final hurrah before being sent to the breaker's yard. On board, David whipped out a delicious portrayal of a blundering civil servant alongside A.E. Matthews, Brian Reece, Ronald Shiner and Peggy Cummins supporting in good British-comedy style. Given his advancing age – he was by then 87 – Matthews hesitated before accepting the role of Admiral Sir Maximillian Godfrey. 'What happens to your costs and timing schedules if I don't last out the film? It's a big part,' he mused loudly.[3] Although he took it on, Matthews refused to sign a contract or commit to the film company until shooting was completed. Only then did he phone his agents: 'Job finished – alive. Contract signed. Next please.'[4]

Val Guest thought Matthews a very 'wicked old man', with wicked sense of humour. He also recalled:

Another classic story, at one of the Royal Command Film Performances, Larry Olivier came over to him. Larry said, 'You probably won't remember me.' Matty said, 'Yes I do, yes I do, don't tell me,' and he thought for a moment and said, 'Yes you used to play double bass on the *Berengaria*.' That was the sort of humour he had, he swore he really thought that but I don't believe it for a second.[5]

David's humour could be equally subtle. Character actor Sam Kydd remembered witnessing David's flare for comedy during a hospital scene, where he was an attendant and David a patient:

I'm playing solitaire at the beginning of this scene and there's a lovely bit where David suggests I move a card so that the solitaire resolves itself. It was completely spontaneous but worked beautifully. So we kept it in every take. We didn't do many. We didn't need to. A terrific comedy actor who I was to get to know well during *Up the Creek* and *Further up the Creek*.[6]

Val Guest later fumed that Betty E. Box's husband, Peter Rogers – who went on to produce the hugely successful series of *Carry On* films, pinched the title from *Carry on Admiral*. 'That was my original title, and nobody has ever said thank you or come to the opening night or anything,' Guest explained. 'George never registered that title, so they just stole it.'[7]

Given a huge blast of publicity, *Carry on Admiral* generated ample ticket sales both in Britain and abroad. 'A nautical and insistently naughty farce which has the saving graces of David Tomlinson and Peggy Cummins and a little wit (though not very much of it)' was the verdict of the *Illustrated London News*, while the regional press were also enthused. 'Tomlinson has never been seen in a more hilarious role,' the *Broughty Ferry Guide and Advertiser* opined. 'Minter has made an excellent film of this famous play. Comedy is nicely paced throughout. It is eighty-odd minutes of fun. You won't be disappointed if you take the family along to see it,' was the verdict of the *Clitheroe Advertiser and Times*.

After a long run of work, the Tomlinsons headed for a stretched out working vacation in South Africa to appear together in Roger MacDougall's

Escapade at the Hofmeyr Theatre in Cape Town. 'It was an exciting prospect for both of us,' Audrey remembered as they took the chance to indulge in a vast amount of reminiscing with David's brother Peter, who lived in the city. 'Peter and I hit it off from the word go,' Audrey says, adding that, 'Peter was very close to my husband, he was only 11 months older. I adored him. He was a lovely chap, and an adorable brother-in-law.'[8] Away from the theatre, the couple amused themselves on the busy social scene and embarked on a pre-planned excursion, guided by Peter, along the vast southern coast toward Port Elizabeth.

Back in Britain, David's vigorous return to work was interrupted abruptly when he crashed a Tiger Moth aircraft 100 yards from Brook Cottage in April 1957. All hell broke loose and, as Audrey recalled it, the incident became local legend, spun in some circles with elaborate detail. 'But for David, it was a tormenting ordeal.'[9] Initially, after a swerve and nose dive, his plane hurtled earthwards and smacked into the moist turf at the end of his garden, sending a spray of mud, dust and smoke in all directions. But for the grace of God, both he and his passenger, Robert Paterson, a distant relation, had a remarkable escape from death. The next morning, Audrey fumed at the front-page banner headline: 'Wife sees flying film star crash', on a story by the *Daily Herald*'s Ken James in true tabloid fashion. His report described how Audrey 'watched horrified' as the plane came hurtling toward Brook Cottage crashing through a line of trees, just missing three boys, then spinning into a copse by the cottage garden:

> Villagers raced to the wreckage. They pulled Tomlinson out of the shattered fuselage. But he was only dazed and muttered: 'What happened? It's a nightmare.'

After visiting hospital, Audrey told reporters: 'David had a blackout and that is why he crashed. The accident did not happen because he was concentrating on waving to me and our son in the garden.'

The family's delight at DT's narrow escape was somewhat blunted when four summonses concerning reckless flying in a populated area arrived. David simply didn't know how to react to the accusations, which were aggravated by 'witness accounts' in the press alleging he operated an aircraft in a negligent manner, with one teenager claiming to have seen him 'looping-the-loop and pretending to dive-bomb his own house'. He was deeply hurt as he read the charges, which included endangering life or property, flying over a congested settlement below 1,500 ft and conducting an acrobatic flight over a populated area. 'David was very proud of his flying and very upset by the accident as he took it so seriously,' says Audrey. 'As a flying instructor he knew the dangers.'[10]

David pleaded not guilty at Aylesbury Quarter Sessions, insisting he crashed after blacking out and not due to dangerous risk-taking. He explained to the judge how while flying the plane he did not feel well and told Paterson he was returning to the airfield: 'My first recollection is of lying on my back in the hall of my house.' Paterson concurred, saying just before the crash, David's head slumped forward, but until the last minute, it did not seem possible he was not conscious. In court, David's lawyer, the eminent QC Frederick Lawton, built a picture of his client, his background and position:

> You must not think for a moment that because he earns his living play-
> ing the fool in entertainment, he plays the fool when he is at home. He
> is married and has two young children. The last thing he is going to do is
> risk his life – as prosecution witnesses have said.

The jury left the court for just forty-two minutes before finding him not guilty. Summing up, the chairman said, 'Mr. Tomlinson was an experienced flyer and was not likely to have done stunts over his own house to show off.' In almost comedic fashion, as the case was thrown out, two women jurors hurried over and requested David's autograph on the sheet setting out the charges!

Asked if he would give up his aeronautical adventures, DT replied: 'I don't think so. I'll very likely be flying again soon.' However, the ordeal left a bitter taste and was presumably why David embarked on a plan to sell Brook Cottage and quit Mursley. 'If I ask less than £20,000 I shall be losing money,' he told the William Hickey writers on the *Daily Express*. 'It has taken five years to convert it into the lovely house it is, a combination of eighteenth century and Regency. It's a gem.' But when the first prospective buyers came to see it, and indeed made an offer (which was accepted), the Tomlinsons had second thoughts and cancelled the sale – the prospect of moving, it seemed, was too depressing.

Exasperated by the entire business, the Tomlinsons left for a holiday in a quaint village near Le Lavandou on the Côte d'Azur, which, Audrey recalled, despite its lush golden beaches and turquoise waters, had been spared the incursion of package tourism:

> We had a lovely time there. Toward the end of our stay a friend came to join us, and we all packed our bags with the intention of going to Italy. Well, on our way we decided to have a bathe at Hotel du Cap-Eden-Roc, which was on our route. When we arrived, David found so many friends there including William Douglas Home and Michael Medwin. It was so lovely, absolutely luxurious.[11]

Hotel du Cap-Eden-Roc, of course, was accustomed to celebrities. Perched ethereally on a cliff overlooking miles of ocean, it attracted Charlie Chaplin and Rudolph Valentino in the 1920s, while the Duke of Windsor and Wallis Simpson sought solitude there in 1937 after the abdication. It was also widely rumoured that German star Marlene Dietrich embarked on a steamy affair with Senator Joe Kennedy at the hotel just prior to the Second World War. Guests could step out their cars, engage a porter for their luggage and stroll through the courtyard and into the serpentine green tiled pool.

Although the Eden was a centre of gravity for luminaries from the world of entertainment, Douglas Home and his wife Rachael were, in fact, renting Aly Khan's nearby villa with their close friends 'the two Jacks' – Jack and Jackie Kennedy. Khan, the playboy son of the Aga Khan, was known on the Riviera for his relentless pursuit of pleasure. 'Willie invited us round for supper on the terrace and showed us where Rita Hayworth had been sleeping with Aly Khan!' Audrey giggles. 'Willie had said to us that Jack would be the next president of the United States and we rocked with laughter.'[12] As day descended into evening, the Kennedys joined the group for supper:

> He – JFK – was quite a dazzler; he was very good looking and a good host. It was a very jolly time. I mentioned a song that everybody was singing called 'Volare' and Jackie jumped up and said, 'I've got it!' and put it on the record player. Rachael and Jackie were really good pals – it was their responsibility to do the weekly shopping![13]

Audrey remembered that David had another encounter with JFK on a floating platform moored off the coast of the Hotel du Cap-Eden-Roc. 'On the raft one day was Jack Kennedy and David – who had swam out, not knowing who was out there – but he found he was on the raft with JFK and they had a nice chat.' David Jr remembers his father saying that as the two men bathed in the sunshine:

> DT said to JFK that some of the US generals were making too many hawkish noises off and on and needed to be told to dial down the rhetoric. The first thing Kennedy did when he became President was shut up the generals, Dad proudly proclaimed for years afterwards.

There were other pleasures too during this rest period including a visit to British novelist Somerset Maugham's Côte d'Azur villa. 'He was tucked away actually,' Audrey laughs. 'He didn't want to see visitors! It was the most extraordinary holiday really – the Kennedys, Maugham – remarkable.'

On returning to Britain, director Jack Minster invited David to star in Jack Popplewell's *Dear Delinquent*, the sort of racy, light comedy he adored. 'Actually,' David said, beaming, 'I dreamed up the title of that play, which is rather good I think!'[14] The production at the *Westminster Theatre* proved an instant hit and tells how Anna Massey – giving a superb portrayal of an Irish burglar – breaks into David's apartment but then falls in love with him and is persuaded to reform from her life of crime, much to the dismay of her father, played by Laurence Hardy, who gave a series of brilliant performances.

To everybody's surprise and amusement, Clarence came out of the shadows and was regularly seen milling around in the lobby, solicitously extolling the merits of the production. The critics were positive too, and a photograph of David clutching Massey adorned the cover of *Theatre World*, which, back then, was the ultimate accolade. A prized cutting came from the pen of the *Birmingham Daily Post*'s drama critic, who described a pleasant old-fashioned waft from the 1930s that the 'audience received it with gentle pleasure, and included Noel Coward, sitting benevolently in the stalls'. The *Tatler* opined that *Dear Delinquent* had the 'advantage of Mr David Tomlinson as its hero, and Mr Tomlinson is as near the stage equivalent to Bertie Wooster as can be imagined'.

David Jr, who was later a pageboy at Massey's wedding to Jeremy Brett, vaguely recalled a matinee performance:

All I really remember is my father being very cross and standing in front of a cupboard shouting: 'Come out of there!' A rather frightened looking Anna Massey would then emerge and my father would carry on being cross with her. Later, Mum took me round to Anna's dressing room and as we approached the door I shouted: 'Come out of there!' and my rather embarrassed mother shushed me up!

Although Massey enjoyed a happy friendship with David and Audrey, it was a project she later regretted. 'If only I had the confidence to say, "No this is not for me," I would have been spared a mammoth setback to my career,' she lamented, seemingly frustrated with the 'tortuously long' run. 'The choice of play did my reputation great harm. She complained that, from then on, people thought of her as a lightweight comedy actress.[15]

Massey eventually found countless roles to match her talents, ranging from parts in Michael Powell's cult thriller *Peeping Tom* to her BAFTA-winning performance in *Hotel du Lac*.

Meanwhile, David's reputation as Britain's leading exponent of permanently perplexed characters was about to be solidified. In theory, he should have been able to ease up on his gruelling work schedule, but jumped at the chance offered by Val Guest of a part in *Up the Creek*, alongside Peter Sellers, a rising star with marquee value. Author John Warren had dreamed up this sea-bound farce during a Sunday stroll through Acton Park. 'Wouldn't it be funny,' he said to his writing partner Len Heath, 'if a destroyer of the mothball fleet was up a creek somewhere with a small maintenance crew on board receiving the rations of a full ship's complement, and yet no one knew under whose responsibility the ship came? And of course, the crew was in all the rackets with the nearby village.'[16]

With the script finished, the next few weeks were dominated by a whirl of read-throughs and wardrobe tests. Production commenced proper on three sets that emerged on the sound stages of New Elstree Studios and on board an ex-corvette of the Royal Navy laid up at a breaker's yard in Essex. In the movie, David breathed life into Lt Humphrey Fairweather, a nervy, happy-go-lucky naval officer, while Sellers delighted as the sharp-witted artful bosun on the HMS *Berkeley*. Shaking a finger at David during the first morning of rehearsals, Sellers giggled and said: 'I knew we would make a film together some day! I knew it!'

It was a moment forever etched in David's memory, as he recalled their magical screen chemistry:

> I'll never forget the first day of working with him. I thought if this man isn't going to make it as a film actor, I will be very, very surprised. That film, which was made for very little money, and incidentally wasn't the first time I'd met Sellers, but the only other time I worked with him. I remember how brilliant he was; he played a crooked bosun with crooked spectacles – Irish.[17]

Once the cameras began rolling, David gave a stunning portrayal as the befuddled officer conducting a series of daft experiments with a guided missile, causing him innocently to fall headlong into a lower-deck racket on a frigate full of fiddlers, who from their sloop moored up the creek supplied half of Sussex with bacon and eggs from the Berkeley Piggeries, operated the Berkeley Same-Day Laundry, and delighted the natives with Auntie Berkeley's Homemade Goodies.

Making a promising debut, waiflike actress Liliane Sottane provided the romance as the French niece of the local publican, while David's old chum Wilfred Hyde-White – famed for his silken elegance – filled the shoes of a wily old admiral. However, according to David's son Jamie, it didn't take long before the production sailed briefly into choppy waters:

> Hyde-White had not prepared himself for work and did not know his lines. Despite being senior in age, Dad apparently got quite cross with him. That sort of unprofessional behaviour would have really got up Dad's nose. It was quite a spat with Wilfred, obviously being in the wrong, defending the indefensible. It was a way that you could mess up your fellow actor by finally getting the take right and the prepared actor being not quite so good.

In any case, the blot on Hyde-White's copybook was erased soon after and the two remained firm friends. A few years later, Hyde-White was catapulted to fame alongside Audrey Hepburn and Rex Harrison in *My Fair Lady* and, like Robert Morley, he could usually be found in the crowds at Newmarket racecourse. 'He's never made the mistake of taking acting seriously, dear boy,' Morley opined when asked about the secret of Hyde-White's success. 'He has warm and gentle good humour.'[18]

Work progressed quickly on *Up the Creek*, which actress Vera Day thought a rather cheerful business, with lots of giggles. She gave a customary glamorous performance as Lily, the village barmaid pulling pints at the Pig and Whistle:

> For me it was only a few days' work but it was great fun, I enjoyed every minute of it, even though I was again cast as a barmaid but we were a very close group. We had a few little scenes in the pub, David was nice to act with, and he was a notoriously daft face-puller and really quite a funny man on and off screen, so we did have some laughs. His personal acting style was economical, almost crisp because he never wasted a single moment on the screen, a delicious personality. What I do remember is that he always gave his best performance first try. Re-takes and repetition always seemed worse.[19]

As for David, he thought *Up the Creek* was so professionally put together and 'made in the way one should make films. It was shot in ten weeks and everything they promised was right.'[20]

Although Vera Day had worked alongside a parade of matinee idols, she never understood Seller's notoriety for being a difficult actor. 'Some of the crew expected he'd be temperamental. He wasn't. They expected he'd lord it over them. He never did.'

David, too, was perplexed by his co-star's reputation, which, as it happened, didn't stop the two men becoming firm friends. In fact, Val Guest later revealed the admiration was mutual, as he was only able to obtain the services of Sellers by ensuring David played Fairweather.

During breaks in filming while soaking up the sun in canvas chairs on the deck of HMS *Berkeley*, David learnt Sellers had set his heart on shaking off his comic persona to embark on a career as a serious actor. Being a student of the occult and supernatural, a clairvoyant had assured Sellers that cinematic fame was looming.

'He took offence at imaginary slights,' David remembered, saying the most extreme example of his personality was a fear of others taking advantage.[21] 'Peter swallowed up a lot of devotion to those close to him,' making friends and enemies by the score.[22] His life was a series of adventures – he had a huge appetite for women, hamburgers, foreign travel, strong drink and large cigars. But despite his quirky traits, few denied his genius. He could be insanely generous and was crazy about gadgets, as David Jr remembered:

> Peter anonymously sent an Elizabethan tape recorder to the stage door of whichever theatre Dad was performing in at the time. It was a huge bit of kit and certainly state of the art. Sellers also sourced a car for us to run around in, a sort of minor shooting brake called a Ford Esquire.

As Audrey put it, 'Peter was a gentleman and a brilliant mimic – he was articulate and kind.'[23] She still laughs out loud when recalling how Sellers once phoned the cottage at Mursley pretending to be cricketer Geoffrey Boycott. 'I fell for it. Peter said to me – in a thick Yorkshire accent – "Hello Audrey, its Geoff. I've broke'n me back!"'[24]

It was 'the stuff of bloody legend,' Boycott says, attesting to how the gag was elevated to Tomlinson family folklore:

> Peter bloody Sellers! He could do a superb, impassioned impression of me but I never got to hear it personally. Audrey was from near my part of the world coming from Barnsley – a Yorkshire lass – so, I'm surprised she never rumbled him, but then that shows how good he was. I know David thought Peter was a genius. Sadly, I never met him.[25]

By the time *Up the Creek* opened, David had played his fair share of befuddled characters in half a dozen movies, but his portrayal of Fairweather remains his gold standard. *Up the Creek* sailed into cinemas, packing establishments from Glasgow to Grimsby to the rafters. Even across the Atlantic, the critic A.H. Weiler saw it during a limited run at the 55th Street Playhouse in New York and rattled off a largely positive 600-word notice. 'David Tomlinson enters into the wacky spirit of this hare-brained escapade,' he wrote. 'Although his material is not especially inspired, he appears to be giving his all for the writers.'

The success of the movie threw down the gauntlet for Bryon Films and Hammer to produce a similarly ambitious follow-up. David could not resist returning as Fairweather in *Further up the Creek* to fight the shenanigans on board HMS *Aristotle*, where the crew put to sea with paying passengers, all deluded into thinking they're on a luxury cruise. This half-hearted attempt to make a second buck on old work reunited the original cast except one obvious change; Frankie Howerd – a master at milking laughs out of innuendo – replaced Sellers. 'We couldn't get Sellers and they particularly wanted to do a sequel. I got David and I got my old friend Frankie in,' Val Guest explained.[26] Other signings included the glamorous Shirley Eaton and Thora Hird as her gossipy mother. Eaton remembered producers pinning their hopes on another box office hit. 'I worked with David twice,' during two brief, but happy encounters, Eaton reflected. 'On that film David was nice to be around … it was a fun picture to make.'[27] She expressed amused admiration for a cameo from Stanley Unwin, the inventor of his own language, known as 'gobbledy-gook'. 'Isn't he funny?' David laughed. 'A man who talks a lot but never says anything!'[28]

You need eagle eyes to spot him, but the film gave Jess Conrad his first speaking part and he never forgot hurrying from make-up to watch the deck scenes:

> I learned a lot by observing David. With people like John Wayne, you like the way they walk and that makes them iconic. The crew was riveted on him. You see, the thing that made David such an iconic actor is because he was what they call 'very watchable',' which means you never quite knew what he would do next, he was a charismatic star … when he was on set, you never looked at anyone else in the scene. He was very creative in his characterisations. He had a painter's eye.[29]

Oddly, although the picture had plenty of laughs, a number of critics panned it, one calling the casting of Frankie Howerd misguided. 'His great gifts of pantomime are wasted,' wrote Ernest Betts in the *People*. 'His brilliant timing and slapstick scarcely get a look in.' In fact, Howerd was also upset with the finished product, but blamed a rushed schedule. 'The trouble,' he later surmised, 'was that *Further up the Creek* was made too soon – a matter of months – after the original, and so the public had not had a chance to work up an appetite for it. It followed on far too quickly.'[30]

More seriously, at the close of production, shooting was interrupted for 'real-life' drama when £2,000 in wage packets was stolen during the lunchtime break at Bray Studios. The cashier had locked the cash up in a cupboard in his office while he went for a quick lunch but on returning found the cupboard open and the money missing. After extensive questioning, Maidenhead detectives concluded it was an 'inside job' and took the fingerprints of about 100 people. A local reporter, scribbling the details onto a pad, noted David and Frankie Howerd extracted some humour from the situation by jokingly encouraging the detectives to direct their suspicions on each other.

When radio stardom eluded David after he quit *Life of Bliss*, a second chance to shine 'on the air' came in late 1957. With television's popularity soaring, BBC radio managers fought against dwindling audiences and asked David to try his hand on the panel of *Does the Team Think?* alongside Jimmy Edwards and Peter Haigh.

Edwards dreamed up the half-hour show, which 'invited members of the public and invited personalities to put questions to a team of distinguished experts'. The panel responded with improvised jokes, one-liners and impressions to keep up the flow of laughs, but always ensuring their responses were reasonably accurate. As Edwards ran his fingers through his handlebar moustache, he poked fun at the panel, audience and producer. To listeners, Edwards came across, as one critic opined, 'with the subtlety of a battering ram, flattening resistance and sweeping the audience on wave after wave of hilarity'. The show became an immediate hit. Nicholas Parsons argued it was the forefather of *QI*, as panellists tried to be both witty and smart at the same time. Although David brought with him an endless supply of gags and ad-lib patter, he departed after the first series, handing his chair to flamboyant comedian Tommy Trinder, who remained ensconced in it until 1971.[31]

Unusually for the era, David displayed little love for sound broadcasting – it was all too cut-and-dried for his taste – instead, he put his skill to earning a crust treading the boards or on the closed sets of a film studio. He didn't mind hosting the occasional live event either and was delighted to present Yvonne Mitchell with a gong at the Variety Club Silver Heart Awards – a glitzy affair featuring appearances from Alec Guinness, Sir Tom O'Brien and Richard Attenborough. Despite the smiles and back-slapping from the film community, the industry was in crisis – lurching from calamity to calamity.

After an unprecedented box office drop – helped by the rise of television – Rank went on a cost-cutting jag at Pinewood, along with shelving a raft of productions. Lord Rank's call for a reduction in entertainment tax fell on deaf ears. 'So long as the cinema has to live on its present narrow margin, with an occasional crumb of relief from the Chancellor the attrition of the cinema cannot be arrested,' he declared.[32]

Succumbing to the same pressures, John Davis – a man always keen to make cuts – declared almost every Rank cinema was up for sale as the business sniffed out more lucrative investments.

11

New Horizons

During the summer of 1959, David was on cracking form playing scatter-brained civil servant Dick Lanchester in the farce *Follow that Horse!*. 'Milestones have long passed, but I will never forget that old chestnut,' says co-star Mary Peach, her memory still as fresh as if she had shot it the week before.[1] For the project, William Douglas-Home adapted a yarn about a battle between civil servants and foreign agents over a secret micro-film swallowed by a racehorse. 'Shooting schedules were extraordinarily tight. It wasn't a momentous feat, but it was important for me because that is the film I met my husband Thomas Clyde on, he produced it,' Peach reflected. 'It was a time when there were a lot of good English character actors, and they were all packed in that movie.'[2]

Peach says the set at Associated British Elstree Studios certainly wasn't a politically correct environment, but a typical product of pre-feminist days:

> David was fine, very pleasant, he had nice timing and we worked well together but he was absolutely not PC. He would have done very badly in the world today, bless him. He would have got into big trouble but you know in those days you just took it in your stride.[3]

She also confessed to being responsible for an 'unfortunate episode' during the making of the film:

> We had this big set-up at the races, and they'd hired the course, filled it with extras, had the horses – it was quite a big set-up for a little picture

like that, because we didn't have a huge budget. At that time I had a Frenchman called Andre, who had taken a great shine to me, and he had an aeroplane and knew that I was filming there, so he was circling over the racecourse. Now in those days, if there was any noise, the sound men would not record and everybody was going absolutely bloody mad because of this aeroplane, and I knew it was Andre up there! My beau was completely putting the whole schedule out! David said a few words about that plane … I kept very quiet! [4]

The film made back its modest cost within a fortnight of release and went on to reap impressive profits. Ernest Betts, always an astute commentator, said:

You wouldn't imagine so slender an idea could produce eighty minutes of picture and that most of it would be funny. But with such seasoned troupers as David Tomlinson, Cecil Parker and Richard Wattis, supported by a good script, this modest cracker goes with a bang. [5]

The *Daily Mirror* decided that after a year of gloomy films 'this typical David Tomlinson comedy was good natured, harmless and often very funny'.

That summer brought a new role in the theatre – and the arrival of a new addition to the Tomlinson clan, William. 'Audrey presented me with our third son – an especially beautiful, especially perfect little boy,' David beamed, an event made even more memorable as William arrived on his birthday. 'David and Jamie were delighted to have another brother.' [6]

On the strength of *Follow that Horse!*, producer Frith Banbury, working with the Robin Fox Partnership, offered David the lead in Wynyard Browne's comedy *The Ring of Truth* at the Savoy, alongside Shakespearian actress Margaret Johnston, who was making a rare venture into comedy.

First night reviews praised Arthur Lowe as a glib, helpful, hurt insurance official, while Brian Wilde, who later found fame in *Last of the Summer Wine*, won applause as a self-important policeman. But while critics were unanimous in praise – bookings remained sluggish and the smell of disaster began to permeate the production.

However, as Banbury was preparing an autopsy report after weeks of half-empty houses, something remarkable happened. No lesser a force than Prime Minister Harold Macmillan inadvertently led the salvage effort by announcing a snap election – and in the same breath – said he was off to see *The Ring of Truth* that very evening. The result was a full house, a delirious cast and warm words from David who, flashing a toothy smile, made an unabashedly gushing speech: 'I hope it won't be considered partisan if we send our warmest wishes to the most distinguished person in the audience tonight, our very greatly respected Prime Minister.'[7]

Banbury recounted the publicity led to more fine reviews: 'It's a chromium-plated domestic comedy. Crisply played by a polished cast – it really rings the bell,' wrote Ross Shepherd in *The People*.

During this period, Harold Macmillan wasn't the only important visitor to the Savoy. One evening, David received a message that Walt Disney was in the audience and 'would love to have a drink' or even better go out to supper. Disney had touched down in London to sign a five-film contract with Hayley Mills, the 14-year-old daughter of John Mills. David recounted:

> Anyway, he came round and he was terribly nice. I thought the pen is going to come out any minute with a contract. He took me to dinner at a very posh joint with quite a lot of other people who sort of joined us, including the man who owned the Beverly Wilsher Hotel and his attractive South American wife and one or two other characters.
>
> After dinner Walt said to me, 'Where ya going now? You must come and have a drink.' He paid the bill and we crept off to the Dorchester, where he was in the Oliver Messel suite. What was so touching was that when we got there, there was an old pair of hair pyjamas and a brush with a comb and nothing else. So we chatted and talked and he told me what he thought of the play – he thought I was lovely in the play – and I said thank you very much.[8]

Much to David's disappointment, there was no golden offer or contract. The evening ended with Walt saying, 'It was a great pleasure and I hope we are going to meet again.' And that was that.

It was during *The Ring of Truth* that David became aware as to the full extent of his father's extraordinary deception. Quite by chance, his brother Peter stumbled across the family secret from the top-deck of a bus while passing through Chiswick. Glancing across the street, he was thunderstruck to spot Clarence sitting upright in bed, sipping tea in a strange house. Before long, the great family mystery unravelled as the Tomlinson brothers discovered that their lives, as they knew it, were based on a few extraordinary falsehoods.

They were astonished to learn Clarence had lied about virtually every aspect of his 'weekday life' and had been keeping a secret second family – a mistress named Audrey and their seven children – in London for decades.

After their initial shock, the Tomlinsons further discovered that Audrey was aware of his duplicity from the start, while Florence had found out in 1917 after Clarence mistakenly sent a letter intended for Audrey to her when she was heavily pregnant with David.

Oddly enough, while discoveries of such secrets typically bring on tumultuous crises, Clarence continued the relationship with both women after the First World War. Audrey changed her name to Tomlinson by deed poll so they could pass as a married couple, while Florence endured the humiliation in silence. David revealed:

> Although we in Folkestone knew nothing of the London family, they were aware of us. Of course, the whole story did not spill out at once, but as we acquired the bones of the story, Michael's genealogical researches filled in the blanks for a time.[9]

Whilst David was neither surprised nor terribly shaken by the revelation, having suspected for over a decade; Peter – with a face as black as thunder – angrily confronted his father with his duplicity. During an intense encounter, Clarence showed little emotion and no remorse. 'I don't consider myself immoral, I loved two women. That's all,' he shrugged.

Looking back on the saga, Henry said that, understandably, David's life narrative was affected by the revelation. 'I would think subconsciously that discovering about this relationship had to have an impact. But, Dad absolutely adored him. I hated him. I thought Clarence was a ghastly old man. I remembered saying to my mum he never smiled with his eyes.'

David Jr explained that, after the initial shock, it was further revealed that at least two of Audrey's children were born before Clarence married Florence:

> I think that the eldest was John born maybe in 1912, a highly intelligent retired army colonel. Whilst Clarence didn't encourage my father and his brothers to go to university, I am pretty sure that a couple of the children on the other side of the family did go to university, which he (Clarence) must have funded. Clarence, in fact, managed to educate all eleven children privately.

Conversely, he added, the children of the other family were told that their father was off playing golf at weekends and all Bank Holidays. 'It must have been very strange for them to be told at Easter and Christmas that their father preferred to go and play golf than spend the holiday with them.'

From then on Clarence withdrew more and more into his shell, but this unhappy scenario continued to affect Florence into her twilight years. David Jr remembers that she suffered a breakdown whilst visiting Peter in South Africa in the early 1960s, and thereafter spent more time at Brook Cottage:

> Years later my mother told me that my grandmother was seriously contemplating divorcing him at this time. Then in 1964, my grandmother had a serious heart attack. Our much-respected local GP made it to our home in Mursley before the ambulance arrived and gave her a life-saving injection.

From the late 1950s to the pre-psychedelic '60s, David had tried, mostly successfully, to steer clear of appearing on television, a medium he disliked as much as radio. But with *The Ring of Truth* wrapping up, he plunged into a small-screen drama alongside Gwen Nelson and Edith Sharpe. George More O'Ferrall, an old friend then producing *Play of the Week* for ITV, wanted star clout for 'The Happy Man', a play about 'an occasion when a lot of women get together and there are not enough men to keep them in order'. When it aired, the programme ranked in the top ten ratings, with the *Daily Mirror* noting David's television drama debut was better than the first plunge of many a big name. 'When nervous or flustered he gave a wonderfully funny performance; his little speeches when firing a midwife and a French governess were Tomlinson gems.' Calling it a 'triumph', the *Coventry Evening Telegraph* wryly asserted that David 'probably made more money out of being harassed than any other actor in Britain'.

In part, because of dwindling film production, David, with great reluctance, accepted an offer by impresario John Gale to star in *Boeing-Boeing*, an off-the-shelf French farce that brushed up against more than a few slamming doors and bedroom clichés. 'I thought *Boeing-Boeing* was the worst play I had ever read,' David howled, but was later heartened to learn Jack Minster, who had directed him in *Dear Delinquent*, was involved.[10]

'Jack's first choice for the starring role was David Tomlinson, who was a comedian par excellence,' Gale revealed.[11] 'He was a wonderfully funny man and we persuaded him. He was always a very, very difficult man to deal with, David, as comedians sometimes are. They're not at all funny in their private lives.' Gale said it took an interminable time to persuade David to do the play:

And I remember saying to him, 'David, if you don't make up your mind, we'll get somebody younger to play the role.' And that seemed to galvanise him into action and he decided he'd do it.

When casting was completed, Terence Alexander, Andrée Melly, Julia Arnall and Elisabeth Murray took the main supporting roles. In this typically French farce, the action unfolds around an old-school drinker and philanderer in Paris (Alexander) with three mistresses (Melly, Arnall, Murray) each one an airline hostess on a different route. However, storms over the Atlantic spoil his timetable calculations and all three arrive at the same time. As this is happening, a friend (David) arrives, is astounded by the skill and ingenuity of the scheme and becomes involved.

'Dad did not like doing farce,' says son Jamie. 'But he was very good at it partly because he was not over the top – he had perfect timing and was funny without trying.'

The show went out on tour and wasn't very successful. Gale remembered:

There were moments in it that one could see the possibilities, but it didn't play as well as it should have done. And part of it was we had miscast the part of the maid, and it was a dreadful decision I had to make to sack the girl who was playing the maid and re-cast it. And David recommended an actress he'd worked with before called Carmel McSharry, who came in, and the moment that Carmel came in it was transformed and it became a huge success.

There were other changes too. By the time the show reached London's Apollo in February 1962, Patrick Cargill – who had also appeared in *The Ring of Truth* – replaced Terence Alexander. The *Illustrated London News* noted, 'It does not pretend to be more than nonsense, a joy in these over-portentous days. Jack Minster, the director, keeps the pace going.' However, the most spectacular notice came from the *Financial Times*: 'There is nothing routine about Mr Tomlinson's comedy. It has that touch of artistry which comes from imagination and inventiveness.'

The good notices – and a recommendation from the Duke and Duchess of Kent – warranted a visit from the Queen in November 1962, who, according to onlookers, was seen laughing throughout the entire performance.[12]

During the run of *Boeing-Boeing*, the Tomlinson family continued to grow. David and Audrey celebrated the birth of their fourth son, Henry, an event that led John Gale to give his star a short break. At the same time, 8-year-old David Jr, kitted out with a satchel, blazer and sports pumps, was enrolled at Swanbourne House School, where he remembered the headmaster Harold Evans, a lay preacher, was so strait-laced that he regarded the Beatles as a sort of abomination of the Devil:

Almost immediately an older boy said to me, 'Ah, the son of the actor!'

This was within years of Dad's trial at Aylesbury Quarter Sessions, a Tiger Moth that he had piloted having crashed in a wooded area close to our home: in fact my parents later purchased this spinney and years later my father went for a walk in it and found one of the tips of the shattered propeller. However, already by 1962 the story was doing the rounds that he'd actually contrived to dive the plane under London Bridge. Several boys at my prep school were quite convinced of this and that he'd stood up in court and proved his innocence: only the very last bit was true. Being too young to remember the crash and the trial, which Dad didn't care to talk about too much, I was none the wiser and ran it past my Mum, who of course confirmed that the boys were talking poppycock.

During the summer of 1962 – when the Rolling Stones made their debut and Telstar beamed the first live transatlantic television signal – David Tomlinson decided to take a well earned break for some sporting fun. On one occasion, David scored 101 for the Keystone Cops All Stars against Oxford University in the grounds of Blenheim Palace, where, according to the local newspaper, his 'boots were so painful that he discarded them and scored 101 in his socks' – Leslie Crowther acting as his runner.

Jamie remembered:

> Dad was a very good ball player … hand-eye coordination. I was pretty
> good, but if I'd had his hand-eye coordination I would have made it as a
> professional cricketer. Dad's main game was squash, which he excelled
> in. Also rackets. He played tennis well and if he had played golf regularly
> would easily have had a single-figure handicap or better.

In addition to his own sporting exploits, Wimbledon was always a firm date
in the Tomlinson calendar. That year, he joined Peter Ustinov, Rod Steiger,
Peter Cushing and Leo Genn to watch Rod Laver successfully defend his
title defeating Martin Mulligan in the final, 6–2, 6–2, 6–1.

Sir Laurence Olivier had also been in touch and asked David to hand
over a £4,500 bungalow in Bognor to Monica Schlotter, a 26-year-old
clerk, who won it in a shilling raffle organised by the Chichester Festival
Theatre. During August, 2-year-old William and his month-old brother
Henry were christened at a joint service at Mursley Church with cricketer
Colin Cowdrey being one of the godparents. David Jr recounts:

> At Henry's christening Robert Morley gave James a £5 note! It would
> have bought 90 litres of petrol and goodness knows how many sweets in
> those days. For the best part of forty years after *The Little Hut* ended its
> run, Robert and Dad talked constantly of working together, but never did.

However, Morley did persuade David to try his hand at TV light entertainment, where he made a few guest appearances on *Juke Box Jury* – a
show in which panellists voted new music singles a hit or a miss. Before the
unblinking eye, he created the role of the seemingly disinterested partici-
pant. 'I wish,' an irate viewer in Liverpool wrote to the BBC, 'that some of
this programme's panellists would concentrate a little more on the job in
hand, and a little less on being personalities. David Tomlinson, please note.'

12

role of a lifetime

At the beginning of 1963, David plunged straight into yet another film, which took him to locations in the west of England to add a touch of comedy as the twitchingly nervous roué Lord Fellamar in *Tom Jones*, alongside Albert Finney as the happy-go-lucky Tom, with Susannah York playing Sophie and Hugh Griffith as Squire Western, her hard-drinking, rough-riding, loud-mouthed father. Based on Henry Fielding's enduring novel, this rousing historical comedy was beautifully directed by Tony Richardson, an artist with a great feel for dramatic timing. 'It was a hoot,' David recalled referring to a scene where he was required to ravish Sophie. 'Put your hand up her skirt,' Richardson barked, from behind the camera. 'Poor Susannah was not pleased and somewhat anxious but I was able to reassure her by word and deed.'[1] The scene climaxed with Griffith bursting in on the encounter, rolling his eyes and blurting out some of the lustiest dialogue in the film:

Sophie Western: Father!
Lord Fellamar: Your father?
Squire Western: Yes, and who in the hell are you?
Lord Fellamar: I, sir, am Lord Fellamar. I'm the happy man whom I hope you will accept as your son-in-law.
Squire Western: You're a son of a whore, for all your fancy falderals!
Lord Fellamar: I resent your tone, sir.
Squire Western: Resent, my arse! I'll teach you to father-in-law me.

The sight of Hugh Griffith – overweight, huffing and puffing, tipsy and slovenly – became the main attraction for David. 'What a magnetic presence. He used to arrive at 6 o'clock in the morning with 17 dogs in a white Roll's Royce!'[2] In fact, it was whispered that Griffith was totally inebriated through much of the shoot. In one scene, in which his horse accidentally fell on him, he was probably saved by virtue of his condition.

David recounted:

An enormous success wasn't it? I didn't have much to do in it but I rather enjoyed that film. They (the producers) were rather worried that it was taking too long and costing too much money, you see, every foot of *Tom Jones* was shot on location, all found by Ralph Brinton who knew Thomas Hardy country very well. It was a good film, though. Albert Finney was excellent.[3]

A batch of sparkling notices ensured success at the box office, resulting in ten nominations for Academy Awards – it won four.[4]

'The somewhat sprawling, bawdy and vivid screenplay of John Osborne provides some meaty acting opportunities and the thesps grasp their chances with vigorous zest,' wrote *Variety*, while the *Buckinghamshire Examiner* praised the 'guest appearance of David Tomlinson, which adds a touch of comedy to this sexy film'.

However, even after basking in Oscar glory, Tony Richardson remained unhappy. 'I felt the movie to be incomplete and botched in much of its execution,' he complained in his memoirs. 'I am not knocking that kind of success – everyone should have it – but whenever someone gushes to me about *Tom Jones*, I always cringe a little inside.'[5]

Throughout the early 1960s, variety kept David going. However, as 1963 unfolded, life took an unexpected turn when a meeting with Maud Spector from the Walt Disney Company threw the Tomlinson household into flux.

'Finally my long-awaited Disney ship came in with an offer to join the cast of *Mary Poppins*,' David joked at a time when Disney's benediction was pure gold. 'I couldn't believe it. I clutched the script to my bosom and hurried home to Audrey.'

By then, well into his forties, and by no means a matinee idol, his face had developed more folds and creases, leading Noel Coward to quip that he 'resembled a very old baby'. David, though, insisted he looked more like a disappointed spaniel. 'In any case, I was young enough to play the father,' he said, referring to his character Mr Banks in *Mary Poppins*, an elaborate adaptation of P.L. Travers' book starring the young English stage star Julie Andrews.

Typically, this overnight success story came after years of hard work and a combination of factors. David Jr said:

> Firstly, there was research by Disney himself – he, as you know, had watched David perform on stage in *The Ring of Truth*. Then, there was the *Poppins* producer Bill Walsh researching British actors and getting the reels of *Up the Creek* sent over to California, which he showed to Disney and other executives.

Disney watched about fifteen minutes. 'Yeah, that's our guy!' he said, not letting on to Bill that he'd seen David on stage some five years previously. Finally, if it needed any further pushing, the incorruptible casting director Maud Spector was on hand to tell the Disney organisation that David was perfect for the part. All of that was achieved without an agent in sight![6]

In fact, Spector was among the first casting directors to work independently of major studios. She first met David at Denham in the late 1940s before branching out on her own, sealing her reputation by casting Elizabeth Taylor in *National Velvet* and, as she claimed, suggesting Sean Connery for the role of James Bond.

With David's impending departure for Hollywood, Leslie Phillips – who had built up a reputation as a polished light comedian – was installed as the leading man in *Boeing-Boeing*, which was approaching its 500th performance.

At the end of April 1963, David briskly ascended the steps of a BOAC 707, smiled for a photographer from the Rex news agency and vanished into the night sky. Audrey would follow later with the kids:

> David went ahead of me – he always did – I never joined him when he was filming. Some actors needed their wives, but David didn't like to be near the family. I understood it very well because I would have felt the same. But the minute he was finished, I used to join him.[7]

After a brief stop in New York, David was greeted by palm trees against a bright blue sky on touch down at Los Angeles International Airport. Less than an hour later, he was ensconced in a plush hotel room, with its comfortable 'king deluxe' bed, twenty-four-hour service, sunken bath and rose-scented towels – all courtesy of Uncle Walt. 'When I got to Hollywood,' he said sheepishly, 'Americans gave the impression that you are the only person they have ever wanted to meet … they have been keeping themselves well for all these years, just for this big moment. It was an exhilarating, joyful experience.'[8]

David would use his time in Los Angeles to wander around the city unnoticed, loving the incognito life. In due course, there would be plenty of time to enjoy a good deal of tennis, swimming and the Hollywood social scene. Iconic restaurants popular since the 'golden age' were still open, Patsy D'Amore's for Italian, Chasen's for seafood, Romanoff's (Spencer Tracy's favourite) for steaks and Don the Beachcomber, the best spot in town for Asian cuisine.

Walt Disney, who was in the first stages of a cancer that would later kill him, bounded forward and gripped David warmly by the hand for a spot of Hollywood schmoozing on his first day at work. Known as an unostentatious and reserved man, Walt was loved by his loyal band of staff and although he avoided the spotlight, he adored the attention he received when visiting his beloved Disneyland.

Born in Chicago in 1901, his father had Irish–Canadian roots, while his mother was of German–American origin. As a child, he revealed a talent for drawing and after the First World War took up commercial art in Kansas City. In 1923 he left with his brother Roy for Hollywood, working on a shoestring budget producing cartoon films, but it was not until 1928 with *Steamboat Willie* that he achieved real success. Thereafter the Mickey Mouse cartoons and, little later, the *Silly Symphonies* – which burst into colour in 1932 – were in demand the world over and Mickey Mouse became a household word, together with Minnie, Pluto and Donald Duck.

Soon after, Disney produced a series of glorious features including *Snow White and the Seven Dwarfs*, *Bambi* and *Pinocchio*. Things went steadily for a while, until *Dumbo* – the story of a baby elephant born with enormous ears – became an international box-office smash, elevating the company to global success.

Jeffrey Kurtti, author and Disney historian, said that after the Second World War, Disney turned his attention to non-cartoon films such as *Treasure Island* and *The Swiss Family Robinson* and built his studio accordingly. He explained:

Unlike the other Hollywood studios, which typically felt like factories, the Walt Disney Studios in Burbank had been purpose-designed by famed Southern California industrial designer Kem Weber, under the supervision of Walt himself.

It was intimately scaled, with handsomely appointed buildings and special attention to details such as lawns and landscaping. Its pleasant surroundings were intended to reflect the warm and familial feel of the Disney culture. To most visitors, in fact, it most closely resembled the look and feel of the campus of a small college. There were only four sound stages on the lot in 1963, and each of them was occupied by some aspect of the production of *Mary Poppins*.[9]

Firing up a Lucky Strike, 'Uncle Walt' pledged that *Poppins* would be the greatest movie ever made when briefing David on the plot: Mary Poppins – a no-nonsense, fun-loving nanny who could work miracles – takes charge of two kiddies, turns their Dad (David) from a pompous stuffed shirt into quite a lad, and then with her mission accomplished, disappears on the next wind.

Kurtti said that Disney knew from the start that only David Tomlinson could plumb and dissect the complexities of George Banks:

Disney saw the fundamentals needed for a role in a musical – a lightness, solid comic timing, a bit of bluster, and a deft spoken musicality. But Walt must have been aware that his screen story was actually about George Banks, not the titular magical nanny; and for the audience to engage with him, Tomlinson brought the necessary gravitas, warmth, and a remarkable ability to emote through sheer reaction and facial expression. In casting male roles, and particularly fathers, Walt Disney was constantly creating surrogates of his own life and his *own* role as a father, whether it was Fred MacMurray in several films, or John Mills in *Swiss Family Robinson* – fathers and father figures got Walt's attention.[10]

Robert Sherman, the son of *Poppins*' composer Robert B. Sherman, served as editor on his father's autobiography *Moose: Chapters from My Life*. He quoted an unpublished passage from the manuscript, showing how his father and uncle Richard (known as Dick) distinguished the 'Disney George Banks' from the children's father first mentioned in the original Travers book:

In that first *Poppins* book, 'Mr Banks' is quite literally dismissed at the bottom of page one. But in our movie, it is Mr Banks whose inner journey becomes primary. Indeed George Banks serves as no less than the film's protagonist. Dick and I believed that for *Poppins* to be a viable film musical, appealing to everyone across the age spectrum, the story needed to centre around an adult character, not just the children and their magical nanny. Choosing who would play our protagonist needed to be done with utmost care. Selecting the right actor for 'Mr Banks' would prove as critical a choice as that of Julie Andrews, who took the titular role. We needed to get it right. Credit for casting David Tomlinson must go to Walt Disney. Walt had a great nose for talent, especially when it came to untapped potential. Walt was already familiar with David's light British comedy work from the Forties and Fifties, David having spent a career playing the quintessential bumbling Englishman. Ironically, it was our very American production that produced the 'Bumbling Englishman' role for which David will ultimately be best remembered. David brought a multi-dimensionality to 'Mr Banks'. David's 'George Banks' exhibits pathos and humour, charm and awkwardness, ferocity and vulnerability all delightfully wound together in one peculiar bundle of Edwardian eccentricity. Getting to know David over time, I became convinced that much of what makes us love his 'Mr Banks' was born out of his own, often harrowing story.[11]

Remarkably, even the notoriously waspish author Travers found no fault with David, acknowledging he was 'absolutely right' for the part. The transition from a literary figure to a screen character had been difficult for Travers to comprehend, but ultimately she came to understand that the two could exist simultaneously.[12]

Julie Andrews had already been in Hollywood for a month with her husband Tony Walton by the time David arrived. Although a great Broadway and London stage star – having gained recognition as Eliza Doolittle in *My Fair Lady* – she had never appeared on film:

I was petrified at the thought. When Mr Disney asked me to play Mary Poppins, I was so flattered, so excited, I forgot to ask about a screen test. Afterwards, I began to worry. I'd known actresses who were lovely on stage and off, but when they stepped in front of that camera lens, they

photographed miserably. Mr Disney never mentioned a test and finally
I shrugged and thought, if he's not worried why am I?[13]

Her anxieties were further soothed when Disney dropped in for a set visit
and enthused about her work. 'I always had a secret desire to make a film,'
Julie confided at the time, 'but I felt that I should wait for the right role
before taking the plunge. That role came along in *Mary Poppins* and now
I'm glad I waited.'

Andrews basked in the 'sunny ease' of working at Disney, recalling that
from their very first scene together – the job interview between Banks and
Poppins – it was often hard to keep a straight face, as David's readiness to raise
a laugh on set knew no bounds. She loved his 'upside down eyes' and affabil-
ity. She confessed in a recent DVD commentary that she thought David 'so
right' in his character that her responses to him came quite naturally:

> It was easy to be snippy with him or quick with him because he was so
> wonderfully vague and out of it. There was also a slight Clouseau quality
> about him wasn't there? He was slightly pompous – he knew he was good
> – he knew how good he was but was never unpleasant with it. I admire
> him so because he always nailed every 'take' so well.

Dick Van Dyke agreed, 'He was delightful. He would have made a great
Clouseau, he was wonderful.' Van Dyke, then a popular TV entertainer,
played Bert, a nimble, cheerful chimney sweep, saddled with a twangy
Cockney accent. Using all his stamina, Van Dyke managed to film his
role between seasons of his popular CBS situation comedy, *The Dick Van
Dyke Show*. Colleagues remember an intense, driven man who cut a wide
swathe in the Hollywood of the early 1960s. David remembered that 'Dick's
Cockney accent' was a heavy topic of debate from the outset:

> Walt said to me, 'Will you give Dick a hand with the accent.' I arrived a
> little after and Dick had already shot a day or two on the film. I did have
> a go; it is a very difficult thing for an American to speak Cockney. It's
> easier for a Cockney to speak American or something. And I thought he
> was very good actually. And anyway, Walt said, 'What do you think?' And
> I said, 'I think he's doing very well.' And he said, 'Well, Mr Tomlinson,'

he was always very formal, 'It doesn't matter too much if his Cockney isn't too good, because I am not making the film just for East London.'[14]

The picture had a large cast. In addition to David, Andrews and Van Dyke, Glynis Johns, the star of *Miranda*, delighted as Winifred Banks, the easily distracted wife of George Banks and a happy-go-lucky suffragette. The sterling actor Reginald Owen, a veteran of the stage and screen, best known for his performance as Ebenezer Scrooge in the 1938 film version of *A Christmas Carol*, was forceful and magnetic as Admiral Boom, the Banks' eccentric neighbour. In typical Disney fashion, the shooting script was laid out like an architect's sketch, with frame-by-frame drawings with the entire picture shot indoors on all four sound stages, with Cherry Tree Lane, St Paul's Cathedral and the park spreading out over Stage Four.

Composers Robert and Richard Sherman presented David with a list of musical numbers, as Robert recalled:

The songs that were selected were really the very crème of everything we were doing. One of my favourites, of all the songs in the picture, is two reprises that we use near the end of the film, when the father (David) and Bert (Van Dyke) have a conversation and the father is feeling his life is falling apart because he's been fired from the bank for causing a ruckus.

Each song had a story and part of the story was being told through the song. The whole thing is sung, the whole thing is musical comedy ... and that's the way we were writing it.[15]

As the shoot progressed, David continued to find the people delightful:

They pay you well, and treat you like the Aga Khan. I absolutely loved it. It is different, but wonderful. And I like 'Have a nice day'. You see, you don't get 'Have a nice day' in England. If you want 'Have a nice day' in England, forget it. But in America they say, 'Have a nice day.' I made friends with the producer, Bill Walsh. Interesting character; I was very fond of him.[16]

As filming wrapped up, Audrey and the children flew into California and were immediately seduced by the lifestyle. 'We were treated like royalty,' Audrey remembered. 'They were so impressed with the work he'd done on *Poppins*. They were bowled over by him.' Even as a curious 9-year-old, David Jr remembers a feeling of importance and excitement at being introduced to Walt Disney:

I had no idea what to expect having never seen a photo of him: I had a sense of anticlimax as he seemed so old. The office was tidy and not at all ostentatious. He was smartly dressed without being showy. It was quite formal, though he seemed genuinely pleased to meet us. Though he was a smoker and had little more than three years to go before the cigarettes killed him, he certainly didn't smoke in front of us and I don't remember any ashtrays or the office smelling of cigarettes. We knew that he was going to arrange for his private plane to take us to stay at one of his homes in Palm Springs. Another time we drove to Disney's ranch to stay for a few days with the *Poppins'* producer Bill Walsh and his family. Each time we had these homes to ourselves as Disney wasn't there himself. At his office Walt had a model of the plane on his desk and was delighted when James asked him to magic it up to its life size. 'I would, but the room's too small Jamie,' he drawled.

Thanks to the script, the Sherman Brothers, Walsh's direction, Disney's guidance and the cast's finest artistic instincts, *Mary Poppins* emerged as a triumph of the cinema stuffed with fine scenes, such as David's finale performance singing 'Let's go Fly A Kite', which Robert Sherman thought unforgettable. 'People were crying at the end of the picture. Why? Because it's so pretty, it's a beautiful statement. It's one thing to go out and buy a kite and fly it, but if you make a kite, it's really yours and it's a piece of you up in the air.' For Jeffrey Kurtti, there were four standouts in David's performance:

There is a reason that Robert Stevenson holds the camera on Tomlinson rather than Dick Van Dyke as Bert scolds Banks in *A Man Has Dreams*. A truly cinematic performance as Tomlinson hears, and listens, and reacts to the admonition being served up (by an inferior!) – it's a character's complete resolution and transformation, and Tomlinson does it all without saying a word.

After returning the tuppence to her father, Jane turns and asks, 'Does that make everything all right?' Tomlinson's expression and the delivery of the simple, 'thank you' is not only heart touching, it's the first sign of the character actually relating to his children.

On his lonely walk to the bank to be discharged, Banks stops at the steps of St Paul's. Tomlinson looks where the Bird Woman sits, then gazes heavenward. Is he looking at the edifice, or is he asking for guidance?

The range of acting and true emotional resonance in his discharge scene is remarkable. From the moment he finds the tuppence in his pocket to his exit from the board room is a small tour de force that resolves the entire character arc and storyline.[17]

With the live-action filming complete, animators embarked on post-production to create the special effects and two-dimensional animals for the 'Supercalifragilisticexpialidocious' and 'Jolly Holiday' musical scenes. Audiences never knew, but David also provided the voices of a penguin waiter, a turtle helping Mary and Bert cross a stream and a huntsman's horse. David's voice even delivers the scolding Mary Poppins receives about her affection for the children by her parrot-headed umbrella.

Despite having just taken part in a cinematic masterpiece, David often dined out on the story of seeing a rough-cut while sitting alongside Walt Disney in a dimly lit screening room:

> I thought it was the worst film I had ever seen, the most sentimental rubbish. And I practically said to dear darling Walt, 'Well, you can't win them all, Walt, can you?' I'm not always right![18]

Thankfully there was enough encouraging comment for Disney to realise that he had a hit on his hands. In an unusual piece of public relations, the head of Disney's music publishing firms, Jimmy Johnson, arranged for the album *Duke Ellington Plays with the Original Score of Mary Poppins* to be recorded in Chicago and set up Louis Prima's version of 'A Spoonful of Sugar' – the idea being to generate radio airplay. However, it was the original soundtrack album, including David's performances of 'Let's Go Fly a Kite', 'Fidelity Fiduciary Bank' and 'The Life I Lead', which appeared on the Billboard LP chart, selling more than 2 million copies in the first year. 'It was David Tomlinson's performance as the father that glued the whole picture together,' Johnson noted in his memoirs. 'He was eminently believable and if he had not been, the picture wouldn't have been believable either.'

Furthermore, Johnson tallied total sales – including singles, storyteller records and other musical promotions – as topping 5 million units. To David's great wonderment, *Poppins* sold more character merchandise, books and records than any other live-action feature Disney had ever made.

Although nobody was offering anything better on his immediate return from Hollywood, David wisely turned down an invite from Louis Bardoly of Cornelius Productions to star in a three-act Hungarian farce with Diane Hart slated for presentation in London and Broadway. He had his doubts when offered the script that, by a strange twist of fate, was based in an apartment off Sutton Place in New York, the scene of David's romance with Mary back in 1943 – whether that bitter coincidence had anything to do with his decision remains unknown. Written by Ferenc Dunai, the production was first titled *Penny's French Pastry*, then renamed *The Sunday Man*. Eventually, the project rose from the ashes with David Brooks in the lead at the Morosco Theatre in New York on 13 May 1964 – it was a ball-crushing disaster, closing on the first night.

As David Jr, Jamie and Henry sprouted into lively kids, David and Audrey's third child, William, was exhibiting troublesome behavioural patterns, such as frustration and tantrums. David explained at the time:

He would spend the morning in the garden and we thought what a splendid, independent chap he was. We thought he just liked to be alone. But he did not seem to develop. He stayed withdrawn. The more I tried to give him affection the more he rejected me. We didn't know then that he couldn't communicate.[19]

At first, doctors believed he was hearing impaired because he didn't respond when spoken to. But the Tomlinsons weren't convinced and embarked on a search for a proper diagnosis. 'It was unbelievable really,' Audrey recalls. 'Just prior to going to California for *Mary Poppins*, William had been tested by two deaf specialists in the UK. The conclusion was that he was deaf but very bright from the tests he was given.'

Audrey, though, was sceptical and tested William herself in the car going home. Jamie remembered:

Dad was in his pomp and working so Mum had to cope with much of this single handed. Walt Disney took a great interest. Walt and Spencer

Tracy first founded and were then both on the board of a clinic for the deaf in California. Tracy's son was deaf. Walt and Dad had discussed concerns about William. When we were all in California, Walt arranged for William to be seen by the specialists at the clinic, who said that there was a problem but he was definitely not deaf.

The family took comfort in the certainty of a child psychologist in London, who knew something was wrong and diagnosed William as partially deaf but with a high IQ. 'The frustration for William knew no bounds,' Jamie recalls. 'He vented his anger like a donkey ... with his back to a door and kicking in the panels with his heel.' To begin with, William was sent to an institution in Oxford for problem children, which, Jamie says, did him no good. 'A sweet story was Mum packing his bag to go back to Oxford and William taking the bag away from the front door ... in other words, "I don't want to go back to Oxford."'

'There was never any question over William's future,' David Jr says. 'Dad and our mother were determined to get the best for him and resisted the subtle pressures that it may be best to just park him somewhere and forget about him.'

Fortunately, the pioneering dedication of a woman in West London turned things around, as Jamie explained:

An angel appeared in the form of Sybil Elgar. A nursery teacher, Mrs Durrant, who had looked after both William and Henry, had kept William longer than she should have done and he was starting to disrupt the Nursery School. William was about 7 at the time and totally out of control. Miss Durrant had heard about autism and Sybil, who had been a Montessori teacher. Sybil had met a beautiful young boy, Joe Allison, who had been totally out of control and had taken him on. The word autism was new. Someone in America had recognised the condition. Having spent time learning about the condition, Sybil then opened a school in Ealing, keeping Joe. The children boarded four nights a week.

To the amazement of family members, Willie's transformation at Elgar's school was swift, as David explained in 1973:

Before he went to school he had never willingly drawn a pencil across a piece of paper. Now he can write, is fastidiously clean, folds his own clothes, sings and plays in the school band. I brought him a set of tools and he can plane a piece of wood beautifully smooth.[20]

Operating from an old railway hostel, the facility in Ealing eventually became a pioneering residential school teaching forty children with autism. David saw that Elgar had the ability to 'get through the barriers' to autistic children and described her as a 'genius and a saint'. Over time, Willie even managed to utter a few words, much to the delight of his family. 'It seemed to me that William's life was transformed almost instantaneously,' says Jamie.

Gerald de Groot, one of the founders of the National Autistic Society, became friends with David. He recalled the outstanding fundraising help provided by the Tomlinson family – and David's goonish sense of humour. 'I think his role in *Mary Poppins* gives you some idea of what he was like in real life! He was also a wonderful mimic. He once phoned me using Sybil Elgar's voice and I thought I was talking to Sybil – until he started laughing!'

David made his first appearance on stage at the Grand Hotel ballroom in 1927, alongside his brothers Peter and Michael. (Mark Hourahane)

Clarence 'resided' at the sumptuous Junior Carlton Clubhouse in Pall Mall, a popular bolt-hole for Members of Parliament, lawyers and the aristocracy.

David with his brother Paul and an unknown female friend in the early 1930s.

David enlisted with the Grenadier Guards and arrived at Caterham Barracks. 'I discovered for the first time in my life just how quickly human beings can travel without leaving the ground … the foreign legion would have been a holiday camp compared to life in the Guards.' (Tomlinson Family Collection)

The site of the Leas Pavilion today. David won an apprenticeship with the Arthur Brough Players here, an opportunity he 'seized with a nose-to-the grindstone' attitude. (Mark Hourahane)

David zoomed skywards to discover a whole new passion in his life, scraping together every spare farthing to pay for instructional flights and lessons in an Avro Tutor with Flying Officer David W. Llewelyn.

R.M.S. "Andes", 26,000 TONS.   COPYRIGHT ROYAL MAIL LINES LTD   3364

Heading to Canada turned out to be a memorable trip. David spent a gruelling eight-day voyage on the Royal Mail Ship *Andes* in some of the most appalling weather conditions imaginable.

David was posted to the 34 EFTS RAF Flying Training School at Assiniboia in the prairie lands of the west.

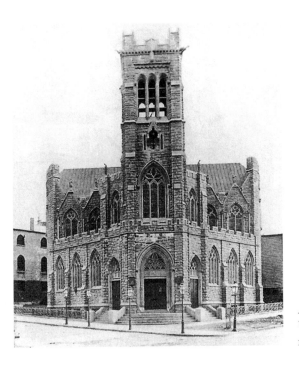

All Angels' Episcopal Church on the Upper West Side, where David and Mary married on 29 September 1943.

MARRIAGES

No. 9

Date September 29, 1943

Place All Angels' Church, New York City

GROOM

David Cecil Mac Alister Tomlinson

BRIDE

Mary Seton Hiddingh

BACHELOR OR WIDOWER?

Bachelor
161 New Bond Street

MAIDEN OR WIDOW?

Widow
404 East 55 Street

Age 26 Residence London, England

Age 34 Residence New York, New York

Parents: Clarence Samuel Tomlinson
Florence Elizabeth Tomson

Parents: Lewin Seton Owen
Gwendoline Owen

SIGNATURE OF GROOM:

DC Tomlinson

SIGNATURE OF BRIDE:

Mary Seton Hiddingh

SIGNATURES OF WITNESSES

We, who have subscribed our names below, were **Witnesses** of the marriage of the above-named parties, at the place and time stated:

L.C.W. Figg

Nancy Hill Lindsay

SIGNATURE OF OFFICIATING MINISTER:

Ralph W. Meadowcroft.

The wedding certificate from 1943. Sheffield-born vicar Ralph Sanders Meadowcroft officiated, with L.C.W. Figg, the British Consul in New York, and Nancy Hill Lindsay acting as witnesses.

14-STORY LEAP KILLS WOMAN AND 2 SONS

Wife of RAF Officer Ends Life After Attempt to Join Husband Is Thwarted

IDENTIFIED BY BROTHER

Police records show Mary rose from bed, unlocked the sliding windows in her fifteenth-floor room and plunged to her death at 8.05 a.m. along with her two sons.

David shot his scenes for *The Wooden Horse* at Luneburg Heath in Germany. The film told the tale of an audacious PoW escape using a vaulting horse to conceal a secret tunnel.

Brook Cottage, the derelict house David discovered in the village of Mursley, ending his quest for a countryside retreat in 1950.

Brook Cottage.

Petula Clark and David on location during the making of *Made in Heaven*.
(Tomlinson Family Collection)

Audrey Freeman aged 17 as the juvenile lead in Emile Littler's *Annie Get Your Gun*. (Tomlinson Family Collection)

David and Audrey married at Ealing Registry Office in 1953. Under the banner, 'Audrey weds in secret,' the *Daily Mirror* carried the story on its back page. (Tomlinson Family Collection)

The proud parents with David Jr. (Tomlinson Family Collection)

Audrey and David at the record player. He picked out classical compositions from Puccini and Verdi – as well as works by Gertrude Lawrence, Joan Hammond and 'Whispering' Jack Smith during his *Desert Island Discs* appearance in 1953. (Tomlinson Family Collection)

Audrey and David with their first child, David Jr, at Brook Cottage. (Tomlinson Family Collection)

In the summer of 1957, Jack Minster invited David to star in Jack Popplewell's comedy *Dear Delinquent* alongside Anna Massey. The two are seen here on the cover of *Theatre World* magazine.

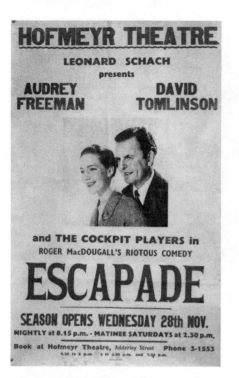

During a trip to South Africa, Audrey and David appeared in Roger MacDougall's *Escapade* at the Hofmeyr Theatre.

David's headshot from *Boeing-Boeing*, which he reckoned was 'the worst play I had ever read'.

After a long provincial run, *Boeing-Boeing* reached the London's Apollo in February 1962. (Tomlinson Family Collection)

Julie Andrews with David. Although a great Broadway and London stage star, Andrews had never appeared on film until *Mary Poppins*.

David and Julie Andrews tackle a jigsaw puzzle during the filming of *Mary Poppins*. (Tomlinson Family Collection)

The Tomlinsons at Wrightwood Drive, their home during the filming of *Mary Poppins*. (Tomlinson Family Collection)

David with Mr and Mrs Disney.
(Tomlinson Family Collection)

David and Julie Andrews by the pool. She had
already been in Hollywood for a month with
husband Tony Walton when David arrived.
(Tomlinson Family Collection)

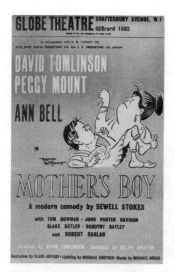

David starred with Peggy
Mount in *Mother's Boy*. 'Peggy
would bring her knitting to
rehearsals and I never knew
knitting needles could be
quite so loud or expressive,'
says Ann Bell.

David was especially active in raising funds for a pioneering
residential school for the teaching of forty children
with autism that offered termly and weekly residential
accommodation.

Actor Friedrich Schoenfelder – the 'voice of David Tomlinson' in Germany and Austria.

Relaxing with composer Robert Sherman during the filming of *Bedknobs and Broomsticks* in June 1970. (Tomlinson Family Collection)

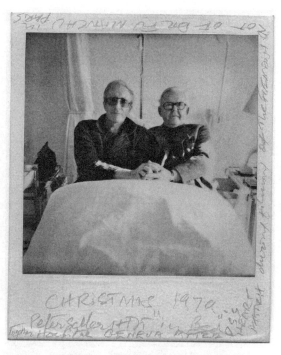

CHRISTMAS 1970

David returned to South Africa in 1973 and starred in Noel Coward's *A Song at Twilight* and *A Friend Indeed*.

Peter Sellers wanted to see David, so he flew to Gstaad. 'Peter wanted to show him *Being There*, which they watched together in hospital. Peter in his hospital bed!' (Tomlinson Family Collection)

Robert Longden and David in *Outside Broadcast* in 1986 in Birmingham. (Courtesy Robert Longden)

Robert Morley with David around 1990. David is holding a copy of his autobiography *Luckier than Most*, which was written with the assistance of Margaret Morley, Robert's daughter-in-law. (Tomlinson Family Collection)

David at Brook Cottage in the 1990s, pursued by the family ducks. (Tomlinson Family Collection)

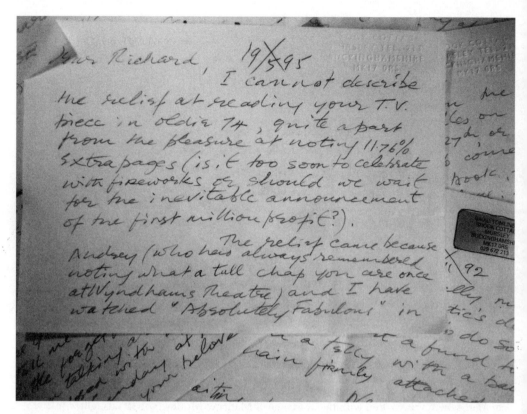

Dear Richard, 19/5/95 I cannot describe
the relief at reading your T.V.
piece in oldie 74, quite apart
from the pleasure at noting 11.76%
extra pages (is it too soon to celebrate
with fireworks or should we wait
for the inevitable announcement
of the first million profit?).
        The relief came because
Audrey (who has always remembered
noting what a tall chap you are once
at Wyndhams Theatre) and I have
watched "Absolutely Fabulous" in

David was a keen letter writer and kept up fluid correspondence with the former *Private Eye* editor Richard Ingrams.

Actor Miles Jupp with Audrey after a performance of *The Life I Lead*. (Tomlinson Family Collection)

Miles Jupp and James Tomlinson with David's beloved Rolls-Royce, registration DT4.

13

WONDrOUS OPPOrTUNITIES

Before David was swallowed up by the hoopla of *Poppins*, he let himself be talked into playing a rich uncle in *The Truth About Spring*, due to commence filming overseas in early 1964. But before that, Sewell Stokes – a writer and close friend of Robert Morley's – called with the offer to direct and star in *Mother's Boy* at the Globe, which turned out to be one of his most unfortunate ventures.

The backdrop for the story concerns a dithering author played by David having 'funny turns' and becoming the character he is writing about: Nero of Ancient Rome.

'My abiding memory of *Mother's Boy* is of continuously rehearsing all the way through the pre-London tour, every day. This isn't unusual, especially when the play isn't working,' recalls Ann Bell.[1] She had finished filming a role in a BBC adaptation of Jane Eyre before joining David and co-star Peggy Mount, famed for her roles as stone-faced mothers-in-law. Bell added:

> So lines and scenes were cut between daily rewrites and scene changes. Then one character, played by the rather wonderful old actor Ernest Thesiger was replaced in our opening week. As someone said, you were never quite sure whose face you'd see on stage in the costume that night.[2]

As the weeks wore on, initial enthusiasm had all but vanished. Bell noted personal tensions too: 'I think it's fair to say by this stage, David and Peggy were not getting on, indeed were not speaking. They would sometimes send messages to each other through me, they co-existed frostily':

> Peggy would bring her knitting to rehearsals and I never knew knitting needles could be quite so loud or expressive. They always increased in volume when David was rehearsing his bits, which of course irritated him beyond measure. He would refer darkly to Madame Defarge sitting in the corner. Then Peggy would collect up her wool and retire to her dressing room, grimly muttering and Peggy's muttering was not sotto voce.[3]

And so it went. For well over a month, Ann observed David at unusually close quarters, he was 'very funny, used a sharp turn of phrase and great charm,' but he could be 'very kind and of course he could be maddening. He had such a wonderful light comic touch. I was very grateful that I worked with him.'

Tensions backstage can't have improved when the *Daily Mirror*'s axe-attack on *Mother's Boy* opened a barrage of poor reviews. 'Sad, and frustrating to see such a waste of talent –David Tomlinson, Peggy Mount and Ann Bell – struggling to get laughs in one of the unhappiest, un-funniest farces I've ever seen,' lamented the paper's anonymous critic who described an orgy of boredom. 'The audience was in a mood to bury this Caesar, for a few boos rang out as the curtain came down.'

Reviewer J.C. Trewin thought it, 'Perhaps the least funny thing that ever happened on the way to the Forum.' Furthermore: 'David Tomlinson prattles away; Peggy Mount hectors. Neither, it seems to me, has a scrap of the period sense that might have done something at least for the scenes in Rome. But in any event, neither of them has the variety to keep such a piece as this going.'

Sitting at the front of the auditorium, veteran critic Collie Knox wondered why David Tomlinson, 'one of our finest light comedy actors, chose to star in and also to direct *Mother's Boy*,' given he had never had a flop.

'*Mother's Boy* is only memorable for two magnificent sets of ancient Rome and Baiae by movie designer Ralph Brinton, his first venture into the theatre, and for an enchanting performance as the author's secretary-doubled in Rome as his paramour by Ann Bell.'

The Stage was kinder, observing that David gave a 'relaxed and easy performance as Ralph and a positively wicked one as Nero'.

Mother's Boy left the West End in a hurry and so did David, who lamented that critics blamed his direction for the poor performance: 'I don't think that was the reason for the failure.'[4] Looking back, Bell never forgot it was:

strange that with all this I can truthfully say I really enjoyed it. Of course, there was no pressure on me as there was on the two of them for it to be a success. I remember Ernest Thesiger coming into my dressing room on our opening night to wish me good luck at the half and I was taken aback by the amount of bright blue eye shadow he was wearing and Carmine lips.[5]

David was packing for Spain to film *The Truth About Spring* when Theo Cowan, the publicity agent from his Rank days, phoned with news that Peter Sellers had suffered a serious heart attack and was in an oxygen tent in the Cedars of Lebanon Hospital in Los Angeles. Cowan had been calling everyone in Peter's orbit that night, telling how he thought, at just 38 years old, Sellers was a most unlikely candidate for a heart attack. 'He is not fat, watches his diet and doesn't eat or drink a lot.'

Cowan kept David informed on events when he jetted off for Sagaro to film scenes for *The Truth About Spring*, a family feature based on the 1921 novel *Satan* by Henry de Vere Stacpoole, the Irish author best known for penning *The Blue Lagoon*. The idea was first broached over lunch between David and director Richard Thorpe, who shared a mutual admiration for each other's work. At 68 years old, Thorpe still had a flair for theatrics but was approaching retirement after a long career. During Hollywood's golden age, he was the original director of *The Wizard of Oz* but was replaced over creative differences and later found famed directing Elvis Presley in *Jailhouse Rock* and *Fun in Acapulco*.[6] Equally important for David was working with John Mills, an actor he had known since the early 1940s – the two got on both professionally and personally.

Seen charitably by *Film Daily* as a 'joyous romp and romance on a boat', *The Truth About Spring* centred on John Mills as a loveable pipe-smoking rogue sailing the Caribbean with his tomboy teenager, played by his real daughter, Hayley. For the part, Mills burst forth with a cringing American accent that frequently lapsed into Irish–Cockney. The more he tried, the worse he got. Mill's approach to acting was unclouded by method or sentimentality – he read the script, then played the part. As shooting progressed, David slipped easily into his role as the wealthy but bored uncle of James MacArthur, the male love interest, who gave Hayley Mills her first screen kiss.

There were fun times on location, with the cast drinking tumblers of whisky at the hotel bar and on the coast where, toes in the sand, there was a chance to enjoy the idyllic beaches and sailing. Although there was a feeling of satisfaction at a job well done, the film curdled, leading John Mills to remark in his memoirs that if the picture had turned out to be half as good as 'the food, the wine, the time and the laughs we had on that location it would have been a sensation – unfortunately it wasn't.'[7] As for David, he laid out his feelings with impressive clarity: 'It was truly a dreadful film but with my new-found Hollywood cachet I was billed as making a "Guest Appearance" in nice big capital letters.'[8]

Back in Britain, David carefully husbanded his energy with a return to the Northampton repertory, where he poured his creative juices into a fortnight's run of *Trouble with Father*, a play written for him by Roger MacDougall, author of *To Dorothy a Son* and *Escapade*, among others. David was pleased, he said, to be working with repertory theatre actors for a change.

For months, David and Audrey had anticipated that the promotion for *Mary Poppins*, which was readying for release, would be a simple affair. The reality was, perhaps inevitably, quite the opposite. As Christmas approached, the Tomlinsons joined Julie Andrews and crowds of enthusiastic onlookers swirling around Leicester Square to attend the gala activities surrounding the première, where Princess Margaret and Lord Snowdon led proceedings. The family was enthralled by the pomp and circumstance of the occasion. The glare of floodlights and popping of flashbulbs provided the customary backdrop for the event, which was covered by newsreel cameras, BBC radio, press and photographers from across Europe.

As predicted, the film had a magical, wondrous effect on audiences – becoming one of the success stories of Hollywood, demonstrating how a single film could buoy up the fortunes of a company. '*Poppins* romped home! It was quite a sensation,' David gushed. 'Everybody came out of that production smelling of roses!'[9]

The film reviewer of the *Coventry Evening Telegraph* said Mr Banks had stamped David in the public memory:

David Tomlinson as the father, who learns to put his values in proper perspective by the promptings of Mary Poppins, and an assortment of other rich characters, help to make this film a success.

Hollywood Reporter critic James Powers opined that it was a triumph of many individual contributions. 'And its special triumph is that it seems to be the work of a single, cohesive intelligence.'

The Academy of Motion Pictures and Sciences were certainly impressed and the picture took thirteen Oscar nominations, winning five, for Best Song, Best Score, Best Film Editing, Best Visual Effects and a Best Actress gong for Julie Andrews. As an amusing sidelight, expatriates and British forces in Germany watching the dubbed version (before the English cut arrived) were left convinced David was a fluent German speaker; such was the uncanny accent and synchronisation performed by actor Friedrich Schoenfelder – a performance that led to him being hired as the 'voice of David Tomlinson' from then on. By this time, Germany already had its fair share of Tomlinson fans, given Rank films had been imported to the country for civilian and military consumption since the Allied occupation in 1945.

David had a low opinion of his sole venture into science fiction but wanted the money offered, so reluctantly signed on to appear in *City Under the Sea*, an Anglo-Amalgamated/American International production opposite Vincent Price, Susan Hart (once described by Bob Hope as the 'all systems go girl') and Tab Hunter. While it brought no critical acclaim, one positive outcome came through his instant rapport with Price, a feverish collector who shared David's passion for art and furniture. Producers had originally hoped to team Price with Boris Karloff, but the latter pulled out due to health issues, so John Le Mesurier filled his shoes. As it happened, David's character was a last-minute addition designed to inject a dose of humour into the story. Endless confabs between writers muddled the plot, which sees Hart, playing an American heiress, kidnapped by humanoid sea creatures and taken to their underwater lost civilisation of immortal Victorian smugglers led by Price. Ben Harris, a nice-ish hero type (Hunter) and Harold Tufnell-Jones (David, playing decidedly second fiddle to his pet chicken) set off in hot pursuit only to be captured and held prisoner.

As all this is happening, a growling deep-sea volcano threatens the existence of the smugglers' underwater empire. It was hardly surprising that Price spent six frustrating weeks grumbling that 'nobody knew what it was about'. David, too, voiced misgivings from the outset, while director Jacques Tourneur, famed for *Cat People*, was rarely willing to compromise, insisting *City Under the Sea* was a 'cinematic carnival' made in the 'Disney tradition in the sense that it's completely fanciful' in the spirit of Jules Verne.

'Tourneur was a marvellous director but he just couldn't get around the bad script,' Price lamented, adding that he didn't see his dialogue until just before shooting began. David Jr said:

> Vincent Price would try to make DT laugh during *City Under the Sea*. Neither of them had much time for Tourneur. 'David,' Vince would sidle up silkily, 'Jacques is going to approach you to give you some direction and I shall be watching you carefully to ensure that you are seen to receive this direction in the proper spirit of mutual respect that it deserves …'

Tab Hunter – a popular bubblegum-pop performer of the era – swallowed his doubts but also suspected the plot was made up as it was being shot. On the upside, he recalled working with David provided a rare thrill:

> David Tomlinson was my sidekick – a wonderful British actor! He was a solid citizen and that's what's important, to work with good people. Tourneur was a very easy going wonderful director to work for because he wasn't in your face and he knew what he wanted – and that's important. I think that picture turned out fairly well for what it was. I do remember the sets were wonderful, I do believe that good set decoration puts you into that atmosphere that you want to create.[10]

Conversely, the lavish photography – shot by Stephen Dade, who had just completed shooting *Zulu* in the Transvaal – received universal praise (underwater scenes were filmed in the Bahamas).

Although a lush-looking picture, *City Under the Sea* sank at the box office, ending up with a limited run in the US and Europe, but it became holiday staple of British and American TV schedules during the 1970s and '80s.

Fortunately, the *Poppins* dividends continued to stack up on the desk of Harry Gunnell in Mursley. MGM-British did not have to push David hard to accept a role in the spicy cold war adventure *The Liquidator*, adapted from the novel by John Gardiner about a ham-handed spy played by Rod Taylor who can't stand the sight of blood but finds himself appointed as MI5's chief assassin. But the heart of the matter is that, although Taylor can handle karate chops and belts in the belly, when ordered to liquidate enemy spies he hires Eric Sykes to do the jobs for him. Trevor Howard co-stars as Taylor's intelligence chief and Jill St John provides the love interest, while David plays the psychopathic but witty Quadrant, seeking to engineer an assassination and filch a secret RAF jet – this was the time when the government of Harold Wilson were about to scrap the TSR2, which was the inspiration for the aircraft portrayed in the film.

Playing out of type, but with tongue wedged firmly in cheek, David blithely dispatches his enemies with a silk cord, or silenced pistol along the way. And when he kills, it is suitably dramatic, as if presenting a magnificent spectacle. John Le Mesurier's subtlety shines as Chekhov, his dour-faced cohort from behind the Iron Curtain. As the plot develops, the good guys seemingly get their revenge on Quadrant – a bullet through the heart while he is in a jet plane speeding down the runway.

'It was a very British story – a spoof on James Bond. It was Jack Cardiff who insisted on David Tomlinson for a role in *The Liquidator*,' recalls screenwriter Peter Yeldham. 'Jack was a famous cameraman who had won an Oscar statuette and numerous other awards, he had turned to directing.'[11]

Yeldham remembered that MGM insisted on the svelte American actress Jill St John for the female lead, 'which was a pity as Jack and I were keen on Diana Rigg, who was brilliant as Emma Peel, so when other important roles came along Jack was very definite they should be British actors'. [12]

Over the two-month shoot, which included filming in Nice, David – along with the entire crew – was left bemused by Taylor, who touched down in Europe with a fully loaded ego and personal protection. 'There were problems with Rod Taylor,' recalls Yeldham, who was on set during the entire production. 'He arrived with what he called his two "hoods", former gangsters who accompanied him everywhere.'[13]

To make matters worse, being Australian it was assumed Taylor would play the lead role with an English accent, but, 'Rod insisted he play it with an American accent. So I had to write a couple of lines that covered a Yank being in the British Army.'

Known for his gentle disposition, Le Mesurier noted in his memoirs that Taylor fancied himself a 'Hollywood great' by having bodyguards 'to put himself somewhere in the league of Brando, with his round dozen, and Sinatra, who seemed to have a fully armed platoon'.

Jill St John can't recall production details but thought David a 'charming gentleman who had the ability to make his acting style look effortless'.

David Jr was 11 years old and remembered the family were packed off to France courtesy of the film company. 'We holidayed at the Negresco in Nice while Dad filmed his bit on location,' he says, recalling meeting Fred Hakim, one of Taylor's hoods. 'He had been badly assaulted in his youth and had more scars on his face than James Bond had on his back – punishment for some misdemeanour that had disappointed the mob.' All went swimmingly until Rod got into an altercation with a moped rider, who ended up in hospital with a massive compress over his eye:

> Fred got charged with assault – we had taken a few days in Le Lavandou and missed it. We came back to hear Harry Fine of MGM say, 'We've got a hood in jail.'
>
> It was a badly kept secret that Rod had almost poked the kid's eye out and poor long-suffering Fred had taken the rap. The production returned to the UK, leaving Fred in an uncongenial Nice prison. Eventually he was allowed out to re-join the crew, not overly impressed with the slopping out arrangements in his overcrowded cell.
>
> I vividly remember within hours of arriving at the Negresco sitting outside facing the sea while my Dad and Mum lapped up the cornucopia of stories that Akim Tamiroff – whom DT and John Le Mesurier murdered in the film – had up his sleeve. Another memory is of John Le Mesurier, with whom we spent a lot of time during the location in Nice. He was a true gentleman and treated Jimi and me like adults. One evening at the Negresco, John opened the lid on the grand piano and played quite beautifully for a good half hour. I was a bit apprehensive because one rather fierce-looking guest kept glancing disapprovingly in our direction. I mentioned this to John. 'Just let her try!' he said grimly, the only time I saw a flash of controlled aggression. No one had the slightest idea of the turmoil in his personal life at this time and fortunately he had the great *Dad's Army* years ahead of him. He also did a brilliant portrayal of

Kim Philby in a TV play circa 1972, proof that most comedians can do the serious stuff as easily as falling off a log.

Despite all the off-set drama and the bonus of a Bond-type theme song incorporating lashings of excited brass and Shirley Bassey, *The Liquidator* failed to elevate Taylor's artistic or commercial standing. Bosley Crowther tartly observed in the *New York Times* that only thing really worth seeing was the scenery.

Ernest Betts was hardly more appreciative in *The People*, where he complained the film came at the tail end of the spy glut and faded into 'one of those absurd Riviera love affairs between Rod Taylor and Jill St John that have nothing to do with the story. I found this film a bit of a bore.'

Back in Britain, the next few jobs came relatively quickly. David was cheered during September 1965 to receive the rare honour of switching on the Blackpool Illuminations – a welcome respite in a hectic schedule. Jamie recalls, 'The memorable thing for me switching the lights on was that Karen Dottrice and Matthew Garber were there too. Karen, David's age, Matti, my age. I remember the four of us tore round the Hotel together doing normal children stuff.'

While in Blackpool the Tomlinson family saw Tommy Trinder and ex-England footballer Stan Mortensen do a hilarious double act in a local night club. 'Trinder was, of course, chairman of Fulham FC and crazy about football,' says David Jr. 'His protégé Johnny Haynes, who lived at Chelsea Cloisters, was the first player to be paid £100 a week.'

Back in London, there was time for David to squeeze in an appearance on *Juke Box Jury* with Katie Boyle and Adam Faith. But upon his return to Mursley it was not quite business as usual as his workhorse routine sent him to Stoke Mandeville Hospital suffering from a mild attack of pneumonia.

14

a BUSY GENTLEMAN

Not long after the coughs and fever subsided, David strode vigorously on to BBC2's *Call My Bluff* as a team captain alongside Thora Hird and radio star Kenneth Horne. Then, an altogether different, more pleasing, endeavour followed in the brief run of the comedy *A Friend Indeed* at the Oxford New Theatre presented by Geoffrey Russell, with Jack Minster directing. The play itself struck David as a work of quality as soon as he obtained a copy from William Douglas-Home, who had devised a meaty, full-flavoured comedy set in a stately home on polling day during the 1945 General Election. 'It read very well,' David remembered, noting his part called for a slight turnabout from his usual image. 'He adored it, he loved it,' says Audrey. 'It wasn't high comedy, it was light comedy.'[1]

The producer Geoffrey Russell lived in some style in a wing of Leeds Castle. David Jr recalled:

> We visited one Sunday during the 1966 World Cup. His wife Susan, believing that Henry had got into difficulties in their swimming pool, waded in fully dressed to fish him out, forgetting that she was wearing DT's Cartier tank watch; her own wasn't waterproof either!

A Friend Indeed helped shore up David's stock. *The Stage* again led the praise, calling it an expertly tailored production:

After a gentle start Mr Home effectively tangles the skeins, in the second act in particular. He provides David Tomlinson, as Sir John, with one very rewarding scene in which he puts through a mock telephone call from Rome to Moscow. Mr Tomlinson has limited opportunity to perform his own sort of part owlish, part blight, type of comedy, but takes all his good moments extremely well.

David's next project came when West End impresario Emile Littler attempted to engage him as the linchpin in *The Impossible Years*, a light, chirpy play about a middle-class, middle-aged father trying to write a book on teenage behaviour but distracted by a band of youths, led by his daughter. For the best part of an evening, Littler painted scenes that would show off David's talent; he invented comic situations and explained a series of hilarious gags.

David thought the appeal of such a play at the height of the promiscuous Swinging Sixties was obvious enough, and so were the risks. 'I am very fussy about the plays I do,' he said emphatically, during an interview. 'I avoid those where girls come on stage and talk about diaphragms. Too much talk about sex and perversion has permeated into the theatre, television, radio, and films.'[2] Despite his mild demeanour, he sounded genuinely aggrieved about the issue:

> It's all good business, we know, but it's also horrid. Believe me, when you have four small children you think very carefully about moral standards. And I don't happen to think that discipline, reticence, and grace are dirty words. Being a parent these days is a most complicated responsibility. If I had daughters instead of sons, I would be pretty worried. Unless you fit them out with chastity belts at the age of 10 you have every reason to be concerned.[3]

Although *The Impossible Years* looked funny on the page, it turned out to be demanding and thankless. And while not averse to turning down roles for which he was ill-suited, Audrey watched David stretch himself. 'He hated that play. He knew he should not have done it,' she admitted, saying the debacle had scarcely faded from her memory. 'But he couldn't reverse course and bow out.'[4]

'Littler persuaded me with money,' David noted in his memoirs.[5] 'He had faith in the play even if I didn't and offered me a non-returnable advance to play the part.'

Casting was completed quickly but, despite the financial benefits, David's energy and spirits were taxed during the short run in Brighton and by time the curtain rose at London's Cambridge Theatre, his physical exhaustion was accelerated by severe back pain.

'The play, from the word go, was absolutely appalling, it was dreadful,' a cast member, who spoke on the condition of anonymity, recalled, adding the show was plagued by snappishness and angry disagreements.[6] 'As David was the star, he was carrying the whole production. If I can give any kind of validation for his behaviour it would have been that he realised very quickly that the play was a no-goer':

> As we became more aware that it was an absolute disaster, during the course of the rehearsals, David took it upon himself to sack the director Peter Cotes and then began directing rehearsals himself, which was a total disaster, and just got worse. All the way through the tour he hid away and didn't have much contact with the cast at all. Eventually, before the play reached the West End, Peter Cotes was persuaded to return. I'm amazed he returned, anyway, the play closed early. He made a hash of it. Everybody was dreadfully sad. David was absolutely dreadful to the rest of the cast. As we were about to close, Mr Tomlinson's parting shot to the cast was: 'I'll work again, but you lot never will.' I just couldn't believe it. Maybe he was in a crisis, I don't know.

It is remarkable to note that, amid such chaos, the production received some praise. R.B. Marriott of *The Stage*, one of DT's most admiring critics, recorded:

> It seems to me that David Tomlinson, as the psychiatrist Kingsley, has never been better. His acting has an incisiveness and wit I have not seen so abundantly displayed before, and despite the frivolity of it all, he draws a recognisable character. Some of the best moments involved Joyce Cummings, giving a superb harassed mother performance.

As *The Impossible Years* approached the end of its short, unhappy run, David's mood was further darkened with news that Walt Disney had died. 'He didn't like being told that he had the common touch, but he did,' David remarked in a short tribute on British radio. When he talked about Disney, he did so with a certain reserve. 'He knew what the public wanted and he gave it to them, and they loved it.'

Though no Tomlinson family members were present at the funeral, flowers and a note of condolence were dispatched to Lillian Disney, who had been so encouraging and gracious during the filming of *Mary Poppins*.

Back at Brook Cottage, David mulled over returning to television when Stuart Allan offered him the starring role in 'Loitering with Intent' on the BBC *Comedy Playhouse*, a mainstay of their schedules. The part presented him as an exquisitely timid solicitor with trouble on his hands when a couple of yobs pitch a tent on his front lawn.

He commented after accepting the part:

> The only reason I have not done more TV plays was because I am not very often offered a script I like. I liked this script as soon as I saw it. For a start, neither Harold Wilson nor David Frost is mentioned in it and I should think this must be a relief to the viewers.[7]

The *Comedy Playhouse* was primarily used as a showcase for writers to produce a one-off, which was presented in a six-part series and one of the six would then be chosen to be one of the following year's new sitcoms. Stuart Allan, who later found fame as the driving force behind *On the Buses*, directed the play, which featured Daphne Anderson, John Nettleton, Barry Fantoni, and Rudolph Walker, latterly known as Patrick Truman in *EastEnders*. Looking back, Fantoni remembered a happy production:

> David had that look and that avuncular voice. He seemed a bit like everybody's uncle – and you can't get more popular than that, it is as good as it gets. I knew the Beatles and everyone else back then, but when I told my mum I was working with David Tomlinson she said, 'Ah, you've reached the big time at last!'[8]

For Fantoni, it was a splendid opportunity, which he seized with gratitude:

The play was weak as a piece, but in the '60s, people wrote plays that included the statutory long-haired hippy. These characters were instantly recognisable as part of the rebellion. I looked a bit like Ringo and could get as much work as I wanted. 'Loitering with Intent' was a very good case in point.[9]

However, according to Fantoni, David must have wondered if the effort had been worthwhile as doubts crept in about the project:

David played a do-gooder figure who had married another do-gooder. He hadn't done much live TV until then and it scared the shit out of him. He was in an absolute state from the very beginning. He had an incredible problem studying; he couldn't remember his lines.[10]

In fact, Frank Muir produced the play and broke it to David rather later than might have been expected that they would be broadcasting live. The *Daily Mirror* reported 'a small panic' just prior to the broadcast, with David telling the paper he had lost his voice due to a bout of laryngitis. 'I didn't know quite what to do. I can't do acrobatics or stand on my head or anything.' Fantoni was certain the laryngitis was psychosomatic, 'because the doctor did look at him and said there is nothing wrong':

He had invented it; we all remembered it because he couldn't speak much. He was terrified, but it showed as a massive star he really wasn't comfortable with television. As the week of rehearsals progressed he got more confident – he felt more secure.[11]

Then, Fantoni explains, the day of the transmission came and, after a dry run in the afternoon, everything was going really well. That evening at 19.30, the red light came on and the studio went quiet:

The show opened in a typical English way – man sits at table reading paper, while wife pours cup of tea. But then … David started his speech with the last sentence of what he was going to say in that scene! So he started at the end. For a couple of terrible moments I saw the colour drain from the director's face. But this incredible actress, Daphne Anderson, incredibly and cleverly picked her way back and gave David lots of little starters to take him back to the beginning … she was brilliant, very clever. Then it went fine after that but the idea that the scene started with the very last sentence sent shivers up everybody's spine. In any case, we enjoyed a thumpingly good post-transmission supper – we all went off to Chelsea, and his voice came back and he was very happy it was all over and it had gone really well in spite of the fluff at the beginning.[12]

Thankfully the critics failed to detect any slip-ups. N. Alice Frick thought it a neat and funny little play, with comic observations and insights in a series that was usually given over to farce:

Comedy and farce were mixed, but the comic thread was the stronger. David Tomlinson as Mr Pinfold was appropriately fussy and earnest. Daphne Anderson, justifiably tart as his wife. Many a woman in Mrs P.'s shoes would have been downright sour.

With 'Loitering with Intent' deemed a success, given it drew the biggest audience of June 1967, attracting 7 million viewers, David found his next project more of a pleasure than a duty, when he took a holiday from decency to play Peter Thorndyke, the sharply scripted villain-in-chief in Disney's lavish Technicolor comedy *The Love Bug*. Film historian Jeffery Kurtti says that after Walt's passing, his creative heirs 'strove to advance with the times and respect the values of Walt himself'.

Creating a sharp, modern comedy such as *The Love Bug* was a tentative step to a new kind of film-making for the studio, and bringing forward 'old friends' in the cast such as David Tomlinson seemed a safe 'endorsement', and a method to reassure purists that Walt's ideas were not being left behind.

The camera began rolling at Burbank on 1 April 1968, on what turned out to be a happy production featuring the clean-cut Dean Jones, Michele Lee and Buddy Hackett, an actor famed for his puppy-dog expressions. By all accounts, David and Jones were a perfect blend as they fought over the possession of a Volkswagen Beetle with a mind of its own. 'David Tomlinson, a unique actor,' Jones said in a filmed documentary. 'I mean understated Englishman and yet he had this outlandish, vaudevillian, over-the-top sense of humour. So the juxtaposition of those two things and his personality made for very interesting punch lines or straight lines.'

Michele Lee was 26 years old when she signed to play Carole Bennet, Jones's love interest and Thorndyke's assistant. Back then, she was also an up-and-coming singer and earmarked to record an LP at Columbia Records while shooting was under way, forcing her to split her time on the film set during the day and at the recording studio at night. Reflecting on the production, which took the cast to shoots at Disney's Golden Oak Ranch and Riverside International Raceway in California, Lee remembered filming was a delight for all:

> David was loved far and wide, just like his teeth! He was magical. This was very early in my career and I was just eating everything up around me and I would watch all the actors. I was learning what was happening on set. Watching David Tomlinson was like watching a comic genius. It was always so truthful that it didn't matter whether it was funny or not … it was always right.[13]

In the midst of filming, David was packing his bag to go to the studio when Audrey called from Mursley and asked him if he was sitting down. His long-suffering mother Florence, who had been battling for her health for some time, had died of heart failure – a heartbreaking blow. Trapped in Los Angeles by obligations, Audrey supervised funeral arrangements and gave comfort to Clarence. 'Only my mother went to the funeral and rather to her relief, Clarence asked her to drive them away from the crematorium. He had become quite an erratic driver in old age,' David Jr recalled with a smile.

Marked by a blitz of TV and press coverage, *The Love Bug* turned out to be a huge success, becoming the third highest-grossing hit of 1968, earning over $51.2 million in the United States.[14] The verdict of the critics was positive too, with David winning especially favourable notices.

'I was immediately attracted to him by his sidelong observation that honesty is a quality not necessarily to be despised,' Michael Billington noted, while Dick Richards in the *Daily Mirror* thought the best thing was the splendid villain 'played with relish by David Tomlinson, who dreams up some unsporting tricks and knavish plots to throw a spanner in the works of Dean Jones and the Love Bug'.

However, the public relish for the movie didn't impress Vincent Canby of *The New York Times*, who shot off a nasty notice entitled: 'Disney Film Offers Ad for a Certain Car', in which he described a 'long, sentimental

Volkswagen commercial about a small car'. He hardly warmed the cockles of DT's heart either with his downright hostile remark that David Tomlinson was 'the British comedian you apparently hire when Terry-Thomas is busy.'

Whilst such biting criticism bruised his ego, his 51-year-old body was also exhausted after six months of arduous filming. David Jr never forgot DT being wheeled in to Stoke Mandeville Hospital for an operation on a debilitating hernia:

> In fact, DT knew he had the hernia before he set off for LA. On arrival in Hollywood he fibbed during his medical before the filming of the *Love Bug* started. It actually gave him a lot of discomfort, for instance getting under the hood of the VW in order to peer through the dashboard and walking frog-legged on his haunches for several paces.

A few weeks after the operation, he was ever so gingerly nudged by Peter Bridge to prepare for a new challenge: starring in the seldom-seen Shaw opus *On the Rocks* alongside Rachel Gurney, Robert Flemyng and Jack Hulbert. The play had been revived by Bridge for a national tour and performance at the Dublin Theatre Festival programme. According to David Jr, this was one of his best performances, playing Prime Minister Sir Arthur Chavender, a part that included perhaps the most impassioned speech of his career. 'It is a very difficult play but he made it look so easy,' says Lawrence Douglas who was amazed to be cast as his son. 'We were on stage in some of the biggest theatres in England – the Leeds Grand and all that – and David just had the whole audience in the palm of his hand, he was such a wonderful player.'[15]

The Observer's critic Merete Bates still recalls watching the play at the Opera House in Manchester. 'There was always something poignant about David's performances, a sense of loss and bewilderment,' she commented admiringly. 'How much the war or the death of his first wife contributed to this it's hard to know but I suspect it was simply his character.'[16]

In her review, she thought the casting intelligent, noting David managed to 'blossom from pout-mouthed senility to spry energy as the Prime Minister'. The verdict of *The Stage* came as a pleasant surprise: 'David Tomlinson provides a splendid study of the Prime Minister, and in the process masters what must be the longest part of his career.'

15

THE 1970S

Hollywood success gave David Tomlinson the freedom to choose his projects without the need to expend his energies rashly. 'Everything has changed, and not always for the better,' he complained, as his mind drifted back to an earlier, more innocent time.

'I think an awful lot of what one sees is not very funny. I'll always do films, provided they pay. I don't really work hard,' he explained on reframing his priorities – very few offers 'pique my interest.'[1]

Although he often rejected work in favour of family life, Harry Gunnell remained a man not to be trifled with. 'If he didn't get the fee he asked for, he wouldn't do it. That simple,' Jamie explains, adding his father spent more time administrating his investments.

Audrey says he was a good businessman, but he couldn't have been a 'top businessman' because he wasn't prepared to gamble. 'He was too careful to be a businessman really. He wasn't prepared to speculate. He was always careful but interested. If he could knock something down in price, he would. He liked to bargain.'[2]

While principled about the fees he expected for artistic endeavours, this attitude might have led to him to inadvertently turn down a few plum roles. 'He made some bad choices, without a doubt,' Jamie adds. 'My mother says he should never have chosen theatre for himself. He would do anything Jack Minster told him to do. If Jack had lived, Mum thinks that he would have insisted on him working in the theatre and guided him very well.'[3]

David Jr also says his father had some awareness that his choices wouldn't necessarily conform to what theatre-goers expected to see him doing:

In the '60s, a delightful neighbour called Jane Palmer typed his and Harry Gunnell's letters. Her husband, David, had been invalided out of the army having suffered a nasty injury to one of his hands, courtesy of a faulty hand grenade. They were a rather glamorous couple with four or five very nice children and when Dad was sent a play he'd sometimes give it to David Palmer to read. Unerringly Palmer would accurately forecast the plays that went on to succeed and those others that were doomed to fail. It became a joke that Dad would routinely ignore Palmer's advice.

The 1970s were a period of intense transition for the British film business. MGM-British, where David had made *The Liquidator*, closed its studio, while John Davis at Rank continued with cold-hearted efficiency to strip the company of its film interests as he attempted to purchase Watney's chain of pubs to beef up the company's leisure subsidiary. In any case, with record profits from its Rank-Xerox copying machine business pouring in since the mid-1960s, movie-making had largely become a footnote in the Rank profile. Writing in the *Daily Express*, Kenneth Fleet observed Davis's vision rankled many in the industry. 'The tragedy is that, except in all too brief spells, Rank has shown itself incapable of reinvesting those [Xerox] millions with much acumen or of managing its own cinema, leisure and industrial operations with much skill. For Rank's decline, John Davis must take the blame.'

With more free time, leisure provided David Tomlinson many pleasures:

What I watch on the 'box' is rather like what I read – never fiction. I've just discovered reading. I've read a biography of Irving. I don't think he was the most fantastic of actors but a generous man. He had humour. I like that. Sir Henry Irving ... I really think my own knighthood is greatly overdue. What a funny business it is knighting actors.[4]

Audrey recalled:

David was interested in everything. He was a man that loved art, he was a collector, he loved architecture he liked going to the law courts, he had such a variety of hobbies, which I found wonderful because it was different for me. From the moment I went into the theatre at the age of 15, I only ever met people who were interested in the business.[5]

While David took an interest in politics, Audrey says he guarded his views carefully, but his attitude was very liberal:

Most actors were at that time left wing. He watched every news bulletin on the telly. Vanessa Redgrave did fundraising for the Autistic Society and they became friends, but he wouldn't have talked politics with her. These were people who were almost communists at one time.[6]

But it wasn't just politics that interested him. David Jr said his father's fascination with the law and courts stretched back to the late 1950s, when he became friendly with the chief clerk at the Old Bailey, a larger-than-life character called Leslie Balfour Boyd:

Boyd would get Dad and friends into the privileged seats behind Counsel in the older courtrooms where all the notorious cases were tried. In 1956 Dad watched Geoffrey Lawrence QC winding up in his defence of the Chief Constable of Sussex, a certain Mr Ridge who had been indicted on corruption charges.

He explained the jurors were obviously pretty mesmerised by Lawrence's forensic skill and found Ridge not guilty. A hapless detective inspector and a sergeant were both convicted and sentenced to long terms of imprisonment:

As was usually the case when police officers found themselves in the dock, the evidence against the junior officers had been stronger than against their chief. Making no bones what he thought of the mixed verdicts, the trial judge Mr Justice 'put 'em down' Donovan commented when sentencing the detectives that their chief constable had set them a very bad example.

On another occasion, David sat open-mouthed as a judge at the Old Bailey wore the black cap to sentence Joseph Chrimes to death by hanging.

Chrimes had murdered 60-year-old Norah Summerfield while burgling her home in Hillingdon in December 1958. 'Dad was very much opposed to the death penalty, though it had been a terrible case involving the murder of a defenceless old lady in her own home,' David Jr said.

During these spells in the real world, Tomlinson trained his sights on enjoying the humdrum of ordinary life and its tiny bedevilments. On his various travels, the blight of new 'eyesore buildings' left him perpetually flummoxed. 'He wasn't keen on modern architecture, I'm afraid,' giggles Audrey. 'He wouldn't have studied it. It just didn't appeal to him. His passion was Georgian and Regency period.'[7]

During a brief visit to Liverpool – which had seen large, monolithic, brutalist buildings spring up during the 1960s – David could not hide his distaste: 'I was shocked by some of the new buildings going up. I think we should look elsewhere to see how rebuilding can be done properly,' he told the local paper.

Liverpool, he argued, was threatened by the menace of 'absolutely repugnant' buildings. On a trip to Birmingham, he was equally vocal while adopting the pose of an interested observer:

> I like old industrial towns like Birmingham or Leeds. The finest thing in the world would be to take the planners and put them all under water for twenty-four hours.[8]

His opinion about London wasn't much cheerier, where the sheer gall of architects ripping the city apart was 'enough to make me weep', he lamented, referring to the West End, which had changed beyond recognition. Leicester Square had been remodelled into a pedestrian precinct, while casinos and graffiti-spattered discothèques with velvet couches and gyro laser lights had replaced the clubs and elegant restaurants he once frequented.

However, amid this modern world, a journalist observed that David remained an eminently reasonable sort, with a no-nonsense air and self-deprecating humour. He said even his car conveyed a nonchalance, which had become part of his almost aristocratic pose: 'His Rolls-Royce was always as spotless and gleaming as his shoes. To an extent he himself looks like an Establishment figure, he affects to be a conservative and his Rolls-Royce fits him well.'

The car in question, a Silver Cloud 1, was the last of the rigid chassis models with a 4½ litre, six-cylinder engine. David Jr explained:

Dad had bought a Bentley from Jack Barclay and traded it in for the Silver Cloud, which from new had belonged to Barclay himself and was only about eighteen months old when he sold it to us. Barclay's sales technique was to say, 'Take the car away and see how you get on with it.' Of course, that made it rather difficult to return. In the late '60s Barclay nearly persuaded Dad to exchange the Silver Cloud for a Silver Shadow, but the shrewd Jimi, who would only have been 12 or 13, rightly predicted that the Cloud would retain a vintage status long after the Shadow was overtaken by other models.[9]

While Henry says, 'He didn't drive around in the Rolls very often because he didn't like getting it wet,' former *Private Eye* editor Richard Ingrams often saw David behind the wheel and thought the car endearingly old-fashioned:

Oh, he loved driving it. He was in full control in that sunken leather seat. I remember particularly going in it with my partner Deborah Bosley, who he was very keen on. David drove us up to see John Wells performing in a play in Bath.[10]

That memory reminded Ingrams of other leisurely passions. 'We used to meet at Boodle's Club for lunch; I always thought it was a pretty stuffy sort of place,' he said, referring to the club on St James's Street founded in 1762 by the Earl of Shelburne:

He liked it because there weren't any other actors in it and he could have lunch relatively undisturbed. He had a certain disdain of pretentiousness of the acting profession, so I don't think he was particularly keen on being surrounded by other actors. Of course, he had his special friends amongst actors but you couldn't say he was a 'luvvie' at all. As far as I was concerned, we had very little theatrical chat with the exception of Robert Morley, he spoke about him a lot. David was very proud of the fact that he insulted the secretary of Boodle's. He'd accosted him on the stairs of the club and said to him, 'I do admire the way you are always so pleased with yourself. How do you manage it? Do you go to evening classes?' He was very proud of that![11]

Much to Audrey's embarrassment, just prior to joining Boodle's, her husband had, in fact, enjoyed membership of the illustrious Garrick Club, whose members included Laurence Olivier, John Mills, David Niven and John Gielgud. 'It was very difficult to get into the Garrick, they were full,' Audrey recalls. 'But the moment he got in, he resigned! Terrible, I'm ashamed of that because of his two sponsors, they were horrified!'[12]

It is feasible that the Garrick restaurant – where liveried waiters served modern cuisine – was the cause of his ire. He often cursed substandard cooking, such as the overcooked vegetables, 'dreary' salads, greasy chips and heavy pastry found in many restaurants. 'Yes, he could be tricky at restaurants,' Audrey laughs. 'People had to have the right expression really. If we got somebody gloomy, it was a bad sign for him … or if they weren't interested.'[13]

The British, David explained to the *Newcastle Evening Chronicle*, were notorious for accepting cold or badly prepared food without a whimper:

> The real test of any cook or English hotel is to order a very plain English dish such as cold sliced roast beef, served with a salad dressing. That's something, you see, that they can't whack up and I'm sick to death of whacked up food … bits of meat heated up and smothered in some ghastly sauce, then covered with pineapples – tinned pineapples at that – well, it's just not good enough.

On the few occasions they bumped into each other socially, Jess Conrad thought David would have made a superb restaurant critic:

> Oh yes, he did have opinions about such things. Like most personalities and actors, he was quite different off, and he was so charismatic and beautifully turned out – always great for conversation and very witty.

16

reTUrN TO HOLLYWOOD

Eager for a new challenge, David renewed his acquaintance with Disney for *Bedknobs and Broomsticks* to play the roguish Emelius Browne in his third Hollywood role secured by Maud Spector.

'Dad took me round to Maud's flat in Mayfair and she insisted on uncorking a bottle of Champagne to toast another project,' remembers David Jr. 'With friends like her, Dad didn't need an agent.'

From the outset, Spector had assured David that Julie Andrews would play the lead role of Eglantine Price but, despite a generous financial offer, she hemmed and hawed, leading to producer Bill Walsh approaching Angela Lansbury, who he tracked down in Germany filming *Something for Everyone*. Key to the role was Lansbury's strong English accent, which, remarkably, she still maintained despite having arrived in America thirty years earlier. 'I think the script has so many marvellous facets, character, humour, heart and an opportunity for rare inventiveness in so many areas,' she scrawled in a short note in response to Walsh's overtures. 'So, all things being equal, I do hope I'm 'Your Girl.' [1]

The final shooting script – Production Number 0108 – was sent by courier to Brook Cottage on 5 February 1970 and featured a plot bursting with action and animation. The project was first presented to Bill Walsh and the Sherman Brothers in the early 1960s. 'Walt [Disney] saw enough of an 'outline' of characters and situations that a similar live action–animation musical fantasy could be crafted by his talented team,' says Jeffrey Kurtti. The story deals with three wartime child evacuees discovering that their guardian Eglantine Price (Lansbury) is, in fact, an amateur witch and between them foil a Nazi invasion of Britain. Robert Sherman thought David's portrayal of Browne, the devilish headmaster of the Correspondence College of Witchcraft, was superb. 'We were going to use Ron Moody, who was a fine English actor. He played Fagin in Oliver,' he explained. 'We had been seeking a solid, English actor who could really do that phoney-baloney and everything.'[2]

To start with, Moody accepted the part, 'but then he decided he didn't want to do it because he wasn't the star – the star being the lady. So, he pulled out.' Hence, David was cast.

As contract negotiations continued, Disney craftsmen were busily constructing London's old Portobello Road in plasterboard on Sound Stage 2, which became the most expensive and largest set the company had ever built. On the scrubland – or backlot – craftsmen completed an equally impressive job of creating the English village of Pepperinge Eye. 'I like surprises,' David told reporters before embarking on the five-month shoot. 'That's why I cannot refuse a Disney picture. Where else can one perform with levitated nannies, driverless Volkswagens and airborne beds?'

However, although he wrote and spoke fondly of *Poppins* and the *Love Bug*, David's expectations of *Bedknobs* dimmed quickly. 'To begin with it was magic,' Audrey recalled but, although filming went crisply, it was not without incident. Before leaving England, David had taken it upon himself to carefully prepare his own costumes, an action which led to an indelicate dilemma.[3]

'That was very unfortunate,' she says tactfully, recalling a spat with writer Don DaGradi. 'David had chosen these natural clothes, which I thought were spot-on really, but Don, who had always worked in magic, didn't get it. David adored Don and had a wonderful relationship with him through *Poppins* and *The Love Bug* but this dispute soured things.'[4]

After some tension and misunderstanding, DaGradi's costumes – a tweed suit, red sweater and elaborately long cape – were used.

To make matters worse, David was upset by a growing lack of rapport with his co-star. 'I knew things weren't going well,' Audrey recalled.[5] For whatever reason – which she has never understood – Lansbury appeared to be intimidated or nervous of her husband:

Well, this is why she was so tricky to work with. It's terrible; it's like an actor on stage that is so frightened that they will upstage you, unconsciously. Because they're frightened of what you're doing, they want to see what you're doing all the time – so they step back and it's called upstaging.[6]

By David's description of what was happening, Audrey thought Lansbury 'an insecure actress' who was determined to be number one:

To behave like that on a film is boring and unnecessary. Lansbury was terrified of him and made it very tough. David should have been flattered, you see, but he wasn't. He found it very awkward. Shame.[7]

Roy Snart, who played evacuee Paul Rawlins – whose possession of the bedknob and the Isle of Naboombu children's book led to the group's adventures – was under no illusion about who was the star. 'The anecdote that my mother always tells about David,' says Roy, 'was that he was definitely the big shot on the set; very popular, very professional but a bit scary. He was always nice to me and naturally, as a small boy, I was oblivious to all the politics':

When I learnt my lines I learnt everyone's lines (that spoke to me) so when David, on one occasion, couldn't recall his lines I had no difficulty reminding him of what they were to help him out. My mother said that the set went deathly quiet and there were looks of horror on the crew's faces – a small boy telling a big star his lines – but he just smiled, thanked me and we shot the scene again. I was completely oblivious to my faux pas until my mother suggested that I didn't 'help out' in future, when we got home.[8]

For the musical numbers, the Shermans provided simple vocal refrains that wouldn't tax David's range, including 'The Beautiful Briny' a song originally written for *Mary Poppins*. 'David was not a singer but he sang his heart out and he was so good. He did a wonderful job,' Robert Sherman remembered. In unpublished excerpts from his autobiography *Moose: Chapters from My Life*, Sherman further recounted the role of Professor Browne was markedly different from that of Mr Banks in *Poppins*:

Mr Banks strove to fit into society while Professor Browne blissfully skimmed on society's outskirts. Like he had done in that earlier role,

David was tasked to play the British 'Everyman'. It's just that *Bedknobs* takes place in a different era to *Poppins*. There was something specifically relevant about the timing of *Bedknobs'* release as well. Like 1940 Britain, 1971 was also an 'Age of Not Believing' and therein lays the special significance of the movie's theme. Like the protagonist he played in *Poppins*, when Professor Browne learns the lesson of the witch he ultimately comes to believe in himself. As the lyric of the song goes:

You must face The Age of Not Believing
Doubting everything you ever knew
Until at last you start believing
There's something wonderful in you

When Professor Browne begins to believe in himself, that's when magical things start to happen for him. Then together with Eglantine, they successfully push back the Nazi invasion.[9]

Hiding behind the stiff moustache he pasted on for the part, David expressed his enthusiasm for the project to journalists touring the set: 'There is much singing and dancing along the way. We finally land at Angela's seaside cottage, where I fix a tasty meal of sausage and mash. I go from "bed" (a pun) to worst you might say.'

Lansbury too gushed publicly, saying it turned out to be 'one of the best things I ever did. It was delightful.' She especially appreciated the nuts-and-bolts aspect of Disney production:

It was acting by the numbers, because they had what they knew as a 'storyboard' at Disney and every shot is pre-decided on and drawn and the director shoots that shot – nothing else. So, the show is actually pre-cut and shot via the storyboard and that's it.[10]

The most ambitious animation sequence transported the cast to the mysterious land of Naboombu on a flying bed. Lansbury said at the time:

So much of the photography is trick stuff, like flying around on wires, or playing against an eerie yellow screen – the animation characters are put in later. One scene has me watching a football game in which David

Tomlinson is the only human player; all others are cartoon figures. I sit in the grandstand conversing with a tiger.[11]

Looking back at the picture, Kurtti thinks David was somewhat miscast as Emelius Browne:

His intelligent warmth and comic timing were certainly utilised admirably, but I think he was perhaps a bit too old to make a credible romantic connection with Lansbury's Miss Price, and his character needs a bit more deviltry and rakishness in order to effectively shed that skin at the end of the second act.[12]

All in all, Audrey says: 'It must have been awful for David, really. He had (the dispute with) Don about the clothes, and Angela Lansbury who sounded impossible – bloody awful.'[13]

Unsurprisingly, the experience left little impression on David and in his memoirs he omitted the film altogether.

By the time of its world premiere in London on 7 October 1971, *Bedknobs and Broomsticks* had become the costliest Disney feature ever made. Peter McGarry, always a perceptive critic, welcomed the old Disney sparkle, adding he thought it 'far more attuned to youngsters than the colourful aimlessness of *Mary Poppins*'.

However, as well turned as the film was, *The New Yorker* complained it had 'no logic' and 'dribbles on for so long that it exhausts the viewer before that final magical battle begins'.

Although Kurtti asserts the resulting film was 'pleasant and commercially successful', he too believes the story meanders with superfluous subplots. 'It never achieved a status such as *Mary Poppins*. There was no longer a Walt, who was the arbiter of taste, the defender of ideas, and the last word in story decisions.'[14]

On David's return to Britain, Disney's publicity department asked him to do all the usual chores that a completed movie required – interviews with magazines, an appearance in a 'Disney-themed' special edition of TV's *Golden Shot* with Bob Monkhouse in which he was the sole guest, followed by a one-off 'Disney DJ slot' on BBC Radio 2, which turned out to be a surprise hit and was rebroadcast in the Commonwealth and on the World Service.

Given his volume of work, it was surprising David managed to help organise another charity drive for the Ealing autistic children's school at the Acton Odeon with Ian Carmichael and Robert Morley, who, in his own unique style, entertained guests with silhouettes of animals on the screen. 'They have been of great assistance to me,' Sybil Elgar told the audience. 'And I appreciate it.' It wasn't long afterwards that David persuaded Vanessa Redgrave – a woman regarded with some alarm by older conservative actors – to present raffle prizes, including a plate of her own home-baked muffins, at another fundraiser for Elgar's school.

For a few months, David successfully avoided having to work, before being persuaded that a spell in South Africa would make for a relaxing winter. The invitation to direct and star in *A Friend Indeed* – the play he had appeared in back in 1966 – came just as Equity, the actors' union, announced it would no longer offer support or protection to performers who choose to appear before segregated audiences. Audrey noted:

> Well, that was no concern for David. He certainly didn't support the colour bar. In Africa he worked for a very nice couple, who were very liberal. I felt he was due for a recharge and that's what happened, it was a lovely time. He had no bad times there, he had white and coloured friends – there were no problems for him. [15]

The play was staged at Johannesburg's Academy Theatre, whose manager, Ray Cooney, was associated with the impresario Hymie Udwin. *The Stage* described the fourteen-week run in Johannesburg, followed by a tour of the country, as a 'tremendous success', as Geoff Boycott recalled:

> I spent quite a bit of time with David in Johannesburg. I think at that time I was still doing a bit of coaching at the King David School during the summer. Because there was no theatre on Sundays, he used to come for lunch at the home of Selma and Jules Browde, both marvellous people. Jules was an advocate, dealing with human rights, and Selma did equally wonderful things, especially in Soweto. [16]

Boycott never forgot long afternoons dining al fresco, swimming, playing tennis and relaxing in the sunshine:

It was a treat for him because he worked at nights in the theatre and sometimes till late. We would talk cricket and theatre, he was passionate about cricket. That's how I got to know him well; there was a lot of fun and laughter – he had an irresistible impulse to raise a laugh.[17]

One night, Boycott recalls, David sallied out to do his bit on stage:

He got me tickets in the front row. Anyway, during the play he winked at me and was adlibbing – I can't remember what he said – but he slipped something in about cricket – I understood the gag but there might have been locals there wondering 'what the bloody hell was that about!' He could be very funny, lovely man![18]

More than anything else, Jamie remembered spending time with another sporting great, the footballer Stanley Matthews, who was working in Soweto at the same time:

Dad and I saw a lot of Stan. I played table tennis with him and narrowly beat him. Only afterwards did Dad say that Stan 'did not like losing at all to me'. Like all professional sportsmen … they can't stand losing, Stan later thrashed me on the tennis court!

Before wrapping up, *A Friend Indeed* briefly played in Salisbury in Southern Rhodesia, where the controversial Prime Minister Ian Smith joined the audience. Relations between Smith and British Prime Minister Harold Wilson had broken down years earlier, leading Smith to unilaterally declare independence in 1965.

David noted in his memoirs that the spat was still brewing. 'I assured Ian Smith,' he said, speaking from the stage with extravagant politeness, 'that I would personally carry any message he would like to send to Harold Wilson.' This unscripted offer received a rapturous round of applause from the audience.

Back in Britain with the part still fresh in his mind, David revived his role in *A Friend Indeed* for Anglia Television. He described the play as 'high comedy': 'I'm not chasing prestige. Intellectuals tend to be contemptuous of such plays. But personally I wouldn't want to go near Hamlet. Far too serious'[19]

During the summer of 1974, with David's encouragement and Sybil Elgar's enthusiasm, the Ealing autism school planned to move out of London. 'When William was approaching his teens, Sybil needed to have somewhere for adult and adolescent autistic people,' Jamie explained. 'Her children were growing up. Dad and Robert Morley raised most of the funds to buy Somerset Court near Weston-super-Mare.'[20]

Set in 26 acres of fields and grounds, it became the first residential home in Europe devoted specifically to adults suffering from autism. To help raise the £120,000 needed to buy the property, Morley even made a television appeal, which raised more money than any other fundraiser had done up to that time. David Jr adds:

Robert Morley was a great help. Even though he was always behind with paying his own income tax bill, he was extraordinarily generous. He never complained about his own crippling tax burden, which stood at around £60,000 in 1969. Because Robert never stopped working, his tax inspector seems to have decided not to kill the goose while it was still laying, and the anxiety never stopped Robert giving his money to good causes. When Somerset Court started and needed some private funding, Robert approached the great and the good. He told Leslie Grade that his twin brother Lew was giving £1,000! So, Leslie gave £1,000 and then Robert went to Sir Lew Grade and said truthfully, 'Leslie's giving £1,000.' In fact, Robert actually nobbled Sir Lew at a drinks party. He was full of some anecdote, which Robert only half listened to. Sensing he'd finished, Robert asked him to cough up. 'Of course,' said Sir Lew testily, 'you'll have it by tomorrow morning at the latest but don't interrupt me again ...' and he carried on with his story. Robert actually introduced John Lennon to Sybil Elgar as well as getting him to contribute. However, even Robert couldn't shame H.M. Tennent's 'Binkie' Beaumont to cough up. Robert felt that Beaumont owed him as Robert had made a success in a play that Peter Ustinov had written but which Robert had substantially altered, thus 'saving Ustinov from himself', as Robert saw it. Beaumont had produced the play and Robert felt that he'd helped him avoid a substantial financial loss. Beaumont refused and though Robert went and sat in an outer office a Beaumont's HQ waiting for him to come in and out and attempting the shake-down each time, 'Binkie' was intransigent.

Back on the work front, the French publicity mill began grinding at fever pitch when David joined Mickey Rooney to feature in *Bons Baisers de Hong Kong*, a French-made James Bond parody.

David portrayed the Lord Chamberlain, while the enormously energetic Rooney played an American megalomaniac who kidnaps Queen Elizabeth II. For some reason, the plot sees the British secret service request assistance from their French counterparts, who, in turn, dispatch four dazed-looking dimwit agents to investigate. The occasional comic line fought hard with a soundtrack that flipped from French organs to Chinese Ruan, depending on which ethnicity was onscreen.

Unsurprisingly, David regarded it a 'bizarre experience', given the lack of comic gravity. Worse still, production in Hong Kong was overshadowed when Rooney was forced to deny persistent rumours that he intended to make singer Jan Chamberlain his eighth wife. Like many cast members, the 55-year-old former child star spent much of the shoot in bed with flu.

'The whole cast and crew got food poisoning or pink eye or both which didn't help matters,' David recounted.[21]

When released, *Bons Baisers de Hong Kong* treated cinema-goers to a flashy milieu of gags, slapstick, kung fu kicks and never a moment of silence. But for all its faults, it enjoyed a successful run in France, however distribution in Britain proved tricky. 'I wouldn't like to show a film making fun of royalty,' Maurice Young, boss of United Artists, said at the time. 'It is a comedy and I don't think it is very unfriendly, but I don't think anyone in Britain will take it.'[22] He was right: it bombed in the UK.

It took David a month to recover from his Hong Kong experience before he returned to the stage as director and star in an English adaptation of Francoise Dorin's French comedy *The Turning Point*, which toured the provinces before reaching the West End.

'This comedy lends itself to English more than most,' David told the *Birmingham Daily Post*, as he described the plot about a middle-aged playwright's lament at the advance of 'kitchen-sink' authors:

Nothing is more different really than a French lady and an English lady – never the twain shall meet. My un-favourite kind of play is when they don't translate it, and the characters call each other Monsieur and Pierre or Georges.

During the *Post* interview, he took a world-weary, or at least worldly, view of the 'theatre of naughtiness':

> The naked body came as no surprise to me. I knew all about it. Of course, there won't be anything of that sort in my play. If I took my clothes off, the theatre would empty in 30 seconds – some say five, but they're being unkind.

Despite strong performances by David, Maurice Roeves and Anne Rogers, the play failed to ignite, as described by Michael Billington in the *Guardian*:

> [A] tricksy, trite, anti-trivial, play … a real turkey. And one can only sympathise with David, whose hooded eyebrows and baleful bloodhound stare have been put to infinitely better uses, and Rogers and Roeves, for getting caught up in such a disaster. It is indeed rather like watching boulevard comedy write its own epitaph.

The Stage critic R.B. Marriott was equally sympathetic:

> David Tomlinson plays the old guard playwright; a very accomplished comedy artist whom it is good to see after a long absence. Yet, in spite of brilliant efforts, he is unable to rescue the play. One watches him with great interest, he is so deft and agreeable without being able to become much interested in the character he is playing.

In April, David returned to the Savoy Theatre, not to relive his triumphs in *The Ring of Truth*, but as a surprise guest alongside 91-year-old Dame Sybil Thorndike, Wilfred Hyde-White, John Huston and Peter Ustinov sharing their memories on a *This is Your Life* special dedicated to Robert Morley. During his tribute, Hyde-White had the audience in stitches as he described Morley's perfect day as 'staying at the racecourse till dark, and the casino till daybreak', while Huston gave a little speech about how Morley once twisted his arm into jointly bidding for a racehorse. Huston explained he was just about to agree when the auctioneer shouted, 'Going, going, gone!' and slammed down his gavel, whereupon the horse Robert so fancied joint-owning let out a last 'neigh … and dropped down dead'.

Not long after, in an attack of bad judgment, David returned to Hong Kong to work alongside the American TV star Jack Lord, a man he later described as among the most arrogant and unpleasant actors he ever had the misfortune to encounter. The two met after the producers of the crime show *Hawaii Five-O* invited him to play an ineffective British police officer in a two-hour episode. David had seen the series several times and was vividly aware of the hoopla newspapers generated about the show. In addition to an attractive financial sweetener, he was cheered to learn he would be reunited with James MacArthur, who had played his nephew in *The Truth About Spring* a decade earlier.

Hawaii Five-O was an all-family crowd-pleaser, whose success had put it right on top of the CBS food chain. Lord, who also acted as executive producer, portrayed Detective Steve McGarrett, pursuing his perennial antagonist Wo Fat, a key figure in the theft of deadly nerve gas. Lord's reputation for rudeness towards colleagues has been well documented over the decades, although Jamie says, 'There was no incident in *Hawaii Five-O*,' just that his Dad, 'Really didn't rate Jack Lord at all. He was naught out of ten as an actor and as a bloke.' Kam Fong Chun, one of the actors engaged on the episode, thought Lord a temperamental perfectionist with a tough-as-nails attitude, 'after work, he had nothing to do with us socially. He considered shooting strictly business and would not tolerate flippancy or horseplay on set.'

To compound difficulties, David remained unenamoured by Hong Kong with its pungent smells, pink eye, soaking humidity and chatter spilling out on to the streets from every window. He remembered noise began at dawn and continued long into the night: the shouting of tradesmen, the rattle of pushcarts and the shriller outbursts of tourists indulging in the local nightlife. That, combined with navigating the muck and bullets of Lord's temper, made for hard work, which David considered the most bizarre filming he'd ever done. Furthermore, David Jr once heard his father speaking of an odd experience prior to shooting that shone a light on Lord's querulous temperament:

It was actually a 'join me in silent prayer' session on the first day of shooting – Jack Lord's language uttered with eyes closed, followed by a prolonged, uncomfortable silence. DT had a lifelong aversion to 'God-botherers' and didn't think that Lord's professed religious beliefs had improved his character. DT liked the Evelyn Waugh/Nancy Mitford story. 'How can you be so nasty Evelyn and say you're a Catholic?' 'Think How much nastier I'd be Nancy if I wasn't a Catholic.' However, Jack Lord didn't have the same appeal to carry off that sort of playful humbug.

After that, David found it hard to summon enthusiasm for the project. 'From then on he couldn't take it seriously,' says Audrey. 'He did his job and left.' A saving grace for both David and Jack Lord was that when transmitted on 22 December 1976, the episode drew a vast audience, becoming one of the top draws on the ITV Christmas schedules.

Returning to London, David prepared for his first important film role in years with a lead in a big-screen adaptation of the hugely popular children's TV show *The Wombles*, about furry creatures that lived underground, collecting and recycling rubbish. But before that, there were celebrations with Robert Morley when their 'bargain filly' Trample – jointly bought for 200 guineas – had no difficulty in supplementing a previous victory at Doncaster in the Romney Nursery Handicap at Folkestone. The Tomlinsons also managed to spend more time with an ageing Clarence, who was treated to a special ninety-third birthday party at Brook Cottage. By this point, despite all the past dramas, David Jr recalls in the final years, 'Dad made the most of him, knowing that he wasn't going to be around much longer.'

Work on *Wombling Free* commenced with location shooting in Wrexham and Gerrards Cross, Buckinghamshire. David took the juicy character role of crusty old father, exasperated most of the time by one thing or another, while Frances de la Tour and Bonnie Langford played his wife and daughter respectively. Nowadays, de la Tour is familiar for playing Madame Olympe Maxime in *Harry Potter and the Goblet of Fire*, but David had spotted her starring in the TV sitcom *Rising Damp* alongside Leonard Rossiter and had no difficulty persuading Lionel Jeffries to cast her as his wife. De la Tour says their friendship blossomed quickly thereafter:

I loved doing that ridiculous film with him and the Wombles! I never really understood why David was so intrigued with us all – my then husband Tom and our children, and all our friends – except for the fact we were all 'very socialist', unlike him!

But an easy rapport was soon established despite some of David's quirks – including his finicky food obsession. One day Frances invited David to drop by her house for lunch where he spotted 'fish in a bag' – a type of boiled fast food – bubbling on the stove:

> He would say, 'Is this actually food?' And I would say; 'Now, you're just being a snob!' After he left, we would say, he's either genuinely very fond of us all, or he's working for MI6! Both probably! But what he really loved was the play Tom wrote called *Duet for One* in which I played a musician struck down with Multiple Sclerosis. He saw it many times and the subject meant a lot to him.

Bonnie, then just 12 years old, was juggling shooting and school work, and recalls sitting her English exams in a Winnebago between takes. 'It was tricky, because it was the summer of '76 we were filming, it was unbearably hot and a lot of the cast were in skins and it was horrific for them really, I don't know how they did it,' Bonnie remembers, recalling the acute discomfort. 'They would faint it was just horrible to see.'

In later life, cameraman Alan Hume seemed to imply that DT grumbled his way through the entire picture: 'I know David Tomlinson wasn't happy. In fact, in his autobiography he totally skips the film, just mentioning it in the filmography.'

However, Bonnie didn't perceive any sense of dissatisfaction particularly; 'I don't think he entered into it with any less spirit,' she says. In fact, he made a huge impression on the child star. 'He was really very approachable, and very generous. I do remember it being tricky; I do remember some re-shooting.'

Despite the occasional hiccup, Lionel Jeffries oversaw a smooth production. The veteran character actor, who had appeared with David in *Up the Creek* back in 1958, had moved into directing and was enjoying great success working on children's features while at the same time expressing – at any given opportunity – his deep-rooted views about violence and sex in the media. 'I never saw Ingrid Bergman taking her knickers off or Katherine Hepburn baring her breasts,' he argued. 'How is it they could present sex on the screen in those days without being sordid?'[23]

Bonnie thought Lionel a lovely man, 'but he didn't explain himself terribly well and I was too frightened of him. I wasn't bold enough to say, "I'm not sure what you are asking me to do," and David would help me and he would come in and he could tell if I was feeling unsure about something.' She adds:

> I was only 12 when I worked with him. I always felt remarkably comfortable with him, he had time for everybody and I always felt that when he was on set there was calmness and peacefulness and a generosity that he gave through his spirit somehow. He created a great sense of calm and attentiveness as well. I felt that he would listen to you, if you said something.

Wombling Free landed with a thud in British cinemas. While most critics agreed a few rough edges could be forgiven, *The Observer* was positively caustic – calling it abysmal. A scathing review penned by Tom Milne in the pages of the *Monthly Film Bulletin* asserted that Lionel Jeffries' proven touch with children's films had deserted him 'and he simply plods stolidly through a flabby script, featuring innocuous but highly unmemorable songs, which takes an unconscionable time to get nowhere by (apart from the brief eruption of MacWomble from Scotland on his clockwork bedstead-car) very dreary routes.'

What helped David make light of this very rare failure was the fact that Jeffries had already invited him to join the Hollywood legend James Mason in *The Water Babies*, another children's venture. 'Lionel had directed *The Railway Children*, which I would think is one of the best English films ever made and it will wear well,' David said at the time. 'Lionel has a gift for this genre and *The Water Babies* is a terrific story.'[24]

After a month of work fashioning the script into an acceptable shape, production began on 12 November 1976 with Jeffries – directing in a deerstalker cap in the Yorkshire drizzle. Attracted by the escapism and fantasy, he dropped three other projects to work on the movie. 'It has a marvellous cast and a bloody good script,' Jeffries said, grinning ruefully as he embarked on the formidable challenge of bringing to the screen what many consider to be one of the finest children's novels ever written.[25] The tale deals with a chimney sweep called Tom, who, after being wrongfully blamed for thieving, makes a run for it with his dog Toby – and ends up jumping into a river and finding an undersea adventure with the mysterious Water Babies.

Referring to the author Charles Kingsley, Jeffries was perplexed how a staid churchman could have dreamed up an almost hallucinatory experience. 'I don't know what he did it on!' David recalled chilling autumn rain soaking the countryside when shooting commenced, 'but I was required to do very little really,' he reflected when talking about his character Sir John.[26] As well as featuring the brilliant talents of James Mason, the film starred Billie Whitelaw, Bernard Cribbins and newcomer Tommy Pender playing a soot-covered chimney sweep. A teenager of smallish stature with a spunky personality, Pender distinguished himself as an affable character and a fine actor. 'Such a charming little boy,' David thought. 'He was very good too.'[27]

In his late sixties, Mason – the self-styled 'dark hero' of the Gainsborough flicks – had lost little of his renowned charm, which was tempered by gentle warmth. There was definitely an on-set friendship with David; they spent much of their free time between takes together. Even when filming wrapped, the pair met in London for dinner at La Poissonerie in Sloane Avenue for a farewell supper.

Not long afterwards, David was invited by Sword and Sorcery Productions to appear in the slender role of a solicitor in *Dominique*, the tale of a millionaire who drove his wife to suicide, then began believing that he is being haunted by her spirit. The film starred Jean Simmons, who had carved out her own career in Hollywood since their last encounter in 1949 on the set of *So Long At the Fair*. The picture also featured Cliff Robertson and was notable for Jack Warner's brief guest role as a stonemason, which marked his last ever screen part. 'It was a trouble-free engagement, but not a great effort,' David later said in typical candour.

The following year, just shy of his ninety-fifth birthday, Clarence died, having survived Florence by ten years. Towards the end of his life, even as his health deteriorated, he had been far more relaxed and amusing than in the past – perhaps at least partly because his 'double life' was over.

'Though he'd stipulated in his will that he wanted "no flowers or mourning" I cried for hours after he died,' David Jr reflected. He also recounted how Clarence could be as financially generous as he was emotionally distant. 'Late in his lifetime he gave each of his eleven children £500, but in his will he disinherited the 'illegitimate' side of the family. Though my father and Michael tried with some success to make friends with their half siblings, it rather faded after Clarence died.'

Given a dearth of engagements during 1978, David sought to lend a hand advising his old chum Geoffrey Boycott on the wording of a 'uncharacteristically mild' press statement in response to his sacking as captain of Yorkshire after failing to win a trophy while in charge.

'Oh yes, he did help me with that,' laughs Boycott. 'You know me – I'm usually frank, forthright and opinionated. If it's diplomatic, it was either David or my wife writing. He was a people person; bless him – and a beautiful writer.'

David Jr recalls his father revelled in the company of sportsmen. 'After a match against Northamptonshire, circa 1964, Dad brought the whole of the Middlesex cricket team back to Mursley for supper. He similarly invited Colin Cowdrey and his Kent team in 1969, the year before they won the county championship.'

17

It's a Wrap

David's last film, *The Fiendish Plot of Dr Fu Manchu*, had a turbulent time making its way to the screen. The invitation to play the part of Scotland Yard Commissioner Sir Roger Avery came during a late-night call from Peter Sellers. 'He was a great phoner, he liked phoning,' David said. Trading jokes and gossip late at night was one of Seller's favourite pastimes. 'He used to ring me up and have long conversations on the telephone from all parts of the world or from a yacht in the Mediterranean. "Is it lovely weather?" I'd say to Peter. "No darling, it's pissing down," he'd say.'[1]

Although relishing a reunion with old friends, there was no repeat of the jovial atmosphere enjoyed on *Up the Creek* twenty-two years earlier. Featuring Helen Mirren, Simon Williams, John Le Mesurier, Stratford Johns and the veteran comedian Sid Caesar, Sellers topped the cast, assuming the guise of Oriental genius Fu Manchu and Inspector Nayland Smith. David Jr recalls how just before filming commenced, John Le Mesurier phoned Brook Cottage to discuss the project. 'Mistaking me for my father, he unleashed a stream of jokey regimental sergeant major-like obscenities. He was profusely apologetic when I said that he'd got the wrong David and only half persuaded that we were well used to it in the Tomlinson household!'

The goonish plot in *The Fiendish Plot of Dr Fu Manchu* centred on the theft of the Star of Leningrad diamond, sparking a bizarre search. The jewel belongs to Russia, which threatens war if the stone is not returned immediately. Worse still is the discovery that the evil Oriental master criminal Fu Manchu is still alive at the age of 168 and is not dead as had been thought. Tweedy English detective inspector Nayland Smith comes out of retirement to investigate. With zany devices such as a flying cottage, Sellers endeavours to track down the ancient oriental and the diamond.

Director Piers Haggard – who had distinguished himself on *Wedding Night*, *The Blood on Satan's Claw* and *Pennies from Heaven* – was left mystified at the plot. In this he was not alone: at every stage of its fractured development, everyone involved was similarly in the dark about what the film was actually about. Almost before the cameras rolled, the picture was in freefall as two directors – Richard Quine and John Avildsen – were both sacked. 'I came to the *Fu Manchu* project late and at high speed, taking it over from Richard, who had been fired after falling out with Sellers.'[2]

Haggard needed a sense of humour to alleviate the tension building on the set, as Sellers simmered and seethed over the script, direction, casting and a string of what he perceived as endless faults. 'Relationships between Peter and me became fraught during the rewrite, about three weeks in, and well before I met with David or shooting started,' Haggard said, remembering endless testy exchanges.[3]

It was into this cauldron that David – fully grey, with sagging jowls and a finely trimmed moustache – arrived to play Scotland Yard Commissioner Sir Roger Avery. 'I knew David Tomlinson, of course, from a number of big-budget films, but I hadn't cast him.' Haggard says.

'When he did join the shoot, David was very pleasant and courteous, and did his stuff very professionally. I was so distracted by the primary challenge of "riding the tiger", i.e. handling Sellers' wayward moods and frequent unpleasantness.'[4]

Throughout the film, the Chicago-born financier and producer Zev Braun maintained a stoical calm and was tolerant of the frequent budgetary breaches.

'In spite of her quite open disloyalty to him,' says David Jr. 'Sellers persuaded Zev to give a phantom executive job to his wife, Lynne Frederick, which paid her an eye-watering sum for doing nothing very much.'

Production notes detail how the oriental make-up applied to reshape Peter Sellers' face involved filled-in brows, lashes coated in mascara and 'gluing twelve moulded sponge appliances in place, and spraying a compound that hardened to form rubbery facial creases and crow's feet in daily sessions that lasted a minimum of two hours'. Despite advice to the contrary, he persisted with the monstrous makeup, regardless of the physical toll it took on him. The rubber mask, foundation and itchy powder were uncomfortable, especially when filming outside or under the blazing hot studio lamps. His face itched, leaving him short of breath – and temper.

Sellers, as noted earlier, had been plagued with heart trouble since 1964 and his deathly white complexion disturbed David, 'He was by this time not at all well; I was shocked by his appearance when I saw him for the first day on the film, I hadn't seen him for some time.'[5]

Sellers, he observed had developed a stoop, appeared smaller in stature and to be underweight. As the star wrestled with heart pangs and stress, filming became a nerve-rattling experience, but David stuck close to his old friend:

> I was very devoted to him. He never bored me for a second – he was fun and fascinating. Although he was well when he was in front of the camera, he did have a little heart attack whilst we were actually making the picture.[6]

David maintained he never personally witnessed Sellers behaving badly but was aware the atmosphere was becoming increasingly strained, especially with producer Zev Braun and Haggard. He never forgot Sellers confessing to being plagued by mental health issues during a dinner in Paris. 'The only time he mentioned his depressions was that night,' David recounted. 'He told me he was a manic depressive and I said, "Come on Peter, you're not!" … "Oh yes I am," he said. And he was.'[7]

Audrey added: 'Apparently, Peter told Helen Mirren after he had been out with me and David, because we were a couple looking "very together", we had this "togetherness", it had depressed him.'

Jamie recalls how, given the lavish expense budget, David installed himself at the Hotel Lancaster off the Champs-Élysées, a favourite haunt of Richard Burton and Elizabeth Taylor:

> Peter, leaning heavily on Dad, asked where he was staying and asked if Dad could arrange for him to move in as well. So Peter had a suite above Dad. 'Can I phone you anytime?' Peter asked. 'Of course,' Dad replied. Dad would be woken sometimes at 4 in the morning. Sometimes they met in the foyer in dressing gowns and slippers and wandered out in

to the Champs-Élysées and sat on a bench. They did spend a lot of time together. Simon Williams told me later that the only time Peter behaved was when David was on the set.

Soon after, David left the film when he'd completed his scenes, 'I loved doing it,' he said. 'We shot it in Paris and in the French Alps and a little bit of location in England. I loved the whole thing, I thought it was marvellous.'[8]

For Haggard, the testy experience continued: 'I had to stick it out almost to the end of the shoot, but was then obliged to retire, defeated.'[9]

As the picture plodded erratically toward completion, character actor David Lodge – who had also appeared in *Up the Creek* – was summoned to rescue the remaining segments. It was rumoured that when Sellers saw the rushes, he actually started to weep.

When released in October 1980, *Manchu* was every bit the mess everyone feared. In the course of researching this book, a supporting cast member requested 'never to be reminded of that frightful turgid experience. I've tried to look on the bright side of *Manchu* but never found it.'

The virtue of *The Fiendish Plot of Dr Fu Manchu* is that David was required for relatively little of it, while the sadness was the misfortune of ending his impressive movie career on such a glum note. As it happened, the film turned out to be Sellers' last hurrah. Soon after filming, he planned a reunion at Brook Cottage with the Tomlinsons. Audrey recalled:

He was coming with Helen – but his daughter arrived from America that very day, so he couldn't make it. Apparently he didn't like green and our sitting room was all green – we had green carpet, green curtains – perhaps that's why he didn't come! He was allergic to green![10]

The next day, Peter collapsed and died at London's Dorchester Hotel after suffering a massive heart attack. 'Curiously enough,' David later revealed, 'Peter phoned me forty-eight hours before he died and talked to me for an hour. Over the last month or so of his life he phoned me quite often.'[11]

'What little merit lies in *The Fiendish Plot* comes from a supporting cast that tries to lend some subtlety and comic aplomb to a script that lacks both, as well as action or real humour,' was the verdict of David Chenoweth in Canada's *Gazette*. 'David Tomlinson as the Commissioner of Scotland Yard and John Le Mesurier as Smith's dour-faced butler provide a quality that makes Sellers' double role seem as it may have been in fact the work of a man whose health impaired both his insight and his technique.' Critic Albert Watson remarked:

> It is a shame that it had to be his swansong. As the climax to a film by the foremost comedy actor of his generation it is, to say the least, inadequate. The whole business is embarrassingly silly. Not silly like the inspired lunacy of Inspector Clouseau or The Goons, but silly in a way that means that a press show audience liberally sprinkled with personal friends of the late genius could hardly raise a titter most of the time.

18

FADE OUT

'I have no regrets,' David said cheerfully when throwing himself into retirement in 1980. 'I don't really ever think I had hard times. I mean a lot of actors struggle, but I was really rather lucky I didn't struggle very much.'[1]

In a characteristically incisive remark, he summed up a desire for a carefree retreat from professional life: 'If I were very rich, which I'm not, I would wander round the world watching all the big sporting, events … but not wrestling.'[2]

Looking back, he was proud of his self-made career and continued to follow the trade press and answer his own meticulously filed correspondence. Retirement, however, came with the caveat that should Walt Disney Pictures come knocking with a part anywhere near as good as the one in *Mary Poppins*, he would not turn a deaf ear. 'It would be nice to do another film there,' he said. 'I'm all packed up and ready to go!'

In the twenty years his life had left, there would be an autobiography, a starring spot on *This is Your Life* and the chance to enjoy the gentle shade of his own quiet life. 'He wasn't grumpy in retirement,' Audrey insists. 'He had no appetite for relaxation. He was an avid collector and that kept him busy. He got wonderful things at marvellous prices before those antiques programmes started on TV.'[3]

Having achieved financial security, Audrey says he felt no pressure or desire to return to acting. 'There would be no late flowering. He didn't want to work. Robert Morley couldn't understand it at all.'[4]

In fact, so much heat developed over the decision that Morley suggested that David star in *A Ghost on Tiptoe* in an effort to coax his old friend back on stage. 'But Dad would not do it,' Jamie adds. 'He proved a tough nut to crack. He shrugged it off. Explain that? So, Robert, with a few rewrites, cast Bill Franklyn instead and it had a successful tour and eighteen months at the Savoy.'

This kind of attitude was no surprise for Audrey, who said retirement made her husband bounce with good cheer. 'He was as free as a bird and probably one of the luckiest husbands really. He could go to London to our little flat in Chelsea anytime he wanted to.'[5]

Furthermore, aided by friends such as the famed art director Ralph Brinton, he enjoyed a substantial portfolio of shares, the dividends of which provided a decent income. Brinton had become an important and dear friend; the two had first met when working on *Hotel Sahara* in the early 1950s. Brinton had enjoyed an exotic and interesting life having joined the Royal Navy as a teenager, survived the First World War and eventually retiring as a commander. David Jr remembers:

He lived with his wife Cynthia and their children in Holland Park. Like many of my parents' friends, Ralph was quite left wing and I'm pretty sure that in the early '60s he and Cynthia went marching on Aldermaston to protest against Polaris. Ralph's sister was Baroness Mary Stocks, a Labour peer, whom my father once arranged to take to a strip club in Soho in order that she could see what it was like before condemning it!

In addition to Brinton's advice, investment management came from the Rathbone Brothers. David had also been an exclusive 'Lloyd's Name' from 1969 but miraculously pulled his investments just before the whole institution was shaken by ruinous losses. Audrey remembered:

He had accidentally pre-empted disaster. For some reason, he didn't like the fact that someone was in total charge of his money, even with a broker he was always in control. And with Lloyd's, he found himself not in control and he pulled out of that just in time without knowing this was going to happen. He had no idea – the timing was lucky. Many people lost money in Lloyds; some had a very sticky time after that.[6]

By this point, the Tomlinson boys had long flown Brook Cottage. All four of them had accomplished the task of carving out their own identities. David Jr was enjoying a successful career in the legal profession; James, like his father, was treading the boards; teenage Henry dreamed of embarking on a career in television production, while William remained endlessly active under the care of the staff at Somerset Court. 'Willie is clever, not to say astute. He is totally responsible for himself and fastidious in everything,' David said at the time. In fact, William had developed extraordinary skills with his hands; had his own home workshop and became an expert wood craftsman.[7]

After a three-year near-total absence from public view, the year 1983 brought David back to the limelight as host of *When You Wish Upon a Star*, a glittering event fondly remembered by conductor Iain Sutherland. 'It was a collaboration between BBC Radio 2 and the Walt Disney Music Company to celebrate sixty years of wonderful Disney music at the Royal Albert Hall,' he explained.

'Although thirty-six years ago, I still have fond recollections of that gala concert, and David. We enjoyed swapping showbiz stories over some bottles of champagne.'

Under Sutherland's baton, the BBC Radio Orchestra performed music from *Pinocchio, Bambi, Peter Pan, Snow White and the Seven Dwarfs* and *Jungle Book* in what the BBC described as the first concert of that type to be staged and broadcast live. Russell Grant, a young star from the BBC's breakfast television service, never forgot singing at the event:

We had our first rehearsal at the Golders Green Hippodrome with the BBC Concert Orchestra. For my call, I was given the wrong time and arrived too late and I only got a chance to run through all my songs once. It was a tall order because I had never sung with an eighty-piece orchestra. David and I were in the same dressing room and he was just the loveliest man – and I don't say this about everybody – he took me under his wing because he could see basically I was shit scared. He came up to me – put his arm around me and tried to calm me down, saying I was going to be fine. He had a great sense of calm; his charisma came from pragmatism. He had the ability to ground you, to protect you, to make you feel safe. If it wasn't for David, I don't think I would have gone on, I would have pulled a sickie![8]

Grant need not have worried; the evening was a roaring success according to Pamela Field, who also performed at the gala. 'It was a superb evening. I loved seeing the characters in costume, which I believe had been flown over from America for the occasion and this provided the perfect setting for us to bring the music of Disney to life.'

David opened the show, still gratefully remembering his Hollywood break. 'The sheer professionalism of Disney productions makes other films seem amateurish. Having been around for a long time now I have worked with the bad and the best, and Walt Disney certainly offers the best in music, characterisation and general artistry.'

There were other late-career high points, like heading a donations drive for the RAF Museum at Hendon by hosting a charity gala night on BBC radio, alongside 1950s pop singer Frankie Vaughan. Then, he burst on to Radio 4's *Week's Good Cause*, attracting valuable attention to education for autistic children and, not long afterwards, he was feted by Roy Hudd on the ITV show *Movie Memories*, the result being a brilliant treatment of his years at Rank. There was a time to catch up with old friends at a special, opulent, star-studded tribute to the life of Sir Michael Redgrave at the Old Vic alongside Joss Ackland, Dame Peggy Ashcroft, Sir John Gielgud, Alan Gravill and Elisabeth Welch.

By 1986, David's retirement looked more like a sabbatical, when Roger Smith, a former collaborator of Ken Loach, coaxed him to star in Peter Woodward's *Outside Broadcast* in Birmingham, a comedy romp through the early days of live television, set in the year of the Coronation. In a woeful miscalculation, given he needed a cane to help steady himself, David accepted the part of Willoughby Brandon, a hammy, egotistical stage star.

Co-star Robert Longden remembered discussing the play at Brook Cottage:

So, the show was at Birmingham. I was to play a bewigged, hysterical BBC producer stumbling through the very first outside broadcast featuring a Donald Wolfit type of old dragon played by David. It was just me and him round the pond, where we talked the day away.

However, niggling doubts soon emerged. David was only sixty-nine but he seemed exhausted: '[He] looked frail. He would also be restricted by his age for this slapstick comedy.'

Longden says that David was resigned to the fact that age and changing times worked against him:

> whilst I was in my physical prime and I ate up the stage as soon as I saw it. I got up to everything. David's role needed aggression, which comes from energy, which he didn't have at this time … he was a big name in the wrong genre. I was worried he might be too old to play the last of a stage monster known collectively as an actor manager.

In fact, it became the least enjoyable enterprise of David's career as his bad back and low spirits led him, at least twice, to the local doctor. To make matters worse, rehearsals became dysfunctional: 'There was a lot of anarchy. Roger was a socialist and I think David was expected to defend himself. He was not up to the bombast required and so the recipe expired and fell into the hands of every man for himself,' Longden said.

However, to everybody's astonishment, the press was benevolent. Fred Norris of the *Sandwell Evening Mail* observed David played well within himself but 'the thunder and lightning roar of a Wolfit setting fire to a scene or two would have made a world of difference.' Furthermore, he reckoned: 'Mr Woodward has found his vein all right but in comic terms he needs to dig deeper before he strikes it rich. His first act in particular wants dismantling and shaking up.'

David's condition forced the cancellation of *Outside Broadcast* after just two weeks. Reflecting on the experience, Longden thought a long run 'may have been a little too much for David. It was sad, because Peter deserved some recognition and the team Roger put together delivered an enjoyable evening.'

More troubling, the driving to Birmingham combined with the energy required for the actual production left David in a fragile state with acute back pain, leading to a spell under the care of the surgeon, Nigel Cobb, who had put motorcycle racer Barry Sheene back together. 'Dad was in a poor way and I'd heard about Cobb through working in hospitals,' Jamie noted. 'I managed to contact his secretary and Cobb saw Dad very quickly. Dad was in a private hospital in Northampton under Cobb where he had to lie on his back and not move for several days until the inflammation had eased.'

A short spell at Stoke Mandeville's orthopaedic unit followed. Walking, even at his slow pace, could be torture. Speaking to the press at the time,

Audrey said he was almost bedridden, unable to walk and in constant agony despite having spent several days resting 'but that doesn't seem to have cured the problem'.

The slow and painful recovery required a month in bed and Audrey seriously never considered he would return to work. In fact, he promised to take several months off and do nothing but rest and relax. However, before too much time had passed, he was back on stage at the Children's Royal Variety Performance presenting the opening segment of the 1988 show. Elegantly dressed with a glint in his eye, he gave a cheerful comic monologue before Princess Margaret and a sea of children's faces at the Victoria Palace Theatre:

> Your Royal Highness, my lords, ladies and gentlemen. Do you like the suit? Now you will realise ladies and gentlemen that they wanted somebody very special to open the show tonight, they were hoping for a charismatic character – clean living, decent, charming, handsome, wonderfully clever – generally speaking an all-round wonderful chap. Well here I am ladies and gentlemen … need I say more? With all due modesty ladies and gentlemen, I do have all those attributes and, of course, I'm well-known for being the only actor living who can swim under water and sing at the same time. Now ladies and gentleman, my small contribution to this evening's performance is to welcome you most warmly to this year's Children's Royal Variety Performance. My wife waved me off today as wives do and said: 'Well my darling, I do hope that they're not all too young to remember you!' But having had a good look at you, most of you are before my time …

And while the distinguished audience barked with laughter, other guest performers including, Bros, Keith Harris, Jimmy Cricket and Michael Barrymore chuckled in the wings. Comedian Cricket recalled:

> It was a great show, but it wasn't the first time I had met David, or experienced his dry wit first hand. That was in the early eighties at the Wellington Theatre in Great Yarmouth during a show called *The Happy Holiday Show*.
> David's son Jamie worked backstage and one evening his dad came to visit him and watch the show. Afterwards I knocked on the dressing

room door of another comic on the show, Denny Willis. Just to explain here, Denny did a wonderful slapstick act with three other guys dressed in hunting gear and him in ill-fitting hunting gear. They all sang a song that included lots of hand waving and kicks. Denny would be at the end of the line getting it all wrong with hilarious consequences and shrieks of laughter from the audience. Anyway, when Denny opened his door none other than David Tomlinson was sitting there and Denny introduced me to him. I found him utterly charming. I mentioned to him about how good I thought Denny's act was and he replied, 'Yes, and he's been so good for such a long time!' Denny had been in the business quite a while by this stage.

For many years David had toyed, on and off, with the idea of putting his story on record. That seed began to germinate one day in 1969 when he got a telephone call from Robert Morley, who, after writing his own memoirs, assured him that publishing deals could not only be lucrative (with advance payments to the authors) but also generate positive publicity. Though his faculties were slowly fading, Audrey thought it the perfect distraction, and representatives from publisher Hodder and Stoughton offered an agreeable contract. However, while most autobiographies share the need for self-revelation, David's book, titled *Luckier than Most*, offered few surprises. Henry, describing a sketchy rather than a comprehensive memoir, said:

> I think to a certain extent he kind of underplayed a lot of things. The autobiography summed him up a bit – it is thin – in terms of what he thought would be interesting, whereas, possibly, there was more he could have said. I think that's another case of him underplaying it.[9]

With a thespian's ear for dialogue, David amassed a few dozen anecdotes, newspaper reviews, and other writings culled from boxes of memorabilia. Through 198 pages, David wafts readers from his childhood in Folkestone to his ambition to act, film stardom and his undying love of flying. Aided by Margaret Morley, the daughter-in-law of Robert, they created a beautifully written work full of gentle charm. A bright glossy still of Mr Banks adorned the yellow cover with a dozen other photos from his childhood and career scattered throughout. Not long after the book hit the shops, David said:

'Well, everybody thought I was dead, you see. And the phone has been going, the autobiography is in demand!'

Although received favourably by most critics – some of which praised his buoyancy and dry wit – the book never passed the first edition. However, it did lead to a flurry of publicity; including David being surprised by *This is Your Life's* Michael Aspel while enjoying a matinee performance of *Snow White* at the Strand Theatre. 'It wasn't easy to keep that secret,' Audrey says, recalling her terror that David would duck out of the programme. 'This eventuality did cross my mind more than once. He had always said he never wanted to be on it, he even told Eamonn Andrews that, I believe.' [10]

As it happened, there was no argument when the 'big red book' was revealed – just an exclamation of 'Goodness Gracious! – followed by a typical big, splashy ITV production that aired nationally in primetime. Through this palaver, David sat and laughed without saying much, but his face lit up the screen when his brothers Peter, Michael and Paul were introduced, followed by other characters that had peppered his life, including Ronald Howard, Glynis Johns and Brian Johnson. Robert Morley – clearly in fragile health – ambled on to the stage to thunderous applause and rejoiced in remarking that after a friendship spanning forty years, David was still 'the second best light comedian in the business', a jibe that led to howls of laughter.

'I thought he was very good in that, amazing really, because he didn't know,' says Audrey. [11] In what was almost a farewell tour of an extraordinary career, film segments interweaved through the programme showed David dancing merrily in *Mary Poppins*, the sparkling moments he sang with an animated fish in *Bedknobs and Broomsticks* and the classic scene where he carried Glynis Johns (and her Dunlop tail) in *Miranda*. Asked by Aspel about his father Clarence, who he observed 'sounded like a bit of character,' David responded: 'Yes, I think he was. But you'll all have to read the book. Hodder and Stoughton, £14.95 – and worth every penny!'

Although there was lots of jolly chat, gossiping and giggling after the show, Jamie thought there was room for improvement. 'It transpired my uncle Michael – Dad's brother – had been involved in much of the planning. I'm sure Roger Moore would have loved to have contributed, even if it was a recorded message.'

A year after *This Is Your Life*, Robert Morley died after suffering a stroke at his home in Wargrave. And although, at 84 years old, the portly star had given life a run for its money, his passing left David inconsolable for weeks. 'This was a blow,' says Audrey. 'It did really upset him.' The funeral at St Mary's in Wargrave attracted 150 mourners – including Robert Hardy, Hillary Minster and Morley's son, Sheridan, who gave a heartfelt tribute to a loving father, gifted actor and a keen gambler.

This terrible moment of grief for David, combined with his own increased frailties, was probably responsible for an unusually crotchety performance on the BBC's *Pebble Mill at One* soon after the funeral. 'David turned up at the studio and came into the green room,' recalled host Judi Spiers, who never forgot the encounter:

We always like to have a bit of a bond before the interview started, and he was absolutely charming and delightful and we sat down together and he told me about his wife, who I believe had committed suicide by throwing herself out of her hotel window.

I mean, he welled up. It was very moving. You know, just the two of us, and he told me that and you can imagine how I felt. As an attempt to say, 'Oh, my gosh, how really traumatic!' I didn't even really know what to say and I ended up saying that I had fallen out of a window years before and broken my back, which is true. We got into this conversation and he was 'Oh, my dear! How terrible,' and you know, it was just very warm and felt very close and, you know, that we bonded and thought, 'Oh, this is going to be a lovely interview!'[12]

However, when David shuffled quietly onto the stage for the live transmission, shielding his eyes from the spotlights, Spiers recounted an uneasy atmosphere. 'He suddenly turned to the audience as if they were his pals and said: "Ha! This one threw herself out of a window!" I looked at him like "What?" He suddenly became really sort of tricky. It was a bizarre experience. And I was just staggered by it.'

There can be no doubt given his track record of being the essence of politeness in previous interviews that David was either under intense strain, nervous – or both. 'It's possible,' says Spiers, looking back. 'It is difficult to know what is happening in people's lives off camera. You know, it happens.

I have a lot clearer memory of Liza Minnelli and Ginger Rogers not being very pleasant and it was for similar reasons.'

As time pushed on, David loved nothing more than to potter in the garden at Brook Cottage, or receive the occasional visit from friends and family, and he studiously avoided anything strenuous. He did his best to retain a sense of humour when pushing the book, earning his greatest exposure on a primetime talk show hosted by Terry Wogan. During Wogan's reign, virtually every Briton with a television set saw his show at some point. At the BBC studios, David encountered comic Simon Day trying out his self-deprecating character Tommy Cockles as a bona fide guest, 'I had just started my career with Cockles. Tommy was a music hall veteran and all-round entertainer, a sort of Leonard Zelig figure who seemed to have performed in every era of show business.'

Day recalled the character mixed up anecdotes featuring everyone from the Rolling Stones to Flanagan and Allen:

I was thrilled to be making an appearance on *Wogan*. Would the septuage-narian audience believe me, would the other guests get it? I was overjoyed to hear David Tomlinson was on the same show with me as he was exactly the sort of showbiz stalwart who I would have put into one of my stories. He was from the strata of English entertainment which was dying out; he had a gentility and almost noble air, which aligned him with David Niven and other 'real' stars.

Before transmission, he met David in make-up at the old BBC Television Centre:

He waved and smiled, having no idea who I was but in my experience real stars are always polite. As I talked to Wogan, David remained on the sofa silent but listening intently – the audience had no idea what was going on as the character is quite surreal. Suddenly, David's shoulders began to shake like Mike Yarwood doing Ted Heath and he laughed and laughed, he actually wiped a tear from his eye. For me it was like I had been accepted into the Royal family of show business!

I will never forget that moment because of his class and standing, who he was, I knew then I was on the right track. At one point he slapped his knee and said, 'I think you'll do very well Tommy!' As I left the BBC, he greeted me in his Bentley with his chauffeur wearing a fur coat! *A fur coat!* What a delightful kind man. Dressed immaculately, he tipped his hat and the car purred away. And I was on the way.

Even now, legions of DT admirers watching the interview on YouTube remark on what they perceive as awkward encounter between a Hollywood legend, modern comedian and Irish host. 'Tommy went straight over their heads, but David got it completely,' one viewer wailed, whilst another called it dry humour at its driest: 'they are all in on it'. Another commenter thought Wogan 'cringeworthy and clumsy,' after he stated David starred in *The Sound of Music*. 'Often chat show hosts get bored or slightly ruffled when someone who is universally loved is opposite in the chair,' Simon Day says. 'David was so charming and witty he kept turning to the audience and saying, "Why does he hate me so?" And they laughed uproariously … David 'won' the interview'.

Away from the public arena, stimulation came from an unlikely quarter. After making a contribution – along with Hughie Green and Dudley Sutton – to *High Flyers*, a book of reminiscences by former pilots to mark the seventy-fifth anniversary of the RAF, David made some interesting literary friends, including the free-thinking writer Beryl Bainbridge, who was working as a theatre critic on Richard Ingrams' *The Oldie* magazine.

'I very much liked Ian Hislop and the delightful Liz Calder,' David wrote to Ingrams after attending his first *Oldie* literary lunch. 'I didn't follow my eldest son's advice, "Don't talk and just listen." As usual I talked too much. Having rather dreaded the experience, I could not have enjoyed it more.'

During the 1990s, *The Oldie*'s literary luncheons became a thriving institution, attracting an eager audience made up of readers, artists and contributors.

At such occasions, David's greatest admiration was always saved for Bainbridge, who had found fame writing psychological fiction, and twice won the Whitbread Awards prize for best novel; as well as being nominated for the Booker Prize on five occasions. She returned David's admiration in kind, describing him as 'a man cast in the same mould as Dr Johnson, one who observed the absurdities of life yet still loved his fellow man'.

One evening, she recalled seeing David engaged in conversation with Tom Kempinski, who was busily describing the pièce de résistance from his latest play. In his throbbing voice, Kempinski explained how – in a dramatic scene – a woman bit off the testicles of a male captive. But, he added, the whole episode was crafted 'very tastefully'. Characteristically, David took a sip of wine and retorted, 'No darling, it is quite unnecessary. She should see to his balls offstage.'

On another occasion, David took Bainbridge to see a new play starring Griff Rhys Jones. 'What a night,' laughs Rhys Jones, before taking a long breath:

What a bloody night! They occupied a box then decided that they couldn't see it properly and made a huge fuss and called the house manager, who moved them to the front row of the circle. They got halfway through the next act and decided the front row circle was no good either so they got up, made more fuss, and left in the middle of the act and went and watched some of it from the God's and then came down and watched the rest of it in the stalls. All you were aware of the entire first night was this huge kerfuffle breaking out somewhere in the audience![13]

Looking back, Rhys Jones says David was an anarchist in patrician clothing:

I met him first when he came backstage at the Watford Palace, but we only became friends some years later when he stopped me, naturally enough, in Burlington Arcade, to laugh at my coat. Thereafter I bobbed in his not inconsiderable wake around London. After a performance in Farnham, he greeted the distinguished actor and playwright who had particularly invited us to see the play with a sympathetic, 'So brave.' He took me into a pompous cigar shop. He greeted the manager as a top customer and was offered the finest. As we left, David turned to me, 'Delightful! Of course I have never been in the place before.'

Away from the public eye, David turned in some of his finest performances when keeping a stiff upper lip, but when his eldest brother Michael died in 1993 the shock hit hard. 'I have never loved anybody more and I have not managed to get over his death,' he confessed in a letter to Richard Ingrams.

They struck up a friendship that lasted for the rest of David's life, and they exchanged letters on topics including film, politics, and other assorted musings. As their correspondence proceeded, the letters became more avid, revealing and in some cases morose. David wrote dejectedly of his personal frailties:

> I now have impaired reading problems. It is time to say that I have senile dementia and that is not a joke, together with serious loss of memory, impaired eyesight and other frailties about which you will be pleased to know, I will never bore you with ever again. Friends tell me they have the same but a little forgetfulness is not what I am talking about. Subject closed, with apologies. I think I need sympathy.

Memory issues notwithstanding, occasional lighter musings on domestic life crept from the nib of his pen:

> Audrey and I have watched *Absolutely Fabulous* in grim silence and I personally have been wondering if my health setbacks could be the reason for my not being able even to begin to understand why it is said to be 'brillian', 'grea' and 'fantasti' (see end code) which are the only words used singly or together by the junior community to describe anything they find vaguely enjoyable. Older viewers and senior citizens seem to be equally enthusiastic about the programme. Audrey feels as I do, which is not the case. Please promise an old aging fart that you will never miss doing your TV column. I go straight to it when the mag (*The Oldie*) comes through the door. Nobody will do it as well, not even dear Beryl, who is wonderful as the theatre critic.

> Yours ever – David.

> PS. Code for pronunciations. 'Brillian ' – no last 't'. 'Fantasti '– no last 'c', 'grea' – no last 't'. SORRY ABOUT THE WRITING.

In another letter, David opened an oblique window into his views on royalty after Princess Diana embarked on a sudden, unlikely, friendship with columnist Auberon Waugh, hitherto, one of her greatest critics. He pondered:

> I'm concerned about Auberon Waugh and Princess Di. Robert Morley always said she was utterly brainless and I believe she flirts with the boys

but doesn't let them get their leg over. If you have difficulty with this low slang I can translate. Now that's no good for anyone. Poor Will Carling. We might save A.W. Do you agree?

According to David Jr, DT had befriended Waugh at a cocktail party and when hearing his eyesight was causing concern insisted on giving him then and there his own 'wear round your neck' magnifying glass. 'Waugh, whose punctilious good manners have been rather underestimated, wrote him a touching thank you letter.'

While David's mind occasionally drifted, he was not above lashing out at perceived injustices. An incident concerning the purchase of a VHS video from the retailer Our Price caused particular outrage:

'Talk of the Town' is the only video I have ever bought as the one I had of it was wiped. My wife bought one from 'Our Price', a chain of video peddlers, only to learn that W.H. Smith sold it for £12.95 instead of £13.95. Irritated, I wrote and asked 'Our Price' if that was what is called profiteering. I received a thoroughly bogus letter which I might send to Columbia to see how they feel about this sort of thing. Perhaps you think I have too much time on my hands, which is probably true, but I have been a bit under the weather lately. But I do loathe outfits like 'Our Price'.

As more of his contemporaries passed away, the subject of mortality became ever-present. 'I am deeply sad about the death of Peter Cook,' David wrote in a gracious letter to Richard Ingrams in January 1995. Aged 57, Cook's alcohol addiction had sucked him completely into its vortex, killing him with a gastrointestinal haemorrhage, a complication caused by years of heavy boozing.

'I immediately thought of you and I doubt if anybody will be more upset and affected by the surprising news. I leave all else unsaid, except to say that nobody ever appealed to me more.'

Characteristically, whatever grief he may have felt about the passing of his friends and colleagues remained mostly private. On 1 December 1995, when Kathleen Harrison died at the remarkable age of 103, David drove out to her funeral in Chislehurst. David Jr says:

Dad was genuinely moved by the occasion. He and I having arrived fairly early, we had a long talk with the vicar who was really charming and quite funny. There seemed to be quite an extended family. They were all very friendly and after the burial, which was quite low key, we went to a nearby pub. It was a good experience.

Amid the gloom, there were moments of pleasure. David remained spry enough to appear in person on Petula Clark's *This is Your Life*, where he lashed praise, calling the songstress 'a very charming, sweet, clever, talented girl. And I mean it from the bottom of my heart – there's a lot of nonsense talked on this sort of programme – but that is genuine'.

Not long afterwards, journalist Craig Brown recounted having lunch with the Tomlinsons in the Lighthouse restaurant in Aldeburgh. 'My children asked him if he would sing *Let's Go Fly a Kite*, and sing it he did, loud and clear, bringing a stunned silence to the restaurant and drawing a spirited round of applause from everyone present.'

And then, unperturbed after the kerfuffle with Beryl Bainbridge, Griff Rhys Jones sent a special invite to David to watch him star in the opening night performance of *Front Page*, a play set in 1940s Chicago. Rhys Jones remembered:

We went out for a meal afterwards in Carluccio's opposite the Donmar. And we sat there and had a delicious supper and I asked David what he thought of the play.

'Terrible!' David snapped despairingly. 'Absolutely awful. Where did they get all those suits from?'

What?

'Griff, there wasn't a single character wearing an American suit. Every single person was wearing an English suit.'

This observation silenced Rhys Jones momentarily, but he later reflected how the costumes – which ran from blazers to dinner jackets – broadly parodied 1950s styles. 'The point was that if you are an actor in a play in the 1950s, the quality of tailoring that you wore was of vital importance. David was genuinely perplexed and outraged by the quality of tailoring!'

Toward the end of the meal, as coffee was served, the proprietor Carluccio tottered over to the table to say hello. Rhys Jones continues:

'David greeted him by saying, "Signore, have you seen this play that's over the road in that warehouse?"

'"Yes, I see it," Carluccio replied in his thick Italian accent.

"So what did you think of it?"

'"I think it may be too pantomime," he observed, sounding as if he had joined a therapy session.

'"Exactly my point," David said, slamming his hand on the table. "And the suits Carluccio, did you see the suits?"'

Suddenly, a stone-faced man chipped into the salvo from a nearby table: 'Griff, I hope you don't mind me interrupting,' he said, swigging from a bottle of ale. 'I've just seen the show tonight and I thought you were absolutely fantastic and I thought the whole production was amazing – pay absolutely no attention to these two old farts.'

'Do you know who that was David?' enquired Griff.

'No,' he replied with a deadpan veneer.

Demonstrating remarkable restraint, Griff whispered: 'That was Pete Townshend of The Who. And I will never forget this, David had absolutely no idea who Townshend or for that matter, who The Who were.'

By the summer of 1997, David was batting a series of setbacks. 'A blood-less op (cataract) and a bloody one (prostate) – especially with two general anaesthetics are not good for 80-year-olds,' he confided to Ingrams. To compound matters, a series of minor strokes had a major impact on his mobility, as well as seriously impairing his reading and writing. One hand had, however, become paralysed, which caused immense frustration.

As if he wasn't already suffering enough, there was a further blow: 'Bad things come in batches and my beloved brother, eleven years older than me, committed suicide at his home in Cape Town: shattering news for everyone and incomprehensible but nothing more to say to you about that here,' he informed Ingrams, without ransacking his grief for answers.[14]

'There are various special friends who have been kind to me since my health setbacks and this is a good time to thank you also for taking an interest in me together with others after my absolute retirement. It is deeply appreciated.'

Although he confronted the pain with dignity, Audrey says Peter's death was a terrible blow. 'That was very sad. It was a shocking thing that he killed himself. I don't think we really got over it, although we got on with our lives, but somehow – especially for my husband – it hung over him.'[15]

Despite the personal tragedies, his humour was still in evidence during 'A Day with David Tomlinson' at the Aldeburgh Cinema in Suffolk in 1998, where he was interviewed by Griff Rhys Jones before an invited audience. 'We have had a wonderful day, he was very chipper and I think elated by the whole thing,' Jones recalls. He selected *Up the Creek* and *The Love Bug* from the list of his own films to be screened at the event. He told stories to the audience, mostly off the cuff but some from *Luckier than Most*, and ended the afternoon taking questions, even though at some points his voice was barely above a whisper.

Around the start of the new millennium, David went into dramatic decline. After another stroke, his system was finally starting to break down. He suffered from a flare-up of his old back problems, combined with other frailties. David Jr remembered an incident around his eighty-third birthday in May 2000, 'We'd gone with him and Mum to a local pub in Little Horwood. Sitting at the table Dad had an episode with his head in his hands and he got taken back home. He seemed better before we left for London that evening.' As concern mounted for his health, Jamie brought forward a scheduled appointment at the King Edward hospital:

> I was called in to see the resident physician, a very nice younger doctor who with a nurse asked me what I thought was going on with my Dad. I remember being very upset and saying that I thought he was probably dying and this was confirmed. The same doctor had admitted him and Dad had been remarkably sharp and had asked him his nationality. Dad realised he'd caused a small degree of offence and said, 'I've offended you! Please don't be offended I'm delighted you're Egyptian. I can't think of anything nicer.' Dad was so inquisitive and questioning.

David Jr remembers in the early days in hospital he was chatty, but his condition declined as the arteritis took its toll on his blood efficiency and he slipped in and out of consciousness. 'In a way this helped us because just when we'd thought that was it, he would rally and so we got used to the idea of life without him before he finally died.'

The end came early in the morning of 24 June 2000, at the King Edward VII Hospital in Marylebone – 32 miles from where he had been born eighty-three years earlier – David passed peacefully in his sleep. In a welcome kindness of fate, he died just moments after David Jr had left his bedside. 'Timing had always mattered to him as an actor and he managed to neatly squeeze his exit between the departures of Sir John Gielgud and Sir Alec Guinness,' David Jr laughs.

When questioned about his religious faith in 1996, David said that he didn't believe in an afterlife, but had a friend who was convinced that we do meet up with everybody again: 'I always say, "But my dear that sounds terrible. Can't we choose?"'

As word of his passing flashed around the world, Jamie paid a simple tribute to a refined and polished gentleman:

He was a very unusual man who had many talents outside his profession … He was good with his eyes and talked very well. He was always an actor and that was his passion. And although he chose to give it up in 1979 and enjoyed spending time with his family, he stayed in touch with the actors of today. It was extraordinary how people knew who he was 20 years after he stopped working.

The *New York Times* remembered David 'delighted millions as the father of the two children in *Mary Poppins*,' while an obituary penned by John Martland for *The Stage* noted his trio of Walt Disney pictures. 'They constituted a kind of Indian summer for the actor who had already enjoyed a distinguished career, in British pictures and in the West End.' *Private Eye* published an uncharacteristically warm poem in tribute to him: 'So farewell David Tomlinson, noted British character actor. *Let's go fly a kite, up to the highest height.* Yes, that was your catchphrase – and where you are going now.'

His passing also made it on to the pages of *The Tonbridgian* school magazine, sixty-five years after his last entry:

David Cecil MacAlister Tomlinson died peacefully at the King Edward VII Hospital for Officers on 24 June, aged 83. Dearly missed husband of Audrey, a much-loved father and adored grandfather.

David Tomlinson's specificity about his own funeral service was well-known to the family. In typical no-nonsense fashion, he had laid down what was to happen after his death and was adamant that cremation was not an option. 'At first we thought he was joking when he said that he wanted to be buried in the garden at Brook Cottage,' David Jr says. In fact, he even picked the spot on the edge of the woodland, not far from where his Tiger Moth crashed in the 1950s.

'We needn't have followed that really,' says Audrey. 'That was his wish and I always had doubts about that afterwards. At the time you follow somebody's wish, but looking back I don't think it was a good idea. I didn't want to be tied to Brook Cottage in old age.'

Henry recalled that 'Dad wanted "David Tomlinson an actor of genius, irresistible to women" to be engraved on his headstone – obviously, our mum had her own thoughts about that and it didn't quite happen!'

As plans progressed, David Jr thought that the local authority would refuse permission for a home burial, as a stream ran through the garden to a fish farm between Mursley and Swanbourne, but in the event, they posed no obstacle. 'Buckinghamshire County Council was fine with the burial,' he says.

Although a bit overcast, the garden at Brook Cottage was a blaze of colour on the day of the funeral. David Jr says although he professed atheism, his father had been friendly with the Mursley parish vicar, John Kinchin-Smith, who conducted the service:

A few days after his death, Dad having been moved to an undertaker in the nearby town of Winslow, we followed the hearse in DT4 home to Mursley and a small intimate interment. My abiding memory is of John Kinchin-Smith walking the 250 yards down Church Lane from the rectory in his full vestments. William took some rather good photos.[16] A few days later we had a memorial service in the village church. John Kinchin-Smith and Sheridan Morley both did brilliant eulogies. An ailing Lionel Jeffries with Eileen made the journey to the funeral. Lionel maintained a very close friendship up to Dad's death, though they saw less of each other after Lionel and his wife Eileen moved away from Beaconsfield to Bournemouth. My Mum and Eileen, who died last year, also kept in touch with each other. A wide variety of other friends made it including Craig Brown and Griff Rhys Jones who had collaborated on a well-researched and delightful obituary in the *Daily Telegraph*. Beryl Bainbridge sat at DT's desk in his summer-house office, closed her eyes and sat in silent meditation for several minutes. DT's great friend

Colonel Andrew Duncan was one of many retired Grenadier Guards who came to remember him. A wreath of poppies expressing deepest sympathy from the Grenadier Guards Association still hangs above Will's work bench in an outbuilding where with his meticulous attention to detail he continues his carpentry to this day. Once a Grenadier, always a Grenadier.

All in all, it was a glorious send-off.

19

POSTHUMOUS GrOWTH IN POPULarITY

In the 1950s, '60s and '70s you had to wait for classic movies on television or in revival viewings. Then, the advent of satellite film channels and online video opened the doors for a new generation of admirers to discover David Tomlinson. Nowadays, *Talking Pictures*, which works to keep historic British cinema alive, shows his movies on almost continuous rotation to an audience of over 6 million viewers. Many films, including *All for Mary*, *Journey Together*, *Helter Skelter*, *Further up the Creek*, *Three Men in a Boat* and *Carry on Admiral*, which had drifted toward obscurity, are now regular features at prime time. Even *Is Your Honeymoon Really Necessary*, which had been buried for decades, has resurfaced.

Surprisingly enough, David was also treated to a fresh round of recognition when his life was revived on stage in *The Life I Lead*, a biographical solo play starring Miles Jupp. 'I felt tremendous warmth toward David, he was a type of prototypical father to us all,' says author James Kettle, known for his work on the BBC's *News Quiz*.

Kettle was stunned by the enthusiasm surrounding the show, which laid bare in quick, moving strokes David's life's high points to Mary's suicide and his topsy-turvy relationship with Clarence. It premiered at the Northcott Theatre in Exeter in 2019 and gained critical acclaim before transferring into London's West End for eight performances at Wyndham's Theatre.

Looking back at the production, Kettle attributes David's popularity partly to his sophisticated understatement and charm:

The way that he carried himself and the way that he presented himself as David Tomlinson, it was very hard not to feel that warmth toward him because of his wit, the way he interacted with the world around him and his lack of pretension. His unwillingness to talk nonsense about acting, and his very self-deprecating appreciation of his own talent – all these things made it very difficult not to feel that warmth. He could be a grumpy old man – as we are all prone to do when we reach a certain age – but I think there was always a twinkle with David Tomlinson and I hope that is something I managed to get across in the show.

After seeing the first-night performance, Henry Tomlinson thought it a brutally honest production, omitting romanticised visions of a dapper past. 'It was only when we saw the play that we thought, Jesus Christ there was quite a lot happening ... so many things about the production were marvellously right.'

Similarly, at the London premier, *Doctor Who* star David Tennant said:

A one-man show is quite an undertaking; it needs someone with nerves of steel. It's a full-length play, yet the audience is absolutely in the palm of his hand from the off. It's fantastic. He is one of these people you grew up with, David Tomlinson, but I've never really sat to wonder about what his life is.

Actress Keeley Hawes saw people laughing and crying, 'It flew by, and I honestly just wanted it to go on.'

'It was incredibly funny but also very moving,' was the verdict of Ian Hislop:

There is obviously a shared sensibility between David Tomlinson, who's a character from most people's childhood, and Miles, who is slightly old fashioned, even if he doesn't want to be. He has a sort of Englishness which is very authentic and very appealing but he is also capable of undercutting it and celebrating it and that makes an amazing show.

Writing in *Time Out*, Tom Wicker thought, 'It gives us a likeable, funny Tomlinson in whose company it's a pleasure to spend a couple of hours. You could call it a welcome spoonful of sugar right now.'

David Jr flags up a remarkable story about the production during the first performances in Exeter, not a million miles from Dawlish where Sybil Elgar was to eventually retire:

> During a performance, one of Miles' astute production team, Rachel Hewer, noticed a member of the audience visibly react at the mention of Sybil's name. Determined to satisfy her curiosity, Rachel approached her after the performance. Sybil and Jack Elgar's only child Jackie explained to Rachel that she had only come to the play out of curiosity because she had met David Tomlinson when she was a child. She hadn't dreamed of hearing Miles Jupp not only mention her mother, but say that she was the closest thing to a saint.

The Life I Lead came on the heels of *Saving Mr Banks*, a Hollywood feature chronicling the making of *Mary Poppins*, by focusing on Disney's long courtship of P.L. Travers, played by Emma Thompson. 'I think that *Saving Mr Banks* had an effect,' says Henry. 'Suddenly you see the movie and realise that *Mary Poppins* was all about Mr Banks' journey.'

Borrowing a page from real history, the film showed how Travers tormented Don DaGradi and the Sherman brothers with complaints about everything from costumes, songs, script to animation and casting. When released, the film grossed US$9.3 million in its opening weekend in the United States, and performed well overseas.

'I think Dad would have savoured his blossoming posthumous career,' says Henry. 'He would have loved it. What actor wouldn't?'

FILMOGraPHY

Garrison Follies (1940) (uncredited)
Quiet Wedding (1941) as John Royd
My Wife's Family (1941) as Willie Bagshott
'Pimpernel' Smith (1941) as Steve
The Way to the Stars (1945) as 'Prune' Parsons
Journey Together (1945) as Smith
I See a Dark Stranger (1946) as Intelligence Officer
School for Secrets (1946) as Mr Watlington
Fame is the Spur (1947) as Lord Liskeard
Master of Bankdam (1947) as Lancelot Handel Crowther
Easy Money (1948) as Martin Latham
Miranda (1948) as Charles
Broken Journey (1948) as Jimmy Marshall
My Brother's Keeper (1948) as Ronnie Waring
Sleeping Car to Trieste (1948) as Tom Bishop
Love in Waiting (1948) as Robert Clitheroe
Here Come the Huggetts (1948) as Harold Hinchley
Warning to Wantons (1949) as Count Max Kardak
Vote for Huggett (1949) as Harold Hinchley
Marry Me! (1949) as David Haig
Helter Skelter (1949) as Nick Martin
The Chiltern Hundreds (1949) as Lord Tony Pym
Landfall (1949) as Binks

So Long at the Fair (1950) as Johnny Barton
The Wooden Horse (1950) as Philip Rowe
Calling Bulldog Drummond (1951) as Algernon 'Algy' Longworth
Hotel Sahara (1951) as Captain Puffin Cheyne
The Magic Box (1951) as Assistant in Laboratory
Castle in the Air (1952) as Earl of Locharne
Made in Heaven (1952) as Basil Topham
Is Your Honeymoon Really Necessary? (1953) as Frank Betteron
All for Mary (1955) as Humphrey 'Humpy' Miller
Three Men in a Boat (1956) as Jerome
Carry on Admiral (1957) as Tom Baker
Up the Creek (1958) as Lt Humphrey Fairweather
Further up the Creek (1958) as Lt Humphrey Fairweather
Follow that Horse! (1960) as Dick Lanchester
Tom Jones (1963) as Lord Fellamar
Mary Poppins (1964) as George Banks
The Truth About Spring (1964) as Charles Skelton
City Under the Sea (1965) as Harold Tufnell-Jones
The Liquidator (1965) as Quadrant
The Love Bug (1968) as Peter Thorndyke
Bedknobs and Broomsticks (1971) as Professor Emelius Browne
From Hong Kong with Love (1975) as Sir John MacGregor
Wombling Free (1977) as Roland Frogmorton
The Water Babies (1978) as Sir John/Polar Bear (voice)
Dominique (1979) as Lawyer
The Fiendish Plot of Dr Fu Manchu (1980) as Sir Roger Avery

Television

The Birdcage Room (TV Film) (1954) as Lord Tempest
All for Mary (Outside Broadcast of the theatre production, 1954) as Clive Norton
Theatre Royal (1955) – episode 'The No Man' as Tom Pettigo
Theatre Night (1957) – episode 'Dear Delinquent' as David Warren
ITV Play of the Week (1960) – episode 'The Happy Man' as Tom Swinley
Comedy Playhouse (1967) – episode 'Loitering with Intent' as Charles Pinfold
Hawaii Five-O (1976) – episode 'Nine Dragons' as Blake

BIBLIOGraPHY

Andrews, Julie, *Home: A Memoir of My Early Years* (London: Weidenfeld & Nicolson, 2008).

Annakin, Ken, *So You Wanna Be a Director?* (Sheffield, UK: Tomahawk Press, 2001).

Carmichael, Ian, *Will the Real Ian Carmichael …* (London: Macmillan & Co. Ltd, First Edition, edition, 1979).

Crowther, Bosley, *The Great Films: Fifty Golden Years of Motion Pictures* (New York: Putnam, 1967).

Johnson, Jimmy, *Inside the Whimsy Works: My Life with Walt Disney Productions* (Jackson, MS, USA: University Press of Mississippi, 2014).

Jones, Dean, *Under Running Laughter* (Bloomington, MN, USA: Chosen Books, First Edition, 1982).

Holloway, Stanley, *Wiv a Little Bit o' Luck* (London: Leslie Frewin, 1967).

Huggett, Richard, *Binkie Beaumont: Eminence Grise of the West End Theatre, 1933–1973* (London: Hodder & Stoughton, 1991).

Laffey, Bruce, *Beatrice Lillie: The Funniest Woman in the World* (New York: Wynwood Press, 1989).

Lane, Anthony, *Nobody's Perfect* (London: Picador, 2002).

Lawson, Valerie, *Mary Poppins She Wrote: The Life of P.L. Travers* (London: Aurum Press, 2005).

Lees, Gene, *Inventing Champagne: The Worlds of Lerner and Loewe* (New York: St Martin's Press, 1990).

Lerner, Alan Jay, *The Street Where I Live* (London: Hodder and Stoughton, 1978).

McFarlane, Brian, (ed.), *Encyclopedia of British Film* (London: Methuen, 2005).

McGilligan, Patrick, *Alfred Hitchcock: A Life in Darkness and Light* (New York: Regan Books, 2003).

MacNab, Geoffrey, *J. Arthur Rank and the British Film Industry* (London: Routledge, 1993).

Morley, Robert, *A Reluctant Autobiography* (New York: Simon and Schuster, 1st edition, 1966).

Moseley, Roy, *Rex Harrison: A Biography* (New York: St Martin's Press, 1986).

Newquist, Roy, *Showcase* (New York: William Morrow & Company, 1966).

Nixon, Marni, *I Could Have Sung All Night* (New York: Billboard Books, 2006).

O'Hara, Maureen, *To Herself* (New York: Simon & Schuster, 2004).

Noyer, Jérémie, 'Richard M. Sherman on Bedknobs And Broomsticks: a Solid Songwriter!' (Excerpt kindly republished courtesy of Animated Views. www.animatedviews.com)

Peary, Danny (ed.), *Close Ups: Intimate Profiles of Movie Stars* (New York: Workman, 1978).

Powell, Michael, *Million Dollar Movie* (London: Heinemann, 1992).

Probert, Henry, *Bomber Harris: His Life and Times: The Biography of Marshal of the Royal Air Force Sir Arthur Harris, Wartime Chief of Bomber Command* (Barnsley, UK: Frontline Books, 2016).

Pykett, Derek, *MGM British Studios: Hollywood in Borehamwood: Celebrating 100 Years of the Film Studios of Elstree/Borehamwood* (Albany, GA, USA: BearManor Media, 2015).

Sherman, Robert B., Sherman Legacy Archives, Unpublished Excerpts from *Moose: Chapters from My Life*, 2013.

Tomlinson, David, *Luckier Than Most: An Autobiography* (London: Hodder & Stoughton, 1992).

Tomlinson, Michael, *The Most Dangerous Moment* (London: Kimber, 1976).

Took, Barry, *Laughter in the Air: An Informal History of British Radio Comedy* (London: Robson Books, 1976).

Wakelin, Michael, *J. Arthur Rank: The Man Behind the Gong* (Sutherland, Australia: Albatross Books, 1996).

NOTES

All quotes without attribution are from the public record or the author's own interviews.

Chapter One

1   After researching family genealogy, David's brother Michael speculated that the Tomlinsons were descendants of Lord Robert Stewart, son of James V, King of the Scots – the illegitimate half-brother of Mary Queen of Scots.

2   Her stepbrother was Scottish polar explorer Albert Armitage, the navigator and second-in-command on Captain Scott's Discovery Expedition to Antarctica at the turn of the century.

3   *Desert Island Discs*, 20 February 1953. BBC Home Service P1

4   *Ibid.*

5   David was himself a guest on Michael Bentine's *This is Your Life* in the days when it was hosted by Eamonn Andrews in the early 1960s.

6   Tomlinson, David, *Luckier Than Most: An Autobiography* (London: Hodder & Stoughton, 1992).

7   *Desert Island Discs, op. cit.*, P2

8   *Ibid.*

9   David Jr notes: 'Hugh Holden was one of CST's best friends. He bankrolled him when along with his elder brother Dick (Richard Berkeley Tomlinson [1874–1964], their sister Gertie having died young of appendicitis, CST set about getting an estate comprising multiple properties in Chiswick, all of which their improvident father had mortgaged to the hilt, back under their control. DT's eldest brother Michael was to marry Hugh's daughter Pamela, but sadly the marriage didn't survive the Second World War. However, CST remained firm friends with Pam until his death in 1978. He never forgot Hugh's kindness and generosity to him.'

10   *Croydon Advertiser and East Surrey Reporter*, 4 June 1910

11   Grampian TV, op. cit., 1981

Chapter Two

1 Advertisement for Basildon Bond, 1954
2 *Ibid.*
3 Grampian TV, op. cit.,1981
4 *Ibid.*
5 *Ibid.*
6 *Ibid.*
7 *Ibid.*
8 *Ibid.*
9 *Ibid.*
10 *Desert Island Discs*, op. cit., P1
11 *Ibid.*
12 *Ibid.*
13 *Uxbridge & W. Drayton Gazette*, 11 November 1949.
14 *Desert Island Discs, op. cit.*, P2
15 Grampian TV, *op. cit.*,1981
16 *Desert Island Discs, op. cit.*, P3
17 *Ibid.*
18 *Ibid.*
19 *Ibid.*
20 *Ibid.*
21 *Ibid.*
22 *Ibid.*
23 David Jr notes: 'During his Hoover-selling days, DT made a friend in Edinburgh with a similarly uninspired salesman called Bill Dolan. Though they hadn't had a lot of contact since, in 1969, I stayed with DT on tour in Edinburgh where he was playing Prime Minister Sir John Holt in George Bernard Shaw's wordy ironical comedy *On the Rocks*. DT predicted that Bill would get in touch and sure enough he came to the stage door on the first night. Later that week we went out with Bill and his wife, whose name I think was Peggy. Inevitably DT and Bill reminisced about the days when, after an unprofitable door-to-door morning, they would sit on a park bench and watch the world go by.'
24 Grampian TV, *op. cit.*,1981.
25 *The Stage*, 7 January 1954.
26 Tomlinson, David, *Luckier Than Most.*
27 Jamie Tomlinson interview, 2020
28 Grampian TV, *op. cit.*,1981
29 *Ibid.*
30 *Ibid.*
31 Tomlinson, David, *Luckier Than Most.*
32 *Ibid.*

Chapter Three

1   *Ibid.*
2   After the declaration of war, the following Government orders and information were announced: 'All places of entertainment have been closed, including cinemas and theatres, and the ban applies also to sports meetings and similar gatherings.' At the same time, blackout regulations had to be stringently observed both by householders and road-users.
3   *Outake*, Grampian TV, *op. cit.*,1981.
4   David was no great fan of Alan Ayckbourn, who he confided to Richard Ingrams, was 'overrated'. This opinion was probably formed during the 1970s when he spent time with Robert Morley during the tour of Ayckbourn's play *How the Other Half Loves* on his way into London. 'Robert completely rewrote [the play] to Ayckbourn's chagrin but it made a fortune but I suppose the author had some cause for complaint but certainly not failure.' – Letter to Richard Ingrams, 1995.
5   Tomlinson, David, *Luckier Than Most.*

Chapter Four

1   *Ibid.*
2   *This is Your Life*, A.E. Matthews, 5 May 1958.
3   *Ibid.*
4   Tomlinson, David, *Luckier Than Most.*
5   *Ibid.*
6   Grampian TV, *op. cit.*, 1981.
7   *New York Herald*, 16 February 1941.
8   David Jr recalls meeting Mary Morris in mid to late 1960s quite by chance as the Tomlinson family queued to board a cross-Channel ferry to Calais. 'She was in a battered Land Rover and looked quite battered herself in a bird-like way, but she was really bright and vivacious. This would have been around the time of *The Prisoner*, a series that didn't mean much to Dad, but in which she had made a guest appearance as one of Patrick McGoohan's No. 2s.'
9   *Liverpool Evening Express*, 25 August 1941.
10 David Tomlinson to Richard Ingrams, letter.
11 Jamie adds: 'The Spitfire Peter flew was unarmed and had three huge fuel tanks to make the long flight. As I understand it, they tried to do a daylight reconnaissance mission, clear skies required, the day after a bombing raid. This was carried out at a very high altitude, so no great danger in terms of enemy aircraft. The pilot flew over the target and had to flip the Spitfire and take photographs. You did have to switch fuel tanks, which involved opening and closing gate valves manually. I think Peter's engine cut out while changing tanks. Come what may, he could not restart the engine. Coming down from a great height he will have had some time to try to restart the engines, including going into a dive. He left it too late to bail out and actually force-landed on a

German-held Dutch airfield. He remained in touch for the rest of his life with the German Luftwaffe officer who had taken him prisoner and who also refused to hand him over to the Gestapo for interrogation.'

12 David Tomlinson to Richard Ingrams, letter (undated).
13 Since the outbreak of hostilities, Canada had become a principal source of materials for the British war effort supplying armoured vehicles as well as operating a vast shipbuilding programme. On top of that, endless supplies of food – ranging from powdered eggs to corned beef – were shipped to the motherland across the hazardous Atlantic.
14 David Tomlinson to Richard Ingrams, letter (undated).
15 *Ibid.*
16 *Ibid.*
17 Tomlinson, David, *Luckier Than Most.*
18 David Tomlinson to Richard Ingrams, letter (undated).
19 *Ibid.*

Chapter Five

1 Tomlinson, David, *Luckier Than Most.*
2 *Ibid.*
3 *Ibid.*
4 *Ibid.*
5 *Ibid.*
6 *Ibid.*

Chapter Six

1 David Tomlinson to Richard Ingrams, letter (undated).
2 Grampian TV, *op. cit.*, 1981.
3 Forbes, Bryan. *Notes for a Life*, Collins, 1974.
4 During shooting, Denham's backlot, with its huge outdoor water tank, became the scene of one of the most unusual episodes of the war when night-time scenes on a mock-up ship for *The Way Ahead* were illuminated by brilliant arc lights, despite the strict blackout. The excitement prompted locals to stay up to watch the sky glow from a controlled raging fire on board the prop-ship. All lighting was controlled by a master switch so that, in the event of an air raid warning, complete darkness would have reigned in a matter of seconds.
5 Grampian TV, *op. cit.*, 1981.

Chapter Seven

1 *Liverpool Echo*, 17 October 1959.
2 Grampian TV, *op. cit.*, 1981.
3 When J. Arthur Rank visited New York during 1947, a feature in the nationally syndicated *Time* magazine described him as a 'burly grandfather-clock of a man'.
4 Grampian TV, *op. cit.*, 1981.
5 *Daily Herald*, 15 August 1947.
6 *Ibid.*
7 Grampian TV, *op. cit.*, 1981.
8 McNab, Geoffrey, *J. Arthur Rank and the British Film Industry*, Routledge, 1993.
9 *The Australian Women's Weekly*, 19 July 1947.
10 David Jr recalls later meeting Thora at the Duke of York's Theatre in 1974 when DT was in an unsuccessful play called *The Turning Point*, which had been a hit in Paris but, in contrast to *The Little Hut*, hadn't translated well. 'After a Saturday night performance where, thankfully, the house had been pretty full and not unappreciative, she came round to DT's dressing room with her father, stepmother, second/third husband (somewhat younger than her I recall) and a daughter, who was a similar age to me. DT told me afterwards that Thora's father had been an unadmirable philanderer in his younger days, but he had still found it uncomfortable to visit the family in Iceland and tell them that he didn't think it a good idea for him and Thora to marry, because according to DT he had not seriously contemplated marriage. I suspect the family's recall of Thora to Iceland was rather because DT hadn't proposed to her. That was indeed the end of the relationship. However, thirty-odd years on there were no recriminations either way: Thora was very friendly, introducing her daughter to me with an ever-slight twinkle in her eye. It was all typically civilised.'
11 The US film quota could have been higher, but was limited by a statutory screen quota of a minimum of 20 per cent.
12 David Tomlinson, letter to Richard Ingrams, 1995.
13 Nottingham Journal, 27 February 1950.
14 *Ibid.*
15 From an interview with Brian McFarlane in his book *An Autobiography of British Cinema by the Actors and Filmmakers Who Made It*, Methuen, 1997.
16 McFarlane, Brian, *An Autobiography of British Cinema*.
17 Ralph Thomas interview with Brian McFarlane for *An Autobiography of British Cinema*.
18 Grampian TV, *op. cit.*, 1981.
19 MacFarlane, *op. cit.*, p. 357.
20 David Jr says the character Phil Rowe was based on real-life escapee Oliver Philpot. 'I have no idea why the name was changed so that only the "Phil" part of it was retained. The names of the three PoWs who actually made the escape were Lieutenant Michael Codner, Flight Lieutenant Eric Williams and Flight Lieutenant Oliver Philpot. I'm in no doubt that DT played Oliver Philpot, whom my uncle Peter also knew quite well. In 1978, I met Oliver's son, Nick,

who was also a barrister several years senior to me and later a judge. The very first time we met he told me quite uncompromisingly, "Your father played my father in *The Wooden Horse* and was completely unsuitable for the part!"'

21 Grampian TV, *op. cit.*, 1981.

22 *Ibid.*

23 *Ibid.*

24 *Film Parade* 1950 annual, p. 68.

25 Henry Tomlinson interview with Nathan Morley, 2020.

26 Alice Mantle worked as a housekeeper at Brook Street and later Chelsea Cloisters. 'She was almost the same age as David and outlived him by twelve years or so: she was one of the very few guests at my parents' wedding. She lived with her husband Ernie in Battersea,' David Jr noted.

27 Interview with Audrey Tomlinson, 2020.

28 Interview with Cordell Marks, 1973.

29 *Ibid.*

Chapter Eight

1   Tomlinson, David, *Luckier Than Most*.

2   Interview with Nathan Morley, 2020.

3   *Ibid.*

4   Sheridan Morley's eulogy at the funeral of his father Robert, 1992.

5   Henry Tomlinson interview with Nathan Morley, 2020.

6   Interview with Nathan Morley, 2020.

7   *Ibid.*

8   Tomlinson, David, *Luckier Than Most*.

9   *Melodies for You with Sheridan Morley*, BBC Radio 2, 18 July 2004.

10 *Ibid.*

11 The film was completed and shown just before the end of the 1951 Festival of Britain, but it did not go on general release until 1952. A copy was sent to Balmoral at the special request of the King and Queen so that they could see the picture at the same time as it was premiered at London's Odeon theatre, Leicester Square, on 18 September.

12 Audrey Tomlinson interview with Nathan Morley, 2020

13 Interview with Nathan Morley, 2020

14 Tomlinson, David, *Luckier Than Most*.

15 *Liverpool Echo*, 12 July 1952.

16 The film is interesting for David's bathtub rendition of 'There Goes Your Heart' by Barry Gray and Edward Dryhurst, which revealed a pleasant vocal range and timbre that would become well-known a decade later. Sheridan Morley opined that David had an even better 'sing-speak voice' than Rex Harrison.

17 Audrey Tomlinson, interview with Nathan Morley, 2020

18 *Ibid.*

19 Whitfield, June, *At a Glance: An Absolutely Fabulous Life*, Orion, 2009.

20 *This is Your Life*, Petula Clark, 1996.

21 *ABC Film Review*, March 1952.

22 Grampian TV, *op. cit.*,1981.

23 *Belfast Telegraph*, 25 July 1960.

24 *Sunday Independent*, 25 May 1997.

Chapter Nine

1 David's appearance on *Desert Island Discs* prompted a letter from Robert Donat, who revealed that he had yet to see *The Magic Box* so 'the masterly scene we created together still remains a figment of the imagination'. David Jr adds: 'Donat was one of DT's favourite actors, second only perhaps to Gary Cooper. DT never forgave himself for failing to keep the letter Donat wrote him. I suppose no one expected Donat, who suffered terribly from asthma, to die so young.'

2 *A Life of Bliss*, sleeve notes by Leslie Bridgmont, Onesmedia release.

3 *Ibid.*

4 Interview with Nathan Morley, 2020.

5 *Ibid.*

6 Tomlinson, David, *Luckier Than Most*.

7 David Tomlinson's remark in a handwritten note to Richard Ingrams regarding an article on Kathleen Harrison. July 1996.

8 Email to Nathan Morley, 2021/.

Chapter Ten

1 Grampian TV, *op. cit.*, 1981.

2 *Ibid.*

3 *Aberdeen Evening Express*, 14 December 1956.

4 *Ibid.*

5 Val Guest interviewed by Roy Fowler for The British Entertainment History Project, 1988. As a memento of his role, a portrait of Matty in his gold-braided uniform was presented to him by Minter on the last day of filming.

6 From *Just Kydding*, the autobiography of Sam Kydd.

7 *Ibid.*

8 Interview with Nathan Morley, 2020.

9 *Ibid.*

10 *Ibid.*

11 *Ibid.*

12 *Ibid.*

13 *Ibid.*

14 Tomlinson, David, *Luckier Than Most*.

15 Anna Massey, *Telling Some Tales*, pp.64–8.

16 *Hammersmith & Shepherds Bush Gazette*, 23 May 1958.

17 Tomlinson, David, *Luckier Than Most*.

18 *West London Observer*, 7 August 1956.
19 Vera Day interview with Nathan Morley, 2020.
20 Grampian TV, *op. cit.*, 1981.
21 Tomlinson, David, *Luckier Than Most*.
22 *Ibid.*
23 Interview with Nathan Morley, 2020.
24 Sir Geoffrey Boycott interview with Nathan Morley, 2020.
25 *Ibid.*
26 DVD commentary, *Up the Creek*, Simply Media, 2004.
27 Interview with Nathan Morley, 2020.
28 Audrey Tomlinson interview with Nathan Morley, 2020.
29 Jess Conrad interview with Nathan Morley, 2020.
30 Maxford, Howard, *Hammer Complete: The Films, The Personnel, The Company*, McFarland, 2019.
31 David had a genuine fondness for Tommy Trinder. In 1960, he was appalled at a negative notice in *The Stage* and was suitably aroused to make his feelings known: 'Sir, I was interested to read the *Stage* notice of "Jack and the Beanstalk", the excellent pantomime now playing to full houses at the Wimbledon Theatre. I hope you will allow me to comment on the suggestion implicit in this criticism that Mr. Trinder didn't know his lines (when your critic saw the show) and that he hadn't taken the trouble to learn them. I sat with a packed matinee house on Monday, 11th January, and marvelled at the skill of this brilliant comedian. His endearing, funny performance is to me a joy to watch, and I was fascinated particularly by the way he delighted, not only the children and they seemed always to be his first consideration but also the adults in the audience. Mr. Trinder, who is well-known to be a most adept, spontaneous ad lib performer, uses his own material throughout the show, and his natural witty "asides" would seem to me to be an important part of his performance. A lot of Mr. Trinder's skill involves his intimacy with the audience, allowing and indeed, encouraging, their participation. It does, indeed, look remarkably natural and unrehearsed, but this, I suggest, is precisely what raises him amongst the greats and is part of the comedian's genius. I would like to suggest that this ad lib technique is precisely what the audience enjoy, and it is possible that your critic does not appreciate this as much as we, the audience, do. As your paper is regarded by many as "the organ of the profession", may I suggest to your critic that he should think a little more deeply before writing such a notice. Yours faithfully. David Tomlinson Savoy Theatre W.C.2.'
32 *Birmingham Daily Post*, 19 September 1957.

Chapter Eleven

1 Mary Peach interview with Nathan Morley, 2020.
2 *Ibid.*
3 *Ibid.*

4   *Ibid.*

5   *The People*, 17 July 1960.

6   Tomlinson, David, *Luckier Than Most*.

7   *Western Mail*, 9 September 1959.

8   Grampian TV, *op. cit.*, 1981.

9   Tomlinson, David, *Luckier Than Most*.

10 *Ibid.*

11 In an interview with the British Library Theatre Archive Project.

12 David Jr remembered being taken to see *Boeing-Boeing* at the Apollo Theatre. 'Again it was a matinee: We were in a box and I started making clucking noises with my tongue in the roof of my mouth. I saw that a number of irritated faces in the stalls were looking in my direction and then I realised that DT was frowning up at me as well. He chided me afterwards, though I don't recall him being that angry. In any play that ran for a while, actors rather liked a bit of distraction from the routine.'

Chapter Twelve

1   Tomlinson, David, *Luckier Than Most*.

2   Grampian TV, *op. cit.*, 1981.

3   *Ibid.*

4   Furthermore, *Tom Jones* and Hollywood's *Hud* won top honours in the twenty-eighth annual poll of the New York Film Critics in December 1963.

5   David Jr notes: 'Osborne and Richardson tried to be as loyal as possible to Henry Fielding's novel, which remains very readable because all of the chapters are short, rather masking its epic proportions. My impression was that the first half of the film covered the first quarter of the novel and that they had to cram the rest of it into the second half. Within a year or two David Lean made no compromises with *Lawrence of Arabia*. Similarly, twelve years later, Stanley Kubrick had no such qualms with *Barry Lyndon*. Sergio Leone invariably left very little on the cutting room floor. Richardson felt that he had to ruthlessly cut *Tom Jones* and was seldom to be seen on set by the time DT was doing his few scenes as Lord Fellamar. The upshot was a series of brilliantly appreciated chapters, but an overall production that perhaps hastened too quickly to its conclusion.'

6   David carried the following advertisement in the Spotlight casting directory throughout the 1960s and '70s: 'David Tomlinson, Height 6 feet 1 inch. All Enquiries: Brook Cottage Mursley, Bucks. Mursley 213 or 610, Chelsea Cloisters Sloane Avenue London, S.W.3 01 - 589 7303 or c/o The Spotlight.'

7   Interview with Nathan Morley, 2020.

8   Grampian TV, *op. cit.*, 1981.

9   Interview with Nathan Morley, 2020.

10 *Ibid.*

11 Unpublished excerpts from *Moose: Chapters from My Life*, courtesy of Robert Sherman.

12 In a letter to Walt on 1 September 1964, the author wrote, 'I know well that in translating a book to another medium something has to be lost – or perhaps undergo a change. The real Mary Poppins, inevitably, as it seems to me, must remain within the covers of the books. And naturally, as an author, it is my hope that your gay, generous, and wonderfully pretty film will turn a new public towards them.'

13 *Thanet Times*, 22 June 1965.

14 David Tomlinson interview on Wogan, 1992.

15 Radio interview, 1969.

16 *Ibid.*

17 Interview with Nathan Morley, 2020.

18 In 2006, the American Film Institute named *Mary Poppins* as the sixth-greatest American film musical.

19 Interview with Cordell Marks, 1973.

20 *Ibid.*

Chapter Thirteen

1   Interview with Nathan Morley, 2020.

2   *Ibid.*

3   *Ibid.*

4   Interview with Nathan Morley, 2020.

5   *Ibid.*

6   Thorpe was criticised for making Judy Garland wear a blonde wig and 'baby-doll' make-up rather than the plain-looking farm girl dress that won her worldwide fame.

7   Mills, John, *Up in the Clouds*, Gollancz, 2001.

8   Tomlinson, David, *Luckier Than Most*.

9   Letter to Richard Ingrams, 1996.

10 Tab Hunter commentary, *War Gods of the Deep* DVD, Kino International, 2015.

11 Peter Yeldham interview with Nathan Morley, 2020.

12 *Ibid.*

13 *Ibid.*

Chapter Fourteen

1   Interview with Nathan Morley, 2020.

2   *Daily Express*, 23 November 1966.

3   *Ibid.*

4   Interview with Nathan Morley, 2020.

5   David Jr notes: 'DT at the very least tinkered with the *Impossible Years* and its authors felt that the finished article bore no resemblance to their creation. Littler had funded DT's trip to New York to see the play on Broadway. I don't think they ever met again. Mind you, Littler had become pretty impossible himself

and had turned into something of a vexatious litigant. Within the next eighteen months he lost two libel cases, one as a claimant and one as a defendant in something bordering on a 'class' action brought by Coral Browne and at least two other actors. By the time an appeal court over which the Master of the Rolls Lord Denning himself presided had sent him packing, he was left with bills for costs and damages exceeding £100,000. He didn't live too long after that humiliation and it was a sad end to a virtuous impresario whose enthusiasm for the business was wholly admirable and who had generously backed my mother and my father at different times in their careers.'

6   Interview with Nathan Morley.
7   *Daily Mirror*, 23 June 1967.
8   Interview with Nathan Morley, 2020.
9   *Ibid.*
10 *Ibid.*
11 *Ibid.*
12 *Ibid.*
13 Interview with Nathan Morley, 2020.
14 The film opened to rave reviews on 13 March 1969 at Radio City Music Hall in New York, where it scored an Easter week record, with a seven-day gross of $285,258.
15 Lawrence Douglas interview with Nathan Morley, 2020.
16 Interview with Nathan Morley.

Chapter Fifteen

1   Interview with Cordell Marks, 1973.
2   Interview with Nathan Morley.
3   Jack Minster died in 1966.
4   Interview with Cordell Marks, 1973.
5   Interview with Nathan Morley, 2020.
6   *Ibid.*
7   Audrey Tomlinson interview with Nathan Morley, 2020.
8   *Birmingham Daily Post*, 24 August 1974.
9   David Jr adds: 'In his biographical book *PS* [Peter Sellers] *I Love You*, Michael Sellers described as a very young child getting a pot of house paint and innocently decorating the wing of his father's Rolls. Coincidentally, Jamie and I did exactly the same thing and far from innocently, but my father's reaction was rather different to Sellers'. He apparently went into a terrifying rage. We were certainly ticked off, but I rather surmise that if any misbehaviour was the sort of thing my father might remember doing or wanting to do as a child himself, he was pretty laid back about it. The one exception was the sibling squabble. Dad was the third of four brothers and I was the eldest of four brothers. When Jamie and I fought as children, Dad – with a totally straight face – would insist that he and his brothers never fought, a claim that his old nanny Sister Louise Noakes, who helped out in the early years of my childhood, later told me was a thumping great fib!'

10 Interview with Nathan Morley.
11 Richard Ingrams interview with Nathan Morley, 2020.
12 Interview with Nathan Morley, 2020.
13 *Ibid.*

Chapter Sixteen

1   Angela Landsbury handwritten note to Bill Walsh, 22 October 1969.
2   Interview with Jérémie Noyer at AnimatedViews.com.
3   Audrey Tomlinson interview with Nathan Morley, 2020.
4   *Ibid.*
5   *Ibid.*
6   *Ibid.*
7   *Ibid.*
8   Roy Snart interview with Nathan Morley, 2020.
9   Unpublished excerpts from *Moose: Chapters from My Life*, courtesy of Robert Sherman Jr.
10 The Bee, Danville, Virginia. 13 May 1970.
11 *Ibid.*
12 Interview with Nathan Morley, 2020.
13 Audrey Tomlinson interview with Nathan Morley, 2020.
14 Kuratti interview with Nathan Morley, 2020.
15 Audrey Tomlinson interview with Nathan Morley, 2020.
16 Geoffrey Boycott interview with Nathan Morley, 2020.
17 *Ibid.*
18 *Ibid.*
19 Interview with Cordell Marks, 1973.
20 Ian Carmichael, Felicity Kendal and many others from the theatre also helped to raise funds.
21 Grampian TV, *op. cit.*, 1981.
22 *The People*, 8 February 1976.
23 *The Guardian*, 1 November 1976.
24 Grampian TV, *op. cit.*, 1981.
25 The Guardian, 1 November 1976.
26 *Ibid.*
27 Grampian TV, *op. cit.*, 1981.

Chapter Seventeen

1   Grampian TV, *op. cit.*, 1981.
2   Piers Haggard interview with Nathan Morley, 2020.
3   *Ibid.*

4   *Ibid.*
5   Tomlinson, David, Luckier Than Most.
6   *Ibid.*
7   *Ibid.*
8   It was an expensive production, with a budget of US$10million. Filmed at Studio De Boulogne, France, and on location in Paris, London, and the French Alps.
9   Piers Haggard interview with Nathan Morley, 2020.
10   Audrey Tomlinson interview with Nathan Morley, 2020.
11   Tomlinson, David, Luckier Than Most.

Chapter Eighteen

1   Grampian TV, *op. cit.*, 1981.
2   *Ibid.*
3   Audrey Tomlinson interview with Nathan Morley, 2020.
4   *Ibid.*
5   *Ibid.*
6   David Jr notes: 'Frankie de la Tour's husband, Tom Kempinski, was one of several friends who told DT to "get out of Lloyds while you still can!"'
7   Letter to Richard Ingrams, 1996.
8   Russell Grant interview with Nathan Morley, 2020.
9   Interview with Nathan Morley, 2020.
10   Audrey Tomlinson interview with Nathan Morley, 2020.
11   Interview with Nathan Morley.
12   *Ibid.*
13   Interview with Nathan Morley.
14   David Jr notes: 'In fact, Peter was only a year older than DT, as he well knew, a sign that his brain wasn't aligned to his text.'
15   Audrey Tomlinson, interview with Nathan Morley, 2020.
16   William continues to see the family regularly and stays with Jamie and Audrey for extended periods. 'He has his own heavy-duty Victorian work bench salvaged from Sir Thomas Beecham's former home, Mursley Hall, before it was demolished in 1965,' David Jr says.' He is no longer at Somerset Court, but part of a community where he does plenty of stimulating activities. 'He's a fine craftsman, can work a lathe and turns out coasters and salad bowls by the bucket-load. He's always got a larger project on the go, recently making a bespoke desk that he has in his bedroom: it is one of a number of things he's put together without any drawn design: the blueprint is in his head. Will is also into horse-riding and he cooks very well with an emphasis on pasta dishes. Later this year he will turn 60 on the 103rd anniversary of our Dad's birth.'

INDEX

Notes: page references in *italics* indicate illustrations.

YOU MAY ALSO ENJOY . . .

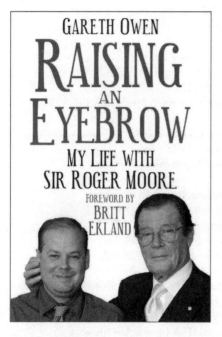

978 0 7509 9751 5

Raising an Eyebrow is a unique insight into life with Sir Roger Moore, written by his PA, co-author, onstage co-star and confidant.

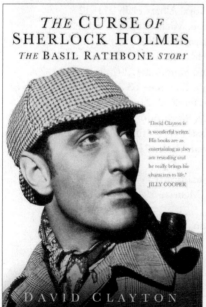

978 0 7509 9747 8

The Curse of Sherlock Holmes is the first definitive account of one of Britain's most loved actors, Basil Rathbone.

The destination for history
www.thehistorypress.co.uk